SHRUBS,CLIMBERS ANNUALS AND PERENNIALS

SHRUBS, CLIMBERS ANNUALS AND PERENNIALS

Your essential guide to planting the perfect garden

RICHARD BIRD

Photography by Jonathan Buckley

HERMES HOUSE

This edition published in 2001 by Hermes House

© Anness Publishing Limited 2000, 2001

Hermes House is an imprint of
Anness Publishing Limited
Hermes House
88-89 Blackfriars Road
London SE1 8HA

Published in the USA by Hermes House, Anness Publishing Inc.,
27 West 20th Street, New York, NY 10011

Publisher: Joanna Lorenz
Project Editor: Emma Hardy
Photographer: Jonathan Buckley
Copy Editor: Alison Bolus
Designer: Ian Sandom
Editorial Reader: Penelope Goodare
Production Controller: Yolande Denny

1 3 5 7 9 10 8 6 4 2

Previously published as *Essential Plants for Every Garden*, and in two separate volumes:
Shrubs and Climbers and *Annuals and Perennials*.

Publisher's note: In the United States, throughout the Sun Belt states, from Florida, across the
Gulf Coast, south Texas, southern deserts to Southern California and coastal regions, annuals are
planted in the autumn, bloom in the winter and spring, and die at the beginning of summer.

ACKNOWLEDGEMENTS
The publishers would like to thank the following for their permission to photograph their plants
and gardens: Hilary and Richard Bird, Ken Bronwin, Mr and Mrs R Cunningham, Chris and Stuart
Fagg, Della and Colin Fox, Christopher Lloyd, Merriments Gardens, Eric Pierson, Mavis and David
Seeney, Lyn and Brian Smith, and the RHS Garden, Wisley.

They would also like to thank the following people for allowing their copyright pictures
to be reproduced in this book:

Key: t = top; b = bottom; r = right; l = left; c = centre

Richard Bird for the pictures on pages: 58 (all), 59 (br), and 97 (br). **Jonathan Buckley** for the
pictures on pages: 1, 2, 3, 4, 5 (tl tr br), 6 (all), 8 (all), 9 (r), 10 (r), 14, 18, 24 (bl), 25 (br), 31 (br),
50, 53 (br), 76, 79 (br), 102 (all), 108 129 (br), 185 (tr br), 201 (tr bl br), 210 (tr), 218 (b), 219 (r),
221 (l), 222 (br), 223 (l br), 224 (all), 225 (all), 266, 295 (all), 302 (r), 307 (all), 322 (all), 335 (b),
380 (r), 388, 408, 409, 412, 413, 415, 416. **The Garden Picture Library** for the pictures on
pages: 26 (t b), 29 (br), 57 (br), 118, 231 (tl r bl), 233 (t), 234 (l), 235 (tl r bl), 237 (bl br), 238 (b),
239 (bl br), 242, 243 (l r), 249 (bl), 258, 259 (tl r bl), 260, 261 (tl r bl), 281 (r bl), 287 (br). **Peter
McHoy** for the pictures on pages:.42, 49 (t), 60, 61 (br), 67 (r), 73 (all), 81, 90, 91, 92 (bl), 93 (t),
113 (tl bl), 127 (br), 145 (tr), 150 (tr), 151 (tr), 158 (tl tr), 160 (br), 161 (bl), 168 (tr), 169 (l), 170
(all), 171 (tr br), 172 (tl tr), 173 (br), 179 (b), 183 (bl), 186 (br), 188 (b), 189 (r), 190 (br), 191
(bl), 192 (tr bl), 343 (t), 381 (tr), 384 (r), 386 (t), 390 (bl tc bc), 391 (t br), 402 (c), and 405 (tl).
Derek St Romaine for the picture on page 117.

CAPTIONS
Half title page: *Aconitum* 'Kelmscott', *Cimifuga racemosa* 'Purpurea',
Helianthus and zinnias .
Frontispiece: *Canna* 'Wyoming' with *Dahlia* 'David Howard' (orange) and
Dahlia 'Hillcrest Royal' (magenta).
Title page: *Echinacea purpurea*, *Scutelaria incana*, *Persicaria amplexicaulis* 'Rosea',
Centranthus ruber var. *coccineus* and *Helenium* 'Kupferzwerg'.
Above: *Erysimum* 'Bowles Mauve'.
Opposite top left: Angelica.
Opposite top right: *Cestrum parqui*.
Opposite bottom left: *Rosa* 'Iceberg'.
Opposite bottom right: *Aconitum* 'Newry Blue'.

CONTENTS

INTRODUCTION

The key to any garden must be its plants. They create not only the form and structure but also provide all the colour and excitement. They are what makes a garden, without them, the garden becomes merely a wilderness.

There is every reason for the gardener getting to know what plants are most suitable for a garden and how to cope with them. They are not only key elements in any design but also give a tremendous amount of joy and pleasure, both in their final appearance and in the satisfaction of growing them. There is an enormous amount to be gained from starting with a packet of seed that appears little more than a handful of dust and ending up with a border full of magnificent plants.

Plants are very versatile. On the one hand there are those that will cope with a damp habitat, and on the other those that like dry conditions. While most like the sun, there are also plenty that like the shade. There are those that can fill large spaces and those that are more

Above: Salvia sclarea turkestanica, Fuchsia versicolor *and* Lychnis coronaria

Above: Anagallis monellii *with* Tagetes *'Suzie Wong'*.

6

suitable for small intimate areas. Most will grow happily in the border, but there are many that can be coaxed into growing in containers, hanging baskets and other similarly restricted areas. The great thing about all this versatility is that you can create exactly the garden that you want; it opens the door to all kinds of possibilities.

Plants fall into a number of botanical types, such as annuals, shrubs and so on. These are convenient categories based on habits of growth, rather than rigid divisions. Some gardeners like to have a bed of just annual plants, but there is nothing to stop you mixing annuals with bulbs, perennials or shrubs, or, indeed, with all three. The plants are there for you to use in whatever combination you choose. However, there are some restrictions. For example, sun-loving plants are usually unhappy growing in shady conditions and will not give of their best and often die, but that is one of the things that this book is about, showing which plants to grow where.

There can be few gardeners who have not grown annuals in one form or another. They have many advantages. They are very colourful which gives them a very cheerful disposition. Their season is a long one with most of the bedding types lasting through the summer and well into autumn, giving very good value for money. They can also be very cheap, especially if

Above: Hyacinthus *'Pink Pearl'* *with pansy Universal series 'Marina'.*

Above: Narcissus *'Unsurpassable' with* Hellebore *and* Muscari.

you grow your own from seed. One big advantage of annuals is that they only last a year. For the following year, you can repeat them if you wish or choose something completely different.

Annuals is rather a loose term. It mainly includes those plants that germinate, flower, set seed and die all within a year. However in gardening terms it also includes other plants that are treated as annuals. For example, biennials, such as foxgloves, which germinate in the first year and flower and die in the second. Short- lived perennials, such as sweet Williams and wallflowers, are normally considered as annuals as they are discarded after flowering. Similarly tender perennials such as pelargoniums are usually started from scratch each year and used in bedding or other such similar schemes.

Most garden centres and nurseries provide a wide range of annuals ready to plant out. On the other hand it is very easy to grow your own hardy annuals from seed, even if you do not have a greenhouse or cold frame. The advantage is that there is a much wider choice of seeds than of young plants. It is also cheaper than buying plants, and often a packet will contain enough seed for you to produce surplus plants to give away or sell.

Perennials form the backbone of the flowering borders. As their name implies they last for several years rather than a single one like annuals. Because of

Above: Colchicum *growing through* Petunia *'Purple Wave'*.

Above: Tropaeolum *'Jewel of Africa' with* Tagetes *'Toreador' marigolds,* Cornus alba *'Elegantissima' and* Anemone japonica alba.

this they are usually used in borders that tend to stay the same from year to year, although minor changes may take place, especially if different annuals are mixed in with them every year. There are literally thousands of different plants to choose from, displaying a wonderful range of colours, shapes and textures. Unlike many annuals which tend to last the whole season in flower, most perennials have a relatively short flowering period. Rather than a disadvantage, this can be an advantage, in that the border is a constantly changing picture throughout the year as different flowers come and go. Many of the plants have attractive foliage, so that even when they are not in flower they still have a role to play in the garden's appearance.

Like annuals, the term perennials is used loosely by gardeners. Strictly, perennials (or herbaceous perennials) are plants (other than bulbs and similar) which die down to ground level and reappear each year. However, some bulbs, such as lilies, and shrubs which are cut down by frosts, such as fuchsias, are often included in the broad definition.

There is an increasing range of perennials available from garden centres and there are plenty of specialist nurseries that grow their own plants and hence often have a very interesting and unusual selection on offer. Many nurseries supply by mail order, which means that gardeners have a wider selection of plants available to them than just those on sale at the local garden centre.

Above: Eranthis hyemalis *produces an array of vivid yellow flowers.*

Above: Alonsoa warscewiczii *with* Browallia americana.

Their catalogues often make fascinating as well as instructive reading.

Propagation of perennials is a little more complicated than that of annuals but the vast majority of plants can be increased by most gardeners without any problems. Like anything else, it is just a question of learning by experience. Greenhouses and propagators are useful but they are far from essential and many gardeners produce all the plants they need without recourse to either, polythene bags and windowsills being sufficient.

Bulbs are, again, plants that most gardeners are familiar with. Many will have known daffodils and tulips since childhood and have a pretty good idea what to do with them. However, there is a much bigger range than just these two, and many of the more unusual ones are well worth growing. Bulbs can be grown by themselves in beds or in containers or can be mixed with other plants. One advantage of mixing them is that other plants will cover and disguise them once they have finished flowering, since the foliage of most bulbs can look tatty at this stage. They can be mixed in with perennial plants to great advantage and left there from

Above: Eranthis hyemalis *with* Helleborus foetidus.

Above: Spires of white foxgloves, *Digitalis purpurea alba*.

one year to another. Naturalizing bulbs in grass or under trees is another long term, trouble-free way of using them. Alternatively they can be mixed with bedding plants and lifted and stored once the flowering period is over.

The definition of bulbs is quite precise in botanical terms, but once again the gardener groups them by convenience and also includes plants that are strictly corms (crocuses for example) and tubers (such as dahlias). Bulbs are usually bought, either from garden centres or from specialist nurseries – the latter usually

have a much wider range of varieties and often produce illustrated catalogues. However, it is also possible to grow them from seed and this is a good way of building up an unusual collection.

Shrubs and climbers are the most permanent of all border plantings. These are generally left in position for many years until their usefulness is over or old age intervenes. Because of their permanence, they are an essential part of the unchanging structure of the garden. Annuals come and go, perennials stay a bit longer but have to be moved every so often, or discarded, but

Above: *Blue* Scilla *planted with yellow buttercups produces a stunning contrast.*

Above: *Mixed* Crocus *in grass including* C. tommasinianus, C. chrysanthus and C. vernus.

shrubs and climbers are always there. Even in the winter when everything else dies back, the evergreens will still form a framework for the garden.

Many shrubs and climbers are grown for their flowers, and many solely for their foliage. The latter is far from restricted to green. There are yellow, purple and grey-leaved shrubs as well as a wide range of variegated foliage, all contributing to the overall effect of the garden. Shrubs can be mixed with other plants, used in a shrub border or planted on their own as specimen plants. Climbers can be used in a variety of ways. To soften the hard structures of the home and garden, or to hide eyesores, they can be grown up walls and over fences. They can be trained up decorative features, too, such as arches, pergolas and arbours, introducing soft foliage and splashes of colour at a higher level in the garden. Climbers can also be grown over and through other plants, such as trees and large shrubs.

Shrubs and climbers can be bought from a wide range of outlets. The majority can also be easily propagated from cuttings and seed. Unlike annuals, perennials and bulbs, most need pruning, but the techniques are easily learned, and in many cases they will need very little additional care.

This book introduces the reader to these key plants and to the enormous range of species and varieties they encompass, and clearly explains how to introduce them to the garden, care for them and increase your plant stock through propagation.

Left: *The yew (*Taxus baccata*), if slow-growing, is one of the best of the hedging and topiary plants, its dark green, needle-like leaves forming a dense, impenetrable thicket. It copes well with wind, pollution and drought, and makes a good boundary hedge. The flowers are barely visible, and are followed by small, cup-shaped red fruits. The leaves are highly poisonous. It grows in any good, well-drained soil, in sun or deep shade.*

Right: *Daphne, a genus of evergreen, semi-evergreen and deciduous shrubs, is largely grown for its tubular flowers which are usually beautifully scented. This* Daphne × burkwoodii *'Somerset', which grows to a height of approximately 1.5 m (5 ft), is a semi-evergreen, upright-growing shrub. It produces thick clusters of highly fragrant white and pink flowers in late spring. Occasionally, there is a second burst of flowering in the autumn. Another species,* D. odora, *has fragrant flowers in mid-winter to early spring. Some species of daphne are also grown for their foliage or fruits, although the seeds are poisonous.*

PREPARATION AND PLANTING

One of the most important of all gardening techniques is soil preparation. It is the foundation of all future growth and success. Inadequate attention to preparation at the outset is difficult to remedy once the plant has put down its roots and become established.

There is nothing difficult about planting, but a few basic points need to be remembered. Most importantly, the situation should as far as possible match the plant's requirements as to sun, shade, wet or dry conditions and soil type. Another consideration, often forgotten, is allowing enough space for the plants to grow. A climbing plant, of course, will need something to climb on, and while some, such as ivy, can attach themselves with modified roots to a brick wall, others, such as climbing roses, need to be tied to wires or a trellis.

Left: Crocosmia *'Lucifer' with* Echinops.

GROUND PREPARATION

Preparing the Ground

There can be no doubt that the soil is the most important ingredient when it comes to creating a garden. Understanding your soil and treating it with care and attention will reap rewards that are impossible to achieve in any other way.

CLEARING THE GROUND

The first task when starting any garden is to clear the ground. The most likely problem will be weeds, but in many new gardens there will be builder's rubbish, which can cause problems by making the soil very alkaline.

If you have recently acquired an older garden, you may well find that all manner of rubbish has been dumped in it over the years by previous owners who were not gardeners. Do not make a half-hearted attempt to get rid of this. Hire a skip, if necessary, and have it all taken away. It may seem a lot of trouble, but once it is done you will be rid of the problem. If you leave rubbish lying around at this stage it will be more difficult to deal with once the garden is planted.

DEALING WITH WEEDS

The next problem is the weeds. Many plants are often in the soil in the same place for several, if not many, years, and if weeds, perennial ones in particular, find their way into the roots of these plants the only sure way of getting rid of them is to dig up the plant as well. If you don't do this, but simply break the weeds off where they enter the plant, they will soon revive and you will have a constant battle on your hands. More people give up gardening or are bored by it because of weeds than for any other reason.

You must get rid of all the weeds properly. There is no point in just scraping them off the surface because they will quickly regenerate from the remaining roots. They have to be either totally removed or killed. If the soil in your garden is light and crumbly, it is possible to remove the weeds as you dig. On heavier soils you can either cover the ground with an impermeable mulch such as thick black polythene for several months, or use a weedkiller. Most gardeners are now rightly unwilling to use too many chemicals in the garden, but, if it is done properly, it will only need to be done once. Always follow the manufacturer's instructions to the letter.

Dig the soil, adding as much well-rotted organic material as possible. If you can, carry out this digging in the autumn and leave the ground until spring before planting. If you do this you will see, and be able to remove, any weeds that have regrown from roots that were missed before.

1 Since flower beds (except for those containing only annuals) will be basically undisturbed for many years, it is important to clear the area of any weeds by spraying with weedkiller.

2 You can also clear the area of weeds by organic means, either by skimming off the surface or covering it with black polythene for several months.

3 Dig the first trench to one spade's depth across the plot and barrow the soil you have removed to the other end of the plot.

4 Fork a layer of well-rotted compost or manure into the bottom of the trench to improve the soil structure and to provide nutrients for the plants.

5 Dig the next trench across the plot, turning the soil on to the compost in the first trench. Add compost to the new trench and then dig the next.

6 Continue down the border until the whole of the surface has been turned. Add some compost to the final trench and then fill it in with the earth taken from the first.

7 If possible, dig in the autumn and allow the winter weather to break down the soil. In spring, take out any resprouted weeds and rake over the bed.

Conditioning the Soil

It is impossible to keep taking from the soil without putting something back. Nature does this all the time, and it is important to emulate this in the garden. In the wild, plants are constantly dying back or dropping their leaves, and as they do so, the previous year's lush green growth decays and rots down, returning the nutrients to the soil. In the normal course of things, little is removed from the cycle and plants have a constant supply of the nutrients that are vital to their health and growth.

RECYCLING GARDEN WASTE
In a garden, however, the careless gardener discards all the old foliage and stems into the dustbin (garbage can) or burns it, and it is not returned to the soil to become available for future generations of plants. Unless action is taken to redress this, the soil becomes impoverished and plants become thin and sickly, and are difficult to grow.

The prudent gardener, on the other hand, recycles as much as possible by composting all garden waste and then spreading or digging it into the ground to return it to the soil. Because gardeners remove some of the plant material in the way of cut flowers or vegetables, they should introduce extra material, such as farmyard manure, to supplement the garden compost. In this way, the plants are provided with the nutrients that they need.

SOIL STRUCTURE
Another important aspect to consider is the structure of the soil. Heavy, compacted soils are not particularly good for growing plants. On the other hand, light,

sandy ones also have their problems in that they tend to dry out quickly and the nutrients are leached (washed) out during wet weather. With both extremes of soil type, it is important that the structure of the soil is modified to provide the best possible conditions. Fortunately, this is possible, although in the more extreme circumstances it will take a number of years before the benefits are really seen.

SOIL NUTRITION
To some extent, feeding and conditioning the soil can be achieved in the same way. The addition of rotted organic material not only provides nutrients but also helps to retain moisture and at the same time it helps to break down the structure of the heavier soils.

It is important that the material is well rotted before it is added to the garden, because waste material actually requires nitrogen during the breaking-down process, and, if it is not sufficiently broken down, it will extract nitrogen from the soil so that it can complete the process; this is the reverse of what the gardener wants.

Above: *By providing the best possible soil conditions, you will enable a wide range of plants to flourish, even when closely planted in a border, producing a magnificent display of blooms.*

ADDING HUMUS

1 As much well-rotted compost or farmyard manure as possible should be added to the bed, especially at the time that it is dug.

2 For an existing bed, top-dress the soil with a good layer of well-rotted compost or farmyard manure.

3 Leave the well-rotted compost or farmyard manure as a mulch, allowing the worms to work it into the soil, or you can lightly fork it into the surface.

SOIL CONDITIONERS

Chipped or composted bark has little nutritional value but it is an excellent mulch.

Farmyard manure is rich in nutrients but it also often contains weed seed. Manure also makes a good soil conditioner.

Garden compost, which can be made from all garden waste and the uncooked vegetable peelings from the kitchen, has good nutrient value and is a good soil conditioner.

Leafmould made from composted leaves has good nutritional value and is a good conditioner and mulch.

Peat is not suitable because it breaks down too quickly and has little nutritional value.

Proprietary (commercial) soil conditioners are of variable quality but are usually nutritious conditioners.

Seaweed is rich in minerals and is a good conditioner.

Spent hops, which are the waste from breweries, have some nutritional value and are a good mulch and conditioner.

Spent mushroom compost is good for mulching but usually contains chalk or lime.

MAKING COMPOST

The best material to use when making compost is undoubtedly what came from the soil in the first place – that is, all dead plant material, grass clippings, shredded hedge clippings and prunings. This can be piled into a heap and left to rot down, although most gardeners prefer the much tidier method of using a compost bin. These are wooden or plastic structures into which all the garden waste is placed. The bins should have holes in the side to allow in air.

Any garden waste can be used, as long as it is not diseased, and any woody material should be shredded. Do not add the roots of perennial weeds, and make sure that all waste is free of seeds. In theory, the compost should get hot enough as it breaks down to kill these off, but, in practice, it rarely does and they are liable to germinate wherever the compost is spread. Vegetable peelings and other non-cooked vegetable waste from the kitchen can also be used.

Do not use the compost too early; remember that it should be well rotted before being added to the garden. A good indication that it is ready is that it no longer smells or has a slightly sweet smell. The compost should be dug into the soil in the autumn when you are preparing the beds and borders. In established beds, it can be worked into the soil around the plants or left on the surface for the worms to carry down.

OTHER MATERIALS

A good substitute for garden compost is well-rotted farmyard manure if you can obtain ready supplies. This is animal waste, usually mixed with straw or wood shavings, although it sometimes includes hay, which can be a nuisance if it was allowed to seed before cutting.

Leafmould is another useful material. Collect and rot down your own leaves; never take leafmould from local woods, because you will break the natural cycle and impoverish the soil. Spent mushroom compost is also good, especially for top-dressing borders, but it usually has lime added to it, so do not apply it where you grow acid-loving plants.

Fertilizers can also be used to add nutrients to the soil, but they do not help improve the structure of the soil in the same way that fibrous material does. There are two classes of fertilizer – organic and inorganic. Organic fertilizers, such as bonemeal, which are derived from live materials, usually release their nutrients slowly. Inorganic fertilizers are derived from minerals in rock. They are made purely from chemicals, and, although they are quick acting, they tend to get washed from the soil quickly.

Very few gardeners attempt to change the alkalinity or acidity of the flower borders, although this is much more important in the vegetable garden. In extremely acid gardens, however, it may be desirable to add some lime. Check the conditions with a soil testing kit and then follow the dosage recommended by the manufacturer on the packet.

It is more difficult to turn alkaline conditions to acid ones, however, and if you want to grow acid-loving plants you will have to grow them in containers, rather than trying to change the pH of the soil in your garden.

ADDING FERTILIZER

The best fertilizer is organic material because it improves the structure, as well as the fertility, of the soil. However, if this is not available, use an organic, slow-release fertilizer, such as bonemeal, to feed the soil.

Fertilizers

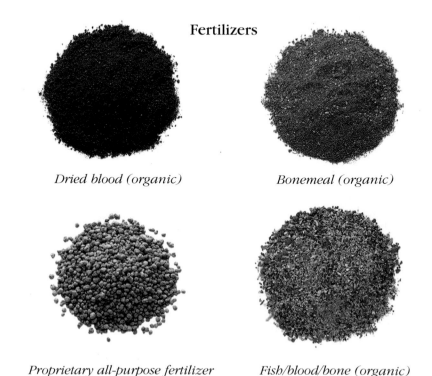

Dried blood (organic)

Bonemeal (organic)

Proprietary all-purpose fertilizer (inorganic)

Fish/blood/bone (organic)

MAKING COMPOST

1 Compost any soft-stemmed garden waste except seed and perennial weeds. Tougher materials, such as hedge trimmings, should be shredded first. You can also add uncooked vegetable waste.

2 Regularly turn the contents of the compost bin and, when full, cover with polythene until the contents have broken down. Alternatively, cover it with soil and plant marrows or courgettes on the top of the bin.

3 The contents should break down, leaving a crumbly, non-sticky, non-smelling compost that is ideal for adding to the soil or using as a mulch.

IMPROVING DRAINAGE

To help heavy soils break down more readily and allow the free drainage of excess water, add sharp sand or fine gravel and fork it into the surface layer.

ALTERING ACIDITY

Although it is not as important as in the vegetable garden, you may need to lower the acidity of the soil. This can be done by adding lime at the recommended dosage.

SOWING AND PLANTING

Advice on Sowing Seed

Growing plants from seed is one of the easiest and cheapest ways of getting a lot of new plants. The techniques involved are not at all difficult, even for those who believe that they do not have green fingers.

THE BEST APPROACH

A packet of seed is relatively cheap when you consider the number of plants you will get from it. There is one disadvantage, however. Plants grown from seed do not always resemble the parent from which the seed was collected. If, for example, you collect the seed of a white hardy geranium, with the intention of growing more, you may find that the whole batch of seedlings produces purple flowers. On the other hand, plants grown by vegetative means – that is, by taking cuttings or by division – always resemble the parent plant. Thus, dividing a white geranium will provide white offspring.

Therefore, if you want to produce a bed of, say, a dozen plants, all of a consistent colour, it is best to use vegetative propagation, unless the plant is known to come true from seed. Remember, too, that it is not only the colour of the flowers that may vary: the colour and shape of the leaves, as well as the size and shape of the whole plant, may also be different.

It is not always a bad thing to grow something unexpected, of course. You may, for instance, suddenly get a blue-flowered form from your white-flowered plant, which may be a plant that is not already in cultivation. It is always rewarding to grow something that no one else will have in their garden. In fact, many of the cultivars we see today were originally chance seedlings that simply appeared in somebody's garden. You may be interested in experimenting in this way, or you may simply feel that a slight variation in the colour and size of the plants does not really matter.

OBTAINING SEED

There are various sources of seed. Many gardeners rely on the major seed merchants, who produce coloured catalogues listing all their available seed. You will get a much wider choice of plants if you order from the catalogues than if you go to your local garden centre, which can carry only a fraction of the bigger merchants' stock.

Another way of obtaining seed is to join a society that runs seed exchange schemes. These often list thousands of species and include many rarer plants. If you want even rarer and more unusual plants, seeds can be obtained by taking shares in the seed-hunting expeditions in the wild that are often advertised in gardening magazines. These work out to be remarkably inexpensive per packet of seed, but you often have to take pot luck about what is gathered.

Having acquired your seeds, there are two ways of dealing with them. They can be sown in the open ground or in pots. For small quantities and the more difficult plants, pots are preferable, but for bulk growing of the more common garden plants, sowing directly into the soil is far less bother and much less expensive because you will not need to buy pots and compost (soil mix).

Many plants can be sown where they are to flower, but it is more usual to sow them in a nursery bed and transplant them to their final positions when they are large enough to transplant.

Left: *Sisyrinchiums are among the many plants that can be sown in open ground.*

Right: *A waterside planting, including* Rodgersia.

Sowing in Pots

Not everyone has sufficient space to devote ground to seed beds, so it is often more sensible to grow the seed in pots. Another argument in favour of pots is that most gardeners need only a few plants; five plants are usually more than enough, unless you have a large garden or you intend to give them away or sell them.

THE ADVANTAGES

Unless you want to grow a huge number of one particular plant, a 9cm (3½in) pot, is a large enough container as this will produce twenty to thirty seedlings. A tray or half-tray will produce hundreds of seedlings.

Whichever method you choose, fill the pot or tray to the rim with compost (soil mix) and then tap it on the bench to settle it. Lightly press down the compost so that it is level. Sow the seed thinly on the compost and then cover it with a layer of fine gravel. Label the pot and water it from above with a watering can or from below by standing the pot in a shallow tray of water. Place the pot in a sheltered spot, away from direct sun. There is no need to use a propagator because most seeds will easily germinate at normal temperatures, although using a propagator will speed up the process. Germination will take from a few days to two or three years, so be patient. The seed of some shrubs needs to have its dormancy broken, and this requires a winter's cold weather before germination will occur. Keep the pots watered.

Most plants can be sown in early spring. Some, however, such as primulas and hellebores, need to be sown fresh – that is, as soon as the seed ripens. This usually means sowing in late summer or autumn.

Below: *Primula seed needs to be sown as soon as it has ripened.*

1 The equipment you will need to sow the seed includes a selection of pots or trays, a good-quality sowing compost (soil mix), a propagator (optional), and your choice of plants seed.

2 Fill a pot or tray with compost. Tap on the bench to settle it and very lightly flatten the surface with the base of a pot.

3 Sow the seed thinly on the surface. If you need a lot of plants, do not sow thickly, but use several pots or a tray.

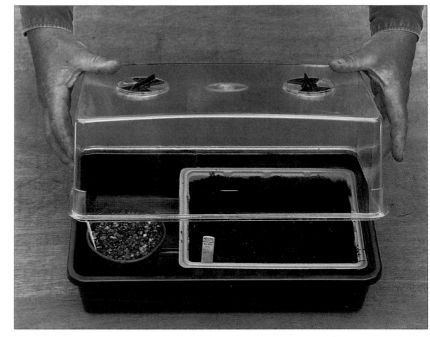

4 Cover the seed with a layer of compost or fine gravel. Gravel will help keep the surface moist, as well as make it easier to water in the seed evenly.

5 Water the pot thoroughly either from above with a watering can or from below by standing the pot in a tray of shallow water.

6 Most plants seeds do not require heat in order to germinate, but the process can be speeded up if the pots and trays are placed in a propagator. Shrub seeds should be placed in the pot outside so that the cold can over-ride any dormancy. Keep the pot watered in dry weather.

7 After a few weeks, in some cases only days, the seedlings will appear. Harden them off by gradually removing the lid of the propagator.

Above: *A number of plants, such as hellebores (Helleborus), will germinate more freely if the seed is fresh, that is as soon it has ripened, rather than waiting until spring.*

Sowing Seed in Rows

Perennials and hardy annuals are often sown in a nursery bed in either spring or autumn and then transplanted to their final positions. For speed, most half-hardy or tender annuals are sown under glass, but many can go directly in the open soil once the threat of frosts is past.

BIENNIALS

Biennials such as wallflowers (*Erysimum*) or sweet Williams (*Dianthus barbatus*) are the type of plant that are most frequently sown outside in rows, in a spare piece of ground, rather than in the positions where they are intended to flower. Since they take a year to come into flower, it is not usually desirable for them to take up valuable bedding or border space during their growing stage when, visually, not much is happening. It is therefore a good idea to find some space for them in the vegetable garden or in specially allocated nursery beds. They are sown in the spring then planted in their flowering positions in the autumn, after the current year's annuals have finished flowering and been cleared away.

SOWING

Before you begin sowing, you need to prepare the ground thoroughly. Remove all the perennial weeds, preferably during the autumn before sowing so that the soil can lie fallow during the winter.

In the spring break the soil down into a fine tilth. Using a garden line and a hoe draw out a shallow drill in the soil.

If there has not been much rain, the soil will be dry. So, water along the drill (alternatively, you can water after the drill has been raked over) and then sow the seed thinly. Rake the soil back over the seed. Mark the row with two sticks, one at each end, and a label. This is important as you will surprised how quickly you forget what you have planted and this will make it difficult to plan planting schemes when you eventually transplant the seedlings.

When the seedlings have germinated, thin out the plants to 10–15cm (4–6in) apart. Keep them weed-free and water during dry spells. In the autumn move the plants to their flowering positions, having first rejuvenated the soil by removing weeds and digging it over, adding plenty of well-rotted organic material.

As well as biennials, perennials in large numbers and annuals to use as replacements in bedding schemes or containers can be grown in this way. The advantage of sowing hardy annuals in the autumn is that they are already in flower at the time the spring-sown ones are being planted out. Combined with the spring-sown plants they create a longer flowering season.

Above: Dianthus barbatus *'Messenger Mixed', a biennial, can be sown outside in open ground and takes a year to come into flower.*

Above: *Pot marigolds* (Calendula officinalis*) come into flower much earlier if they are sown in the open ground during the autumn.*

SOWING IN ROWS

1 Prepare the ground thoroughly, digging it over and breaking it down into a fine tilth using a rake. Do not work the soil when it is too wet or it will become compacted.

2 Using a garden line as a guide, draw out a shallow drill. Use the corner of a hoe, a stick or a trowel.

3 If the soil is very dry, water the drill using a watering can and leave to drain. It should not be muddy for sowing.

4 Identify the row with a clearly labelled marker. This is especially important because when the row is backfilled it will be impossible to see where the seed is until it germinates.

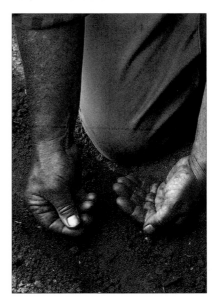

5 Sow the seed along the drill. Sow thinly to reduce the amount of thinning required.

6 Rake the soil back over the drill and lightly tamp it down with the back of the rake. When the seedlings emerge, thin them out to prevent overcrowding.

ANNUALS FOR AUTUMN SOWING

Agrostemma githago (corn cockle)
Calendula officinalis (pot marigold)
Centaurea cyanus (cornflower)
Collinsia grandiflora
Consolida ambigua, syn. *C. ajacis* (larkspur)
Eschscholzia californica
Gypsophila elegans
Iberis umbellata
Lathyrus odoratus (sweet pea)
Limnanthes douglasii (poached-egg plant)
Myosotis (forget-me-not)
Nigella damascena (love-in-a-mist)
Papaver rhoeas (field poppy)
Scabiosa atropurpurea (sweet scabious)

Sowing Seed in Situ

Most plants that are sown directly in the open soil are sown in situ, that is they are sown where they are to flower. This method is usually used for plants that are going to flower in drifts or blocks rather than intricate patterns. It can be used for autumn-sown plants but it is more usually used for seed sown after the frosts have passed in late spring.

PREPARING THE GROUND

Prepare the ground well, preferably in autumn, removing all weeds and breaking it down to a fine tilth. In some cases the planting will be among perennials or some other permanent planting such as shrubs and so the area will already be defined, but if it is a large bed, broken up into several different blocks or areas, then some pre-planning will be required.

Work out on paper the shapes and locations of the various blocks or drifts of plants. The design can be precise or rough, depending on the accuracy you want to achieve. Transfer this outline to the ground by trailing sand, from either your hand or a bottle, around each area. For precise marking first draw a grid over the design on paper then create an equivalent grid on the bed using canes and string. Using the grids as guides transfer the design exactly on to the ground.

SOWING

Once the area has been marked out to your satisfaction, the seed can be sown. There are two methods. The first is to broadcast the seed over the allocated space, simply by taking a handful of seed and scattering it evenly over the soil. The second is to draw out short parallel rows, not too far apart, across the area and sow into these. The first is quicker and creates a natural looking effect, but broadcasting evenly can be difficult and there may be bald areas. The second takes more time but ensures a more even coverage, and also makes weeding easier as you can hoe between rows. Although sown in rows, a random look can be achieved by careful thinning.

If you want the various blocks to merge, scatter a little of the seed into the next area so that the line between adjacent plantings becomes blurred once the plants have matured.

THINNING

Unless you have sown the seed very thinly, you will need to thin out the plants once they have germinated. If you are planning a formal bedding scheme then thin out at regular distances, to create a pattern. Alternatively, for a more natural look, thin at random intervals. If the seed was sown in rows, removing plants at irregular intervals will help break up the lines. Replant a few if necessary to create a more random effect.

SOWING SEED IN DRIFTS

1 Thoroughly prepare the ground by digging the soil and breaking it down into a fine tilth using a rake. Do not work the soil when it is too wet or it will become compacted.

2 If you are planning to use several different blocks of plants, mark out the design on the soil using contrasting coloured sand or compost (soil mix).

3 Broadcast the seed by hand so that it is thinly spread right across the appropriate area. It will probably be necessary to thin out the seedlings when they appear.

4 Gently rake the seed in so that it is covered by a thin layer of soil.

5 Some gardeners prefer to sow in short rows rather than broadcasting. This makes it easier to weed when the seed first comes up. Draw out shallow drills with a hoe.

6 Sow the seed thinly along each row and rake the soil back over them. By carefully thinning the seedlings the resulting overall pattern of the plants will appear to be random and not in rows.

7 Finally, gently water the whole bed, using a watering can fitted with a fine rose.

8 A bed planted with annuals begins to fill out soon after sowing and planting.

Above: *This delightful annual relative of the delphinium,* Consolida ambigua, *can be sown directly into the open border.*

Pricking Out and Hardening Off

Seed that is germinated in pots needs to be pricked out, which simply means that the seedlings are potted up separately. Do this as soon as possible, because the sowing compost (soil mix) is not very rich in nutrients and the seedlings soon become starved.

THE RIGHT TIME

Seedlings are ready to prick out when they have developed the first true leaves (the first pair of leaves are known as the seed leaves; the second pair are known as the first true leaves) or when the seedlings are large enough to handle. Knock the rootball of seedlings from the pot and gently break it apart so that the seedlings can be easily separated out. Fill a 9cm (3½in) pot with good quality potting compost (soil mix) and make a hole in the centre of the pot with your finger.

Pick up a seedling, holding on to a lower leaf (never touch the roots or stems), and suspend it in the hole in the compost. You should be able to see where the soil level was when it was in its seed pot by the mark on the stem. Line up this mark with the compost level in the pot and, with your other hand, trickle more compost around the roots. When the hole is full, tap the pot on the bench and gently firm down. It is a good idea at this point to label each of the pots with the name of the seedling, as well as the sowing date. Water the seedling from below by standing the pot in a shallow tray of water or from above with a fine-rosed watering can.

To ensure that the seedling will recover from the shock of being transplanted and start growing away, the pot should be stood in a closed cold frame or alternatively kept in a draught-free place in a greenhouse. Once you are certain that the plant has become established, it can be hardened off by gradually opening the cold frame over a period of a week to two weeks, until eventually the lid is left open all the time. If the plants are kept in a greenhouse, they can be set outside for increasing lengths of time over a similar period.

Once the plants have been hardened off, they can either be planted in their permanent positions in the border, or they can be left standing in an open cold frame. An alternative solution is to make a plunge bed. This is a simple frame with no lid, built from wooden planks, bricks or blocks. It is part-filled with sand or ashes and the pots are stood on or partially plunged into this mixture. The plunge bed helps to keep the roots cool in the summer and warm in the winter, as well as providing a small amount of moisture through the drainage holes in the bases of the pots.

PRICKING OUT SEEDLINGS

1 As soon as seedlings are large enough, they should be pricked out. Water the pot an hour or so before gently knocking out the seedlings.

2 Gently break up the rootball, finding a natural dividing line between plants. Split into clumps, dealing with one at a time.

3 Gently ease the seedlings away from each clump, one at a time. Only touch the leaves, not the roots or stems.

4 Hold the seedling over a pot by one or more of its seed leaves and gently trickle compost (soil mix) around its roots until the pot is full.

5 Tap the pot on the bench to settle the compost and then gently firm down with your thumbs. Add some more compost if necessary.

6 Water the pots with a watering can or stand them in a tray of water. Keep the plants covered in a cold frame for a day or so, before hardening them off.

Above: *Yellow-flowered* Verbascum olympicum *and hollyhocks* (Alcea rosea*) make a striking planting combination*.

Buying Plants

Growing plants from seeds or cuttings is a rewarding part of gardening, but some gardeners prefer to obtain their plants ready grown. This may be because they have not got the facilities or the time, or simply because growing everything from seed or cuttings does not appeal to them. The easy option is to buy young plants from a garden centre or nursery.

ADVANTAGES AND DISADVANTAGES

There are advantages and disadvantages to buying plants rather than growing them yourself. The main advantage is the convenience of buying plants that are usually ready to plant out. If you have set your heart on a particular plant that you want for your garden now, you may not want to wait while it grows from seed, particularly in the case of a biennial. An established specimen can make an immediate impact in a bed or border.

The main disadvantage is that your choice may be restricted. The choice offered in a seed merchant's catalogue will always be much wider than is available in plants at a garden centre or nursery. Very often you will find that colour choice is restricted. For example, the annual snapdragons (*Antirrhinum*) may be offered as seed in a whole range of single colours, as well as tall or short plants, or even different types of flower. If you buy annuals such as these as plants, you may be offered only trays of mixed colours with no other options.

A wider selection of plants is available if you buy through mail order, and increasing numbers of reputable nurseries are providing this service. Order well in advance because plants sell out. If you are likely to be away when the plants arrive, give the nursery a suitable date so that it does not dispatch the plants before you are ready to deal with them. A parcel of plants that has been sitting on a doorstep in full sun is a sorry sight indeed.

As soon as the plants have been delivered, put them into a cool greenhouse or other sheltered place, out of the sun, in order to allow them to recover. If necessary, pot them on before eventually hardening them off and planting them out.

QUALITY

If you want good-quality plants that are accurately labelled, it is essential to go to a reputable source. Many roadside nurseries and market stalls that sell just a few plants may offer good bargains, but the plants may not always be labelled correctly. If you buy plants that are already in flower, then of course you can be sure of their identity, otherwise you may choose to risk being suprised when the flowers come out - differently to how you expected.

Above: *A group of foxgloves makes a dramatic impact against a background of silver foliage.*

TIPS ON BUYING PLANTS

Above: *Most plants are now sold in pots, although annual bedding plants tend to be sold in cells or strips because of the quantities needed.*

Above: *Although this can be tricky in a garden centre, it is advisable to see if the plant is pot-bound. A plant such as the one on the left will have great difficulty in spreading its roots and growing properly.*

Above: *Buying annuals in strips is a popular method of obtaining large numbers of plants at low cost. Young plants have plenty of room to develop a good root system.*

Above: *Traditionally, perennials were bought bare-rooted, having been grown in the ground and dug up when needed. Bare-rooted plants should be bought only between late autumn and early spring.*

Containers

These days most plants are sold in containers and are available all year round. In the past, and still occasionally today, plants were sold bare-rooted, usually wrapped in hessian; such plants should only be bought between late autumn and early spring.

Annuals and perennials are sold in a range of different containers. Individual pots are the best because plants have room to develop in them, but they are liable to be more expensive. Bedding plants are frequently sold in cells or strips; these are much cheaper, and as long as the plants are not too old or crowded, they should prove satisfactory. Always check your prospective purchase carefully and reject any plant that is diseased, or looks drawn. If possible, knock it out of its pot and look at the roots. Again, reject any that are pot-bound, that is, the roots are wound round and round inside the pot creating a solid mass. Such plants can be very difficult to establish, but if you have no option, you can increase their chances of success by gently teasing out the roots before planting them.

When choosing plants, large, well-grown specimens are obviously preferable, but health and vigour are more important than size. If the plant in question is in flower, you have the added advantage of seeing exactly what colour they are, but do choose one with plenty of buds rather than one which may be almost past its best. If the plants for sale are in a greenhouse or tunnel, harden them off as soon as you get home. Planting them straight into the garden may put them under stress, from which they might not recover.

A wider selection of plants is available if you buy through mail order, and increasing numbers of reputable nurseries are providing this valuable service. Once you have selected the plants you wish to buy, always ensure that you order them well in advance because plants are likely to sell out.

If you are likely to be away when the plants arrive, give the nursery a suitable date for delivery, so that they do not dispatch the plants before you are ready to deal with them. A parcel of plants that has been sitting on a doorstep in full sun is a very sorry sight indeed.

Both annuals and perennials purchased by mail order are liable to come as "plugs", that is individual plantlets either bare-rooted or in cells. As soon as the plants have been delivered, put them into a cool greenhouse or other sheltered place, out of the sun, in order to allow them to recover. If necessary, pot these up and grow them on for a bit longer before planting out.

Above: *Some of the best plants come in individual pots, but they are much more expensive to buy as more work and attention were required to raise them. The plants have more compost (soil mix) in which to grow and can be left in them longer.*

Above: *In packs of plugs, young plants are grown in small cells. These are cheaper than those in larger packs, but make sure they have not become pot-bound, starved and drawn through being left too long in the cells.*

Planting Shrubs

There is nothing difficult about planting a shrub, except possibly making the decision as to where to plant it. One thing that must always be borne in mind is that shrubs *do* grow, and it is a common mistake to underestimate by how much. The result is that shrubs are often planted too close together and then the gardener is faced with the heart-rending decision as to which to dig out so that the others can continue to grow. Avoid this by finding out how big the plant will grow and allowing for this when planting. This means there will be gaps between the shrubs for the first few years but these can be temporarily filled with herbaceous perennials and annuals.

PLANTING CARE

If you are planting more than one shrub at a time, stand them all, still in their pots, on the bed in the places where you wish to plant them, so that you can check that they will all fit in and that the arrangement is a good one. Make any adjustments before you begin to plant, as it does the shrubs no good to be dug up and replanted several times because you have put them in the wrong place.

The actual planting is not a difficult process but looking after the plant once it is planted is important. Water it well until it becomes established. If the site is a windy one, protect either the whole bed or individual shrubs with windbreak netting, until they are firmly established. In really hot weather, light shading will help relieve stress on the plant as its new roots struggle to get enough moisture to supply the rapidly transpiring leaves.

Other aspects to consider in positioning shrubs are discussed elsewhere in the book.

PLANTING TIMES

The recommended time for planting shrubs is at any time between autumn and early spring provided that the weather allows you to do so. Planting should not take place if the weather is too wet or too cold or if the ground is waterlogged or frozen.

However this advice is basically for bare-rooted plants – that is, those dug up from nursery beds. Although container-grown plants are easier to establish if planted at the same time, it is possible to plant out at any time of the year as long as the rootball is not disturbed. If planting takes place in the summer, then avoid doing it during very hot or dry weather. The plants will need constant watering and protection from the effects of drying winds and strong sun.

1 Before you start planting, check that the plant has been watered. If not, give it a thorough soaking, preferably at least an hour before planting.

2 If the soil has not been recently prepared, fork it over, removing any weeds. Add a slow-release fertilizer, such as bonemeal, wearing rubber or vinyl gloves if required, and fork this in.

3 Dig the hole, preferably much wider than the rootball of the shrub. Place the plant, still in its pot, in the hole and check that the hole is deep enough by placing a stick or cane across the hole: the top of the pot should align with the top of the soil. Adjust the depth of the hole accordingly.

4 Remove the plant from its pot, being careful not to disturb the rootball. If it is in a plastic bag, cut the bag away rather than trying to pull it off. Place the shrub in the hole and pull the earth back around it. Firm the soil down well around the plant with the heel of your boot and water well.

5 Finally, mulch all around the shrub, covering the soil with 7.5–10 cm (3–4 in) of bark or similar material. This will not only help to preserve the moisture but will also help to prevent weeds from germinating.

Right: *White frothy mounds of flowers are produced by* Spiraea *'Arguta' during the spring. Since it produces its flowers before many other shrubs come into leaf, it can be planted towards the back of the border where it will show up while in flower but then merge into the background for the rest of the year when it is not so striking.*

Planting Climbers

There are so many different types of climbers that you are bound to be able to choose one that is suitable for any place in the garden. As always, though, the trick is to match up the plant and the planting position correctly.

CHOOSING A POSITION

Probably the most important thing to remember about planting a climber is that it is essential to pause and consider whether you are planting it in the right place. Once planted, with the roots spreading and the stems attached to their supports, it is very difficult to move a climber successfully. Once it has grown to its full size, if you realise that you have got the site wrong, you will have a choice of living with your mistake or scrapping the plant and starting all over again with another one. So, think carefully about the position of any climber you plan to introduce.

As well as considering how the climber looks in its intended position, there is a practical consideration. If you are planting against a wall or fence, the plant should be set a distance away, as the ground immediately adjacent to such structures is usually very dry. Similarly, if a pole or post has been concreted in or simply surrounded with rammed earth, it is best for the roots of your climber to be planted a short distance out and the stems led to the support with canes or sticks.

Most plants should be planted at the same depth as they were in their pot or in the nursery bed (usually indicated by the soil line on the stem). The main exception is clematis, which should be planted 5 cm (2 in)

deeper, so that the base of the stems is covered.

Mulching around the climber helps to preserve moisture and to keep the weeds down. A variety of methods can be used for mulching; any of them will be of benefit at this stage in helping the climber to establish itself quickly.

PLANTING TIMES

Traditionally, climbers were planted, when the weather allowed, between mid-autumn and mid-spring, but most climbers are now sold as container-grown plants and these can be planted at any time of the year, as long as the weather is not too extreme. Bare-rooted climbers have the best chance of survival if planted at the traditional time. Avoid planting any climber when the weather is very hot and dry, or when there are drying winds. In winter, avoid times when the ground is waterlogged or frozen.

1 Dig over the proposed site for the climber, loosening the soil and removing any weeds that have grown since the ground was prepared. If the ground has not recently been prepared, work some well-rotted organic material into the soil to improve soil texture and fertility.

2 Before planting, add a general or specialist shrub fertilizer to the soil at the dosage recommended on the packet. Work the fertilizer into the soil around the planting area with a fork. A slow-release organic fertilizer, such as bonemeal, is best.

3 Water the plant in the pot. Dig a hole that is much wider than the rootball of the plant. Place the soil evenly around the hole, so that it can easily be worked in around the plant. The hole should be away from any compacted soil, near a support and at least 30 cm (12 in) away from a wall or fence. Before removing the plant from its pot, stand it in the hole, to make certain that the depth and width are correct.

4 Place a cane or stick across the hole; the top of the rootball should be at the same level. Dig deeper or add soil to the bottom of the hole, as necessary, to bring it up to the correct height. Remove the plant from the pot, being careful that none of the soil falls away from the rootball. If the plant is in a polythene (plastic) container rather than a pot, cut the bag away rather than pulling it off. Holding the plant steady, pull in the soil from around the hole, filling in around the rootball. Firm as you go, with your hands, and then finally firm down all around the plant with your foot, making certain that there are no cavities or large air pockets.

5 Train the stems of the climber up individual canes to their main support. Tie the stems in with string or plastic ties. Even twining plants or plants with tendrils will need this initial help. Spread them out, so that they ultimately cover the whole of their support. Water the plant in well.

6 Put a layer of mulch around the plant, to help preserve the moisture and prevent weed growth.

Right: *The delicate bells of* Clematis viticella *hang suspended in mid-air.*

Planting a New Bed

Planting up a new bed is one of the most exciting tasks that a gardener can perform. There is a real sense of achievement when it is done and a feeling of pride when the bed or border reaches maturity. That the planting never works out quite as one had imagined – sometimes better, sometimes worse – is irrelevant.

PLANNING THE PLANTING

Some gardeners like to pitch straight in with a collection of plants. Others are more cautious and think about the arrangement for a while before they begin planting. While the impulse method may sometimes work, it usually pays to give some thought to how you want your garden to look and what you can do to achieve your wishes.

POINTS TO CONSIDER

The first step is to plan the border or bed. No matter how badly you think you draw, it is always worth trying to sketch out the arrangement of the plants, and at this stage there are several factors to take into consideration. The first important point to consider is, of course, the colour scheme. You should ensure that plants of sympathetic colours are placed together and obvious clashes are avoided. Then there is the question of height. In general, you will want the tallest plants at the back and the shortest ones at the front, but sometimes it is a good idea to add variety by bringing a few of the taller plants forwards. You might also want to mask a section of the border further down the garden, so that the whole border cannot all be seen at once.

One of the other points to bear in mind when planning the design of a bed is seasonal changes. Not all plants bloom at the same time, as we have noted. Therefore, it is advisable to research the flowering times of your chosen plants in order to spread the flowering from spring through to the autumn, and perhaps include winter, too. Make sure that there are no large areas in the beds or borders that are going to be blank during any of the main seasons – these will only detract from the impact of the other flourishing beds.

Also consider the question of fragrance. Plants that benefit from being smelt close to, or

Left: *The combination of hot, vibrant colours, such as rich crimson, deep purple and sunshine yellow, creates a great deal of impact in this border.*

whose leaves give off a fragrance when they are touched, should be planted near the front of the bed, where they will be accessible.

BUYING THE PLANTS

When you have drawn up the planting plan, try to acquire all the plants before you start planting out. It never seems as satisfactory to plant in batches, because the gaps you leave usually turn out to be either too big or too small. Buy or propagate the plants that you need and then grow them on in their pots, either in a cold frame or plunge bed, until they are needed.

PREPARING THE GROUND

The ground should have been prepared some months earlier to allow it to settle down. Break down any remaining large clods in order to form a fine tilth. Dig out any perennial weeds that have appeared and make sure that you remove every piece of root. The best time to do this is in the spring or autumn, although spring is usually preferable, especially on cold, wet soils. Never work when the soil is wet. Wait until the soil is dry enough for you to walk about and work on it without compacting it. If you have to get on a border when the soil is still rather wet, stand on a wooden plank which serves to spread the load.

If your planting plan is complicated, use string and canes to create a grid over the bed or border. Drawing a similar grid on the plan will help you put the plants in their required positions. Another possibility is to mark the soil by drawing lines on it with sand or peat, which can be trickled through your fingers or put into an empty bottle and poured out in a steady stream as you move around the outlines.

PUTTING IN THE PLANTS

Put all the plants, still in their pots, in their planting positions. Stand back and walk around the border, assessing the effect and trying to visualize the final result. Some plants will need to be moved because of colour clashes or for other reasons. Others will be too close when they are mature and will need to be moved. A few minutes spent doing this, before you begin to plant, will be time well spent if it avoids you having to transplant something that has grown too large for its position.

When you are satisfied with the positions of all the plants, you can begin to plant. Start at the back and move forwards, making sure that the plants are put into the soil at the same depth as they were in their pots. Water in each plant thoroughly, and then rake through the soil to tidy it up as well as to remove any compaction that has resulted from you having to stand on the soil.

It is rare that everything goes right the first time. There is always at least one plant that is not quite the colour you thought it was going to be and clashes with its neighbours, or one that normally only grows to about 30cm (12in), but enjoys the conditions you have provided so much that it grows to 60cm (2ft) and is in the wrong position.

Some plants languish and never really settle down. It may be necessary to move these, perhaps replacing them with other plants or just moving everything around. This is best done in the autumn or in early spring. Dig up the plants with plenty of soil around their roots and, after transplanting, water them in well. You will often find that plants that were unhappy in one particular position will flourish when they are moved only a short distance away.

Above: *Newly planted borders grow away surprisingly quickly.*

The reason for this is often difficult to determine, but there may well have been something in the soil at their first position that disagreed with them.

Planting Bulbs

Bulbs do vary enormously in their requirements, so whenever possible follow the planting advice on the packet or in the catalogue. The advice given here is appropriate for the majority of bulbs, but individual plants may have their own specific needs.

BULBS AND CORMS

Since corms and true bulbs can generally be covered with twice their own depth of soil, a hole 7.5cm (3in) deep is appropriate for a bulb 2.5cm (1in) from base to tip. Often the planting depth is not critical, so there is no need to measure each planting hole once you have an idea of the approximate planting depth.

A few bulbs, late-flowering kinds from warm climates, such as crinums and nerines, are normally planted with the nose of the bulb just below the surface. This helps by exposing the bulbs to more warmth from the sun, but it may mean winter protection in the form of a mulch is required in cold areas. Remove the mulch in spring.

TUBERS

These vary tremendously in size and shape, and it is difficult to generalize about planting depth. Those with a cluster of tubers that meet in a crown at the top are generally best planted shallowly, with the top of the tuber just below soil level.

With some major exceptions, such as tuberous begonias and gloxinias (sinningia), which are usually planted with the top of the tuber sitting flush with the surface of the ground and the top exposed, individual tubers are usually planted so that they are covered with soil equal to once to twice their own depth.

RHIZOMES

Unless the instructions on the packet or in the catalogue advise otherwise, plant rhizomes horizontally, and cover with soil equal to about their own depth. Rhizomatous irises, especially the popular bearded irises of borders, are planted with the top of the rhizome exposed.

PREPARING THE GROUND

Deep-rooted perennial weeds are difficult to eradicate from around bulbs without disturbing the clumps, so make sure the ground is as weed-free as possible before planting.

Bulbs that flower in summer will be growing during the warm months, and they require a generous application of a general balanced fertilizer. This is preferable to something slow-acting, such as bone meal, which is often used when planting spring-flowering bulbs.

Left: *Nerines are among the best of all autumn-flowering plants, but for best results they should be planted shallowly in a warm position. Shown here is 'Fenwick's Variety'.*

DIGGING AND WEEDING

1 Fork over the soil, removing as many weeds as possible before planting. If difficult or deep-rooted weeds are present, remove the roots as you fork over the soil. The hoe is a hazardous tool to use among emerging bulbs.

2 Dig over the soil with a fork or spade. Most bulbs, especially dahlias, will benefit if plenty of organic material, such as garden compost or well-rotted manure, is dug in at the same time. On heavy soil fork in coarse grit to improve the drainage.

3 All bulbs planted in spring will benefit from feeding. Fork, hoe or rake in a balanced general fertilizer.

4 After digging over the soil, rake the ground level before planting, breaking down large clods of soil at the same time.

Spring-flowering Bulbs

With the exception of the few bulbs sometimes transplanted in the green after flowering, spring-flowering bulbs are planted in autumn. Those prepared for early forcing indoors should be planted as soon as they are available, but those for the garden are usually planted once the ground is available.

WHEN TO PLANT

With formal beds, this usually means when the frost has killed the remains of the summer bedding, though when autumns are mild and frost-free it is desirable to clear the summer beds before the first frosts. This is especially true if the bulbs are to be planted between spring-bedding plants such as forget-me-nots or double daisies (*Bellis perennis*), as they are best established in their final positions while the soil is still warm enough for new growth.

Timing is less critical where bulbs are planted in groups on their own. Daffodils generally benefit from early planting, but they will still flower if planted in early winter, albeit perhaps a week or two later than normal. Tulips are usually intentionally planted late, generally in late autumn or even early winter. In very mild climates tulips require a chilling before planting.

PREPARING THE GROUND

Unless naturalizing in grass, prepare the soil before planting. If conditions are appropriate the bulbs will last for many years; if insufficient care is taken they will put on an impressive performance for the first season, then disappoint, or possibly die out within a couple of seasons.

SELECTING A FERTILIZER

Quick-acting fertilizers, especially those high in nitrogen which stimulate rapid growth, should never be used at planting time. The bulbs already contain the reserves they require to flower well in the coming spring. Feeding is best done after flowering to build up reserves for the following year's flowers.

Bonemeal is slow-acting and releases its nutrients over a long period. For that reason it is often used at planting time. Raking in bonemeal is not essential and may make little difference to the spring's display, but it will help to raise soil fertility over time so it is worth using. Wear gloves (latex or vinyl), when applying and rake it in before planting, at the recommended rate.

Controlled-release fertilizers, which only release nutrients when the soil is warm enough, can be used instead.

Above: *Spring-bedding plants such as forget-me-nots help to fill in the base around long-stalked tulips such as 'Warbler'.*

Left: *Mixtures of narcissi can often be bought cheaply, and they make an effective massed display if planted closely.*

PLANTING IN BORDERS

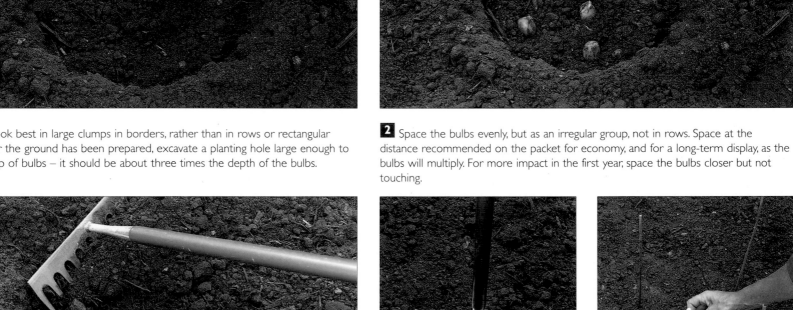

1 Bulbs look best in large clumps in borders, rather than in rows or rectangular blocks. After the ground has been prepared, excavate a planting hole large enough to take a clump of bulbs – it should be about three times the depth of the bulbs.

2 Space the bulbs evenly, but as an irregular group, not in rows. Space at the distance recommended on the packet for economy, and for a long-term display, as the bulbs will multiply. For more impact in the first year, space the bulbs closer but not touching.

3 Draw the soil back over the bulbs with a rake, being careful not to dislodge them in the process.

4 Rake the soil level, taking care not to disturb the bulbs if small kinds are planted shallowly. Then firm the soil with the back of the rake.

5 Use small canes to indicate where the bulbs have been planted if there is any risk of cultivating the area before they appear. A label will ensure you remember what the variety is when spring arrives.

Bulb Combinations

Always make a point of noting successful plant combinations worth copying. These can be groupings of different kinds of bulbs, similar bulbs in different colour combinations, or bulbs with other kinds of plants.

COMBINING BULBS

Attractive bulb combinations include hyacinths and *Scilla siberica*, *Narcissus* 'Jack Snipe' with *Scilla siberica* again, and *Tulipa kaufmanniana* 'Heart's Delight' with *Chionodoxa luciliae*.

Plants with which to underplant bulbs include: polyanthus (primroses) beneath tulips; grape hyacinths with tulips; the red double daisy (*Bellis perennis*) with white, double late tulips; yellow polyanthus with blue hyacinths; blue pansies beneath pink tulips; and aubrieta beneath tulips.

For contrast, consider dark red tulips with pale yellow wallflowers; for a more harmonized effect, pale pink tulips with dark blue forget-me-nots, and for soft colours, pink tulips with yellow wallflowers.

Tall tulips are usually improved by being underplanted with forget-me-nots, which hide the leggy stems and often provide a backdrop of either a contrasting or a complementary colour.

Plant a small area at a time before continuing, otherwise it will be difficult to avoid disturbing the young plants.

Above: *The effect of this formal bed of vivid red tulips ('Arie Alkemade's Memory') and blue-purple hyacinths ('King of the Blues') has been softened with an underplanting of grape hyacinths.*

PLANTING IN FORMAL BEDS

1 After clearing summer-bedding plants and forking over the ground, removing weeds at the same time, rake in bonemeal if the soil is impoverished. This is not necessary if the soil is fertile and the bulbs are to be discarded after flowering.

2 If planting between spring-bedding plants such as wallflowers or forget-me-nots, plant them before the bulbs. Moisten the soil an hour or two before lifting from the nursery bed if you have grown your own supply.

3 Spring-bedding plants can be bought from garden centres. Wallflowers are sometimes sold in bundles without soil on their roots, but whenever possible choose plants grown in pots or containers.

4 Plant an area of bedding first, then position the bulbs between the plants. Work methodically, starting at the back, and planting the bulbs with minimum disturbance to the plants' roots.

PLANTING SMALL BULBS

1 To plant drifts of small bulbs, such as crocuses or snowdrops, lift an area of grass by making an H-shaped cut. If possible, use a half-moon edger rather than a spade, to ensure a straight edge.

2 Slice beneath each flap in turn, then roll or fold it back. If this is done carefully, the grass can be reinstated with minimal disturbance.

3 Loosen the ground before planting. For a small area, a hand fork should be adequate, but if the ground is very hard use a garden fork. It is worth forking in bonemeal or, alternatively, a slow-release fertilizer at this stage.

4 To create a natural-looking group, do not plant in rows. Scatter the bulbs and only respace those that are touching, or to fill a gap. Otherwise, plant where they fall.

5 Large bulbs can be planted using this method of lifting the grass, but usually there is space for just a few. Use a trowel or bulb planter, making sure the bulb will be covered with about twice its own depth of soil when the grass is returned.

6 Firm the soil, compressing it, if necessary, to avoid a raised area when the grass is folded back into position. Relift to make any adjustments as required. Firm the grass down, and water well in dry weather.

Forcing the Issue

EARLY FLOWERING BULBS

One of the joys of planting spring bulbs is that you can enjoy them in mid-winter. This paradox is perfectly possible if you choose suitably prepared or treated bulbs sold for forcing indoors into early flower. Unprepared bulbs may flower a little later, but for true winter flowering plant only bulbs sold for this purpose. Plant prepared bulbs as soon as possible after they come on sale to ensure best results.

Hyacinths are perhaps the most popular choice, but there are others you can try, too, such as narcissi, amarylis and even tulips (*see* opposite).

Above: *For a decorative effect, plant hyacinth bulbs in water in a glass cyclinder. The bulbs rest on large pebbles so that the roots reach down to the water below.*

HYACINTHS FOR EARLY FLOWERING

1 If using an ordinary pot with a drainage hole, use a normal potting compost (potting soil), but for a container without drainage holes use a special bulb-planting mixture formulated for the purpose. In some countries this is called bulb fibre.

2 Place a thin layer of the potting mixture in the bottom of the container – many bulbs can be forced with surprisingly little root-room. Position the bulbs on top; an odd number looks better than an even one.

3 Pack more potting soil around the bulbs, but leave sufficient space at the top for watering. Do not worry if their noses protrude from the soil. Ensure the soil is moist but not wet or waterlogged.

4 Place the bulbs in a cool, dark place until the shoots appear. A suitable place is a cold frame where they can be covered with 2.5 cm (1 in) of sand or grit. Keep moist but not wet, and be very careful not to waterlog containers without drainage holes. A cool, dark cupboard is an alternative.

5 Check the bulbs periodically, and bring them into the light indoors when the shoots are about 2.5cm (1in) high. Clean the container if it has been plunged outdoors, and place it in a cool, light position indoors or in a conservatory. Do not place in a warm room until the buds have emerged and are beginning to show colour.

OTHER BULBS TO TRY

Daffodils The cluster-flowered daffodils such as *Narcissus* 'Paper White' and 'Soleil d'Or' are extremely easy and reliable, but do not place them outside where they could be frosted. Prepared bulbs of ordinary garden daffodils are sometimes available, but they require careful temperature control.
Hippeastrums (amaryllis) These are not hardy and must be kept in warm conditions from planting. Follow the instructions on the packet or in the catalogue.
Lily of the valley (Convallaria majalis) Although the treated rhizomes are likely to be available only from specialist bulb suppliers, they make a fragrant alternative. They are not the easiest of plants to flower indoors, and the instructions supplied should be followed carefully.
Tulips Prepared tulips can flower indoors from mid-winter to spring. Unless growth is carefully temperature-controlled, however, they may not flower when predicted.

Left: *Lilies of the valley,* Convallaria majalis, *are deliciously fragrant and can be forced into early flower indoors.*

CARE AND MAINTENANCE

All plants require some attention from time to
time in order to keep them looking neat and tidy,
whether it be deadheading, trimming, or staking
and protecting. Just a little care and attention
will help plants keep looking their best.
One of the least attractive chores associated with
any garden plant is keeping it free of weeds, but
as long as you keep on top of it, this can be a
suprisingly relaxing pastime, at the same time
improving the long-term health and appearance
of your plants. A weed-free garden can also help
with the problems associated with pests and
diseases, though these can be controlled in a
number of ways. Most plants in the open ground
can look after themselves, but there will still be a
certain amount of watering and feeding to keep
them looking at their very best.

Left: *Border with* Alchemilla mollis, *nicotiana and roses.*

Watering and Feeding

Compared with other gardening jobs, watering is generally not an onerous task, and feeding, too, is rarely much of a problem, as long as the ground has been prepared well in the first place. The key to watering is to make sure that the ground contains plenty of well-rotted humus. This fibrous material holds moisture but does not cause the ground to become water-logged.

THE IMPORTANCE OF HUMUS

If humus is dug into the soil, it will hold the moisture down at root level, where it is needed. Spreading more organic material over the surface of the soil will help to prevent evaporation and thus also reduce the need to water. Black polythene (plastic) can also be used as a mulch, but looks ugly and is best covered with another mulch such as chipped bark. Farmyard manure, garden compost, chipped or composted bark and spent mushroom compost are among the best forms of mulch. If humus is dug in and the soil is given a top-dressing, there will be little need to water even in dry weather.

WATERING METHODS

Sandy soil does not retain moisture, and it may be necessary to water in dry spells. A sprinkler of some sort is undoubtedly the most effective method for a border.

Whatever method you decide to use, always make sure that the ground is thoroughly soaked. If you only wet the surface, you will actually do more harm than good as the plants will tend to form shallow roots, rather than seeking water from deep in the soil. Put a rain gauge or a jam jar within the range of the sprinkler and leave the sprinkler running until there is a reading of at least 2.5cm (1in) of water.

WHEN TO FEED

The same principles hold true for feeding. If the ground is thoroughly prepared in the first place, and then top-dressed with organic material, sufficient nutrients should be available to the plants, and there should be no need for further feeding. Remember that the organic material should be well rotted before it is added to the border, otherwise, in the process of breaking down, it will extract nitrogen from the soil.

Some gardeners who do not have access to much organic material also apply a light feed of a general, balanced fertilizer in spring, but unless your plants are looking particularly starved, there is no need to give them a liquid feed.

1 If they are prepared properly, most borders do not need watering, but in really dry periods a sprinkler is an effective way of covering a large area. Ensure that the ground is thoroughly soaked.

2 Containers are best watered by hand with a watering can. Again, be certain to give the pot a good soaking.

3 Sometimes it is necessary to pep up a flagging border towards the end of a long season. A liquid feed added to a watering can is a quick way to do this. Follow the instructions given by the manufacturer on the bottle.

4 Watering with a hand-held hose is time-consuming, but several manufacturers make fertilizer dispensers that can be fitted to a hosepipe – this is an easy way to supply feed.

5 Early in the season, if insufficient organic material has been used to top-dress the border, a sprinkling of a general fertilizer will help keep the plants in good condition.

Above: *If a border is fed and mulched in spring and autumn, it should not need further watering, except in very dry conditions.*

Staking

One important procedure that should not be neglected, both for the look of the border and the health of the plants, is staking. There are two important factors to remember: make the stakes discreet, so that they are as invisible as possible, and do stake early, before the plants flop.

PLANTS THAT NEED STAKING

Most gardeners find that at least one plant is blown over at some time during the year, and even in sheltered areas, where there is little or no wind, a heavy downpour of rain can cause problems, especially with double flowers, which tend to hold water. Double peonies, for example, have heavy flower-heads, which will often bow down under their own weight. When they are full of rainwater, they topple over as if they were filled with lead.

The key to solving these problems, as with so many aspects of gardening, is to anticipate possible trouble and to stake vulnerable plants before they are big enough to pose a problem. Once a plant has fallen over, it is impossible to stake it in a way that will make it look natural. Plants should always be staked before they are fully grown. This not only affords the plant protection before it is likely to need it, but also allows the plant to grow over its support so that this cannot be seen. Most plants need support between a half and two-thirds of the way up their eventual height, which means that the supports should be in position before the plant reaches half its height. The plant will then be able to grow through the framework.

USING PEA-STICKS

The best staking methods are those that provide some form of lattice through which the plant can grow. One of the most satisfactory methods is to use pea-sticks or brushwood, if available. These twiggy branches are pushed into the ground, right up against the plant. The top twigs are then bent over and interlaced or tied to form a grid through which the growing stems can pass. As the plant grows through the top and sides of this framework, its leaves will cover it, and will eventually hide it completely.

MAKING A CAT'S CRADLE

A similar method is to insert small stakes or canes in the ground and then weave a random cat's cradle of string around them. A more technical method, but one that has the same result, is to use ready-made hoops that have grids of wire welded across them. These are supported on sturdy wire legs at the appropriate height.

Left: *This garden displays a variety of different ways in which plants can be provided with support, including the use of large-mesh wire netting, pea-sticks, and a frame for climbing plants.*

MAKING A CAT'S CRADLE

1 A cheap but effective means of support can be created by forming a cat's cradle of canes and string. Push the canes into the soil around and in the middle of the clumps of plants that need to be supported.

2 Trim off the tops of the canes, so that they will not show above the plants when they are fully grown.

For large areas of plants a similar device can be made by supporting a sheet of large-mesh wire netting horizontally above the plants. The netting can be held in place quite easily, using a series of stakes or canes.

Interlocking stakes, which you should be able to find in most garden centres as well as in many hardware stores, can be placed in any shape, whether regular or irregular, around a clump of plants. A few of these stakes can also be placed horizontally in order to create a grid. They can also be used in a line to provide support for plants that otherwise would flop over a path or lawn. If you do find that you have neglected to stake your plants in time, then these stakes are the best way to lift plants back up again.

STAKING SINGLE PLANTS

All the methods described so far are for supporting clumps of plants. But some tall border plants – delphiniums and hollyhocks, for example – consist of one or a series of vulnerable spikes. These can be staked individually with long canes. If possible, place the cane behind the stem so that it is not so obvious when you are viewing the border. It is rarely necessary for the cane to be as tall as the stem, and a flower stem attached all the way up a tall cane will appear stiff and rigid, giving the plant an artificial look. A better approach is to support the lower part of the stem, allowing the top to move freely. In this way the stake will be less obtrusive, and the plant will appear more natural.

3 Weave string in a random pattern between all the canes so that a mesh of supports is created. At the end of the season, remove the supports from the plants.

Weed Control

One of the least attractive chores associated with any garden plant is keeping it free of weeds. This applies to all plants and shrubs, but as long as you keep on top of it, weeding can be a relaxing pastime. While weeding you are closer to the plants than you would be simply strolling past, so it is hardly surprising that this is when you will often notice detail in the flowers that you would normally miss. It also gives you the opportunity to check that each plant is healthy and not suffering from any pest or disease.

WEEDING

The secret of successful weeding is thorough ground preparation before you sow or plant and then to keep on top of the weeding by doing it regularly. Once you lose control of the weeds in a bed, they begin to take over, after which weeding becomes an uphill battle.

Never plant a bed that has weeds already in it. Clean it thoroughly first. Once you have planted, hoe between the plants regularly to kill any newly germinated weeds. Once the plants begin to fill out, hoeing will be less easy so you will have to resort to hand-weeding. However, by this stage there should be few weeds and it is more a matter of keeping an eye out for the odd weed and pulling it out before it can become too large or start spreading.

MULCHES

You can cut down considerably on the labour of weeding by preventing weed seeds from germinating, and a mulch is an effective way to achieve this, though it will not stop perennial weeds. A mulch is a layer of well-rotted organic material, chipped bark or a similar material, which is placed on the surface of the soil. When applying a mulch, always water first, then cover the soil with a 10cm (4in) layer.

Peat does not have much value as a mulch because it will blow away as soon as it dries out and it adds very little to the soil as it breaks down. Straw and grass cuttings can be used but they are extremely ugly and are best reserved for the back of beds where they are hidden from view by tall plants. Farmyard manure is good but quality varies and frequently it is full of weed seed just waiting to germinate.

HERBICIDES

Try to avoid using too many chemicals in the garden. It may be necessary, especially on heavy soils, to use herbicides to clear the ground initially, but after planting they are best avoided, as they are likely to damage adjacent plants.

EFFECTIVE WEEDING

1 Weeds should be eradicated for several reasons: they make a bed look untidy; they use up a great deal of moisture and nutrients; many harbour pests and diseases.

2 Where plants are close together, the best way of removing weeds is to either pull them out by hand or dig them out using a hand fork. Perennial weeds must be dug out whole and not simply chopped off, or they will soon return.

3 Where there is more room, hoes can be used in a border, but take care to avoid your precious plants. In hot weather hoed-up weeds can be left to shrivel, but it looks much neater if they are all removed to the compost heap.

4 After weeding, rake through the border with a fork, or if the plants are far enough apart with a rake. This will tidy up the bed and level off the surface, removing any footprints and any weed remnants.

Below: *This well-tended border is an excellent example of one in which the weeds are kept at bay partly by weeding and partly by close planting. This technique means that the weeds cannot become established.*

5 It is a good idea to apply or renew a mulch after weeding. As well as helping to prevent weeds from reappearing, this will also preserve moisture. Composted or chipped bark will set the plants off well.

Autumn and Winter Maintenance

A few hours spent working on a border in winter will save many hours the following year. There are a surprising number of autumn and winter days when the soil is sufficiently dry and the weather pleasant enough to get out into the garden and do some work, and you should take advantage of those days whenever you can.

WHEN TO TIDY

Some gardeners like to leave all the work in the garden until spring, and they usually cite two reasons for so doing. The first is that the dead stems of some plants can look attractive in the winter; the second is that they provide food and shelter for birds, insects and small mammals. Both points are undoubtedly true, but the rush to get everything done at the start of the year can be something of a nightmare, especially if the spring is wet. When plants have started into growth before you have had time to tackle them, trying to cut back dead stems without damaging the new shoots is far from easy.

On the other hand, if you work steadily through the winter months, not only will you be ahead of the game, you will also save yourself a great deal of work later on. Weeding in the winter means that you have more time to sit and enjoy the garden in the summer.

REMOVING OLD GROWTH

One of the major jobs in the garden is cutting down and removing the old stems from the previous year's plants. These should be cut off as low to the ground as possible with a pair of secateurs (pruners). Rather than burning or throwing away this material, compost it, shredding it first if it is woody, and return it to the soil once it has rotted down. You will need to prune the live growth of some plants and shrubs rather than simply cutting off the dead growth. Many of these – artemisias and penstemons, for example – are best left until spring.

WEEDING

Once you can see the ground, the next task is to remove any weeds. Avoid using a hoe because you may accidentally damage shoots and bulbs that are just below the surface. Weed by hand, using a hand or border fork. When the border is clean, lightly dig between the plants, but avoid getting too close to them, especially those with spreading, shallow roots. Cover the whole border with a layer of well-rotted organic material, such as farmyard manure.

While you are working through the border, divide any plants that are becoming too congested. Dig them out, divide them and replant them after rejuvenating the soil by digging it over and incorporating humus.

MAINTENANCE TASKS

1 It might seem like an impossible task to turn the overgrown mess shown above into an attractive border, but, if you work steadily throughout the winter, the border will be transformed.

2 Carefully cut back all dead stems as close to the ground as possible. As winter passes, more shoots will appear at the base and care will be needed not to damage them.

3 Some herbaceous plants remain green throughout winter. Cut back to sound growth, removing dead and leggy material.

4 Here, the old stems have been cut off so that they are level with the emerging growth, so as not to damage it.

5 Lightly dig over the soil around the plants and shrubs, removing any weeds. Avoid digging around plants such as asters which have shallow roots.

6 Top-dress around the plants with some organic material, such as well-rotted compost, farmyard manure or composted bark. Avoid using peat.

7 Some plants need some form of winter protection. Here, the crowns of some gunneras have been covered with their own leaves from the previous season.

Dealing with Weather Problems

Weather, in particular winter weather, can cause problems for the gardener. Throughout the year, winds can break branches of shrubs and flatten tall-growing plants. Such plants should be firmly staked. If boughs or stems do break, cut them neatly back to a convenient point. If the wind is a constant problem, it becomes necessary to create a windbreak of some sort to protect your garden.

PROTECTING AGAINST THE ELEMENTS

Frost can cause a lot of damage to plants, especially late or early frosts, which can catch new growth and flowers unexpectedly. Even hardy spring-flowering bulbs are sensitive to cold if planted in exposed containers. Some summer-and-autumn-flowering ones, such as crinums and nerines, are only borderline hardy, and in extreme winter weather they will benefit from a protective mulch. General cold during the winter can be dealt with more easily because it is relatively predictable: either cover the plants or plant them next to a wall, which will provide warmth and shelter.

Drought can be a problem, especially if it is not expected. Defend against drought when preparing the bed by incorporating plenty of moisture-retaining organic material. Once planted, most plants benefit from a thick mulch, which will help hold the moisture in.

There are some plants that do not tolerate wet weather. Most plants with silver leaves, such as *Convolvulus cneorum* and lavenders prefer to grow in fairly dry conditions and lilies in particular hate having their roots constantly in wet soil.

Unfortunately there is little that can be done to protect such plants from the rain, although making their soil more free-draining by adding grit to the soil, or by growing them in well-drained containers usually helps.

Some plants prefer a shady position away from the sun. Many rhododendrons and azaleas, for example, prefer to be out of the hot sun and clematis dislike having sun on their roots. These can either be planted in the shade of a building or under trees or beneath taller shrubs.

WINDBREAKS

If there are perpetual problems with wind, it is essential to create some sort of windbreak. In the short term this can be plastic netting, but a more permanent solution is to create a living windbreak. A number of trees and shrubs can be used for this: *Leylandii* are often used, because they are one of the quickest-growing.

SHRUBS AND TREES FOR WINDBREAKS

Acer pseudoplatanus (sycamore)
Berberis darwinii
Buxus sempervirens (box)
Carpinus betulus (hornbeam)
Choisya ternata
Corylus avellana (hazel)
Cotoneaster simonsii
Crataegus monogyma (hawthorn)
Elaeagnus x ebbingei
Escallonia 'Langleyensis'
Euonymus japonicus 'Macrophyllus'
Fraxinus excelsior (ash)
Griselinia littoralis
Hippophaë rhamnoides (sea buckthorn)
Ilex (holly)
Ligustrum ovalifolium (privet)
Lonicera nitida (box-leaf honeysuckle)
Picea sitchensis (sitka spruce)
Pinus sylvestris (Scots pine)
Pittosporum tenuifolium
Prunus laurocerasus (cherry laurel)
Prunus lusitanica (Portuguese laurel)
Pyracantha (firethorn)
Rosmarinus officinalis (rosemary)
Sorbus aucuparia (rowan)
Tamarix (tamarisk)
Taxus baccata (yew)
Viburnum tinus (laurustinus)

Above: *Hedges are frequently used as windbreaks to protect the whole or specific parts of the garden. Whilst they are becoming established, they themselves may also need some protection, usually in the form of plastic netting. Here privet (*Ligustrum*) has been chosen.*

PROTECTING FROM WINTER COLD

1 Many shrubs, like this bay (*Laurus nobilis*) need some degree of winter protection. This shrub is in a container, but the same principles can be applied to free-standing plants. Insert a number of canes around the edge of the plant, taking care not to damage the roots.

2 Cut a piece of fleece, hessian (burlap) or bubble polythene (plastic) to the necessary size, making sure you allow for an overlap over the shrub and pot. Fleece can be bought as a sleeve, which is particularly handy for enveloping plants.

3 Wrap the protective cover around the plant, allowing a generous overlap. For particularly tender plants, use a double layer.

4 Tie the protective cover around the pot, or lightly around the plant if it is in the ground. Fleece can be tied at the top as moisture can penetrate through, but if using plastic, leave it open for ventilation and watering.

5 Protecting with hessian (burlap) or plastic shade netting should be enough for most plants, but if a plant should require extra protection, wrap it in straw and then hold this in place with hessian or shade netting.

Above: *Late frost can ruin the flowering of a bush. This azalea has been caught on the top by the frost, but the sides were sufficiently sheltered to be unaffected. A covering of fleece would have given it complete protection.*

Right: *Lilac (Syringa) can be affected by late frosts which nip out the flowering buds preventing displays such as this.*

Caring for Climbers

Climbers are relatively maintenance-free and look after themselves, apart from one or two essential things. These essentials are, however, crucial not only to ensuring a good "performance" from your climbers, but also in making your garden safe for you and other users; so don't neglect these jobs, as they are important.

ESSENTIAL JOBS

The most important task is to be certain that the climber is well supported. Make regular checks that the main supports are still secure to the wall or that posts have not rotted or become loose in the wind.

Tie in any stray stems as they appear. If they are left, the wind may damage them. A worse situation can arise with thorned climbers, such as roses, whose thrashing stems may damage other plants or even passers-by. If they are not essential, cut off any stray stems to keep the climber neat and safe.

Throughout the flowering season, a climbing plant's appearance is improved by removing old flower heads. Dead-heading also prevents the plant from channelling vital resources into seed production, and thus frees energy for more flowering and growth.

WINTER PROTECTION

In winter, it may be important to protect the more tender climbers from the weather. Walls give a great deal of protection and may be sufficient for many plants but, even here, some plants may need extra protection if there is the possibility of a severe winter. One way is simply to drape hessian (burlap) or shade netting over the plant, to give temporary protection against frosts. For more prolonged periods, first protect the climber with straw and then cover this with hessian.

Keep an eye on climbers with variegated foliage, as some have the habit of reverting, that is, the leaves turn back to their normal green. If the stems bearing these leaves are not removed, the whole climber may eventually revert, losing its attractive foliage.

ROUTINE CARE

1 When vigorous climbers are grown against a house wall, they can become a nuisance once they have reached roof level.

4 Most climbers will produce stems that float around in space and that will need attention to prevent them being damaged or causing damage to other plants or passers-by. This *solanum* definitely needs some attention.

5 Regularly tie in any stray stems to the main supports. In some cases, it will be easier to attach them to other stems, rather than the supports. Always consider the overall shape of the climber and how you want to encourage it to grow in the future.

6 Sometimes it is better to cut off stray stems, either because there are already ample in that area or because they are becoming a nuisance. Trim them off neatly back to a bud or a branch. Sometimes, such stems will make useful cutting material from which to grow new plants.

2 At least once a year, cut back the new growth to below the level of the gutters and around the windows.

3 Dead-head regularly. If the dead flower is part of a truss, just nip out that flower; if the whole truss has finished, cut back the stem to a bud or leaf.

7 For light protection, especially against unseasonal frosts, hang shade netting or hessian (burlap) around the climber.

8 If the plant is against a wall, hang the shade netting or hessian from the gutter or from some similar support. This is a useful method of protecting new shoots and early flowers. For really tender plants, put a layer of straw around the stems of the climber and then hold it in place with a sheet of shade netting or hessian. Remove as soon as the plant begins to grow.

Above: *The overall effect of tying-in will be a neater and more satisfying shape. If possible, spread out the stems so that the climber looks fuller and less crowded.*

Providing Support for Climbers

When considering the choice and position of a climbing plant, it is important to take into account the method by which it climbs. While an ivy will support itself with modified roots on a brick wall, a rose, which is used to scrambling through bushes in the wild, will need to be tied to wires or trellis that has been attached to the wall.

CLINGING CLIMBERS
Hedera canariensis (Canary Island ivy)
Hedera colchica (Persian ivy)
Hedera helix (common ivy)
Hydrangea anomala petiolaris (climbing hydrangea)
Parthenocissus henryana (Chinese Virginia creeper)
Parthenocissus quinquefolia (Virginia creeper)
Parthenocissus tricuspida (Boston ivy)

CLIMBING HABITS
When buying a climbing plant, always consider the way it climbs and check that it is suitable for your purpose. If you want to cover a wall, and money is tight, an ivy is the best choice as it will cost no more than the plant, whereas the rose will also incur the price of the supporting structure. On the other hand, if you later want to paint the wall, it will be impossible to remove the ivy to do so, while a rose on a hinged or clipped trellis can be moved away from the wall to allow the operation to go ahead.

Above: Hydrangea anomala petiolaris *clings to wall surfaces by putting out modified roots.*

CLINGING CLIMBERS
True climbers are able to attach themselves to their supports. To do this, they have roots or modified roots that grip firmly on the surface of the support. They will attach themselves to any surface, including smooth ones such as glass and plastic. They need little attention, except for cutting them back from around windows and periodically cutting them off at the top of the wall so that they do not foul gutters or creep under tiles. If a wall is in good condition, there is little to fear from these climbers in terms of damage that they might inflict.

Right: *Clinging plants will cover any vertical surface without needing any support.*

CLIMBERS THAT USE TENDRILS

Many climbing plants have adapted themselves so that, although they do not cling to a smooth support, they can attach themselves to branches and other protrusions by means of tendrils. These are modified stems, or even leaves, which curl round the support.

Tendril plants will not climb up a wall unless there is already another plant on it or unless there is a mesh that they can attach themselves to. If a trellis or wires are used and the supporting strands are far apart, the stems will wave about until they are long enough to find something to which to cling; you may need to tie them in, to prevent them from breaking off. Closely woven mesh or another well-branched plant or tree provide the best supports for this type of climber.

CLIMBERS THAT USE TENDRILS

Campsis radicans
    (trumpet creeper)
Clematis
Cobaea scandens
    (cathedral bells)
Lathyrus (peas)
Mutisia
Vitis (vine)
Passiflora (passion flower)

Right: *The overall effect of a wall covered entirely by clematis is a mass of flower and foliage.*

Below: *Clematis puts out tendrils that entwine round a supporting structure, such as wire netting or another plant.*

SCRAMBLING CLIMBERS

In the wild, apart from those that cling to cliffs, most climbers are supported by other plants. While some have adapted themselves to twine or to use tendrils, the majority just push themselves up through the supporting plant, using its framework of branches and twigs as their support. Make use of this technique in the garden by allowing climbers to ramble up through shrubs and trees. The results look natural and there is the added advantage of using the climber to add interest to a shrub or tree that has passed its flowering season.

If the climbers are needed for a more formal situation, such as over a pergola or up a trellis or wall, artificial supports will be required. As the plants have no natural way of attaching themselves to a trellis, you will have to devise means of attaching them. For a wall, either use special lead-headed nails for attaching each branch or stem separately, or erect a framework of wires or trellis to which to tie the stems in with string or plant ties. This latter method is suitable for a pergola too. The tying in should be done at regular intervals.

TYPES OF TIES

There are various different materials for tying in stems. String is the most readily available and the cheapest. Use soft garden string for short-term (up to a year) tying in and tarred string for longer periods. Special twists made from thin wire covered with plastic "wings" are sold for garden use, although the version provided with plastic food bags is just as good.

Above: *Materials for tying in climbers* (left to right)*: heavy-duty plastic tie; plastic twist tie; narrow plastic tie; tarred string; soft garden string.*

These are best used as temporary ties. Of more permanent use are plastic ties, which come in various sizes, from those suitable for holding stems, to those that will cope with small tree-trunks.

1 Use special lead-headed nails to attach the stems of scramblers to walls.

2 The malleable lead head can be wrapped around the stem to secure it.

Right: *Take advantage of scrambling climbers' natural habit of growing through other plants by growing a rose through an old apple tree.*

SCRAMBLING CLIMBERS

Akebia	*Rosa* (rose)
Actinidia (some)	*Solanum* (nightshade)
Bougainvillea	*Thunbergia alata*
Eccremocarpus scaber (Chilean	(black-eyed Susan)
glory flower)	*Trachelospermum*
Fallopia baldschuanica	*Tropaeolum*
(Russian vine)	(nasturtium)
Passiflora (passion-flower)	*Vinca* (periwinkle)
Plumbago capensis	*Vitis* (grapevine)
Rhodochiton atrosanguineus	*Wisteria*

TWINING PLANTS

Some climbers twine their stems round the support as they grow. Plants that adopt this technique can be grown up poles or trellis, or through trees and shrubs. The stems automatically twist round their support, so little attention is required except to tie in any wayward shoots that might thrash around in the wind and get damaged.

Right: *The stems of twining climbers wind themselves round any support they can find as they grow, so, once you have provided the support, they will do the rest.*

Below: *Here, a hop has covered a metal arch with a shower of green leaves, supported by a mass of curling stems.*

TWINING CLIMBERS

Actinidia (some)
Humulus lupulus (hop)
Ipomoea (morning glory)
Lonicera (honeysuckle)
Phaseolus (climbing beans)

WALL SHRUBS

In gardening parlance, the term "climbing plants" is often liberally interpreted to include any plants that are grown up against walls. This can, in fact, include more or less any shrub. Generally, however, there are some shrubs that are best suited to this position, either because of their appearance or because they need the protection of the wall against the vagaries of the weather. Some are strong enough shrubs not to need support, except, perhaps, to be tied the wall to prevent them from being blown forward. Others need a more rigid support and should be tied into wires or a framework to keep them steady.

Above: Pyracantha *is a perfect wall shrub; it has flowers in the early summer and colourful berries in the autumn. Its branches are viciously thorned, making it a good burglar deterrent to plant on walls around windows.*

WALL SHRUBS

Abutilon
Azara
Carpenteria californica
Ceanothus (Californian lilac)
Cotoneaster
Euonymus fortunei
Magnolia
Pyracantha (firethorn)
Teucrium fruticans
   (shrubby germander)

Moving a Shrub

The ideal, when planting shrubs, is to place them in the right position first time round, but, occasionally, it becomes necessary to move one. If the shrub has only been in the ground a few weeks, this is not too much of a problem: simply dig around the plant, lifting it with as big a ball of earth as possible on the spade and move it to a ready-prepared new hole. Moving a well-established shrub requires more thought and planning.

MOVING A WELL-ESTABLISHED SHRUB TO A NEW HOME

If the move is part of a long-term plan, there may well be time to root-prune the shrub first, a few months before you intend to move it. This involves digging a trench or simply slicing a sharp spade into the soil around the shrub, to sever the roots. This encourages the shrub to produce more fibrous feeding roots on the remaining roots and makes it easier for it to become established once it is moved.

Once you have moved the shrub, keep it well-watered and, as with all newly-planted shrubs,

if it is in a windy situation, protect it with windbreak netting to prevent excessive transpiration. Shrubs that have been moved are likely to be vulnerable to wind-rock and so it is important to stake them firmly.

A shrub with a large ball of earth around its roots is a very heavy and unwieldy object to move. This can be a recipe for a back injury, so be very careful. Always get somebody to help, if possible. This will also ensure you don't drop the plant, causing the soil around the roots to drop off, which makes it far more difficult to re-establish the plant.

1 If possible, root-prune the shrub a few months before moving, to encourage the formation of new fibrous roots. Water the plant well the day before moving it.

2 Dig a trench around the plant, leaving a rootball that two people can comfortably lift. Sever any roots you encounter to release the rootball.

3 Dig under the shrub, cutting through any tap roots that hold it in place.

4 Rock the plant to one side and insert some hessian (burlap) sacking or strong plastic sheeting as far under the plant as you can. Push several folds of material under the rootball.

5 Rock it in the opposite direction and pull the hessian sacking or plastic sheeting through, so that it is completely under the plant.

6 Pull the sheeting round the rootball so that it completely encloses the soil and tie it firmly around the neck of the plant. The shrub is now ready to move. If it is a small plant, one person may be able to lift it out of the hole and transfer it to its new site.

7 If the plant plus the soil is heavy, it is best moved by two people. This can be made much easier by tying a bar of wood or metal to the trunk of the shrub or to the sacking. With one person on each end, lift the shrub out of the hole.

8 Prepare the ground and hole as for a new shrub and lower the transplanted shrub into it. Follow the reverse procedure, unwrapping and removing the sheeting from the rootball. Ensure the plant is in the right position and refill the hole.

Right: *Once the shrub has been replanted in its new position, water it thoroughly and mulch the soil around it. In more exposed positions place netting round it to prevent winds from drying the plant out and scorching it. It may also need protection from fierce sun. Moving a shrub in autumn or winter, as long as it is not too cold or wet, will allow it to become established in time for its first summer.*

Pinching Out, Dead-heading and Trimming

Many plants have a long flowering season, often extending from early summer into the autumn and sometimes beyond. Needless to say, they will need a little bit of attention from time to time in order to keep them looking neat.

PINCHING OUT

If left to their own devices, many plants will grow only one main stem. In a bedding scheme, for example, this would result in a forest of tall spindly spikes with large gaps in between them rather than a desirable carpet of flowers and foliage. To avoid this effect, pinch out the growing tip of each main spike. This will cause the stem to produce side shoots. These will make the plants much more bushy, and further pinching out will increase the effect.

DEAD-HEADING

As the season progresses, flowers appear, then die, once they have been pollinated and have served their purpose. The petals go brown and look ugly, spoiling the effect of the still perfect flowers around them. Regular dead-heading keeps everything neat and tidy and looking in much better condition.

Another good reason for regular dead-heading is to prevent seed formation. Producing seed is the natural goal of every flowering plant, and once they have been pollinated, they direct all their energy into forming the seeds, then die. If their fading flowers are removed, they will redirect their energy into producing more flowers for the gardener.

TRIMMING BACK

New flowers are normally produced towards the tips of shoots, so as the season progresses and more and more flowers are produced, the stems get longer and longer. Before too long the plants begin to look somewhat straggly. Cut these stems back every so often so that new shoots are formed, keeping the plant compact. You can do this all at once but the plant may take a while to recover its flowering habit, so it is preferable to cut a few off at a time to prevent any interruption in flowering.

TOOLS

Secateurs (pruners) are the most versatile of tools, especially those that have pointed jaws so that you can get right into the leaf joints. Strong pointed scissors are also useful, especially for small plants. Knives can be used in most situations as long as they are sharp. Many stems can be snapped or pinched out with the fingers or fingernails, but make certain that the action is clean-cut and does not bruise the stem.

1 Many plantswill grow up as a single stem, making rather spindly growth. However, if the tip is pinched out, side shoots will develop and the plant will become bushy and much more attractive. Cut through the stem with secateurs or a knife, just above a leaf joint.

2 The pinched-out plants fill out, creating a solid mass of attractive foliage. Planted together they make an attractive mass planting.

DEAD-HEADING

1 Dead heads left on plants, especially light-coloured flowers as seen here, look very scruffy if they are not removed regularly. Another good reason for dead-heading is to redirect the energy that would normally go into seed production into producing new flowers.

2 Using scissors, a sharp knife or secateurs, snip off the flowers neatly and cleanly where they join the stem. Sometimes the whole head of flowers needs to be removed, in which case cut these back to the first set of leaves. Dead flower heads and other clippings can be added to the compost heap.

TIDYING UP

3 Regular and carefully executed dead-heading produces a much cleaner and healthier looking arrangement. It takes only a short time and the effort is worthwhile.

1 Some edging plants spread out over the grass, possibly killing it or creating bald patches, as has this poached egg plant (Limnanthes douglasii).

2 If the plant has finished flowering, as here, it can be removed completely. Otherwise, just cut back the part that is encroaching on grass. On a brick or stone path, there may be no problem, though it could still cause people to stumble.

Bulb Care

Bulbs, including corms and tubers, have a natural reserve of nutrients that they can draw upon. This is the reason why colchicums, for example, will flower without even being planted, and why hyacinths can flower in water – but they will always respond to extra care and attention.

FEEDING

Even bulbs that give an impressive performance in the first season after planting may deteriorate rapidly in future years unless the plants are given a feed during the growing season. The majority of summer and autumn bulbs can be fed with a general balanced fertilizer that you should use on all flower beds and borders in spring and early summer. Only a few, such as dahlias, require regular feeding throughout the growing season, and even this is not essential for a general garden display.

The best time to feed bulbs is when flowering has finished. From then until the leaves die down the bulbs build up reserves of nutrients for the next season. Apply a balanced garden fertilizer around the plants and carefully hoe it in. Water in dry weather. If possible, hardy bulbs are best left undisturbed, but those used in beds that have to be replanted with summer flowers must be lifted. Once the foliage has died back they can be lifted and dried, ready to be stored in a cool, dry place until planting in the autumn time.

LIFTING BULBS

If the new bed is required for other plants, it may be necessary to move the bulbs before they have had an opportunity to die back naturally. Lift the plants carefully with a garden fork, damaging the roots as little as possible, and retaining plenty of soil on them. Find a spare piece of ground where the bulbs can grow on until they die back, and make a shallow trench with a spade. Gently slope one of the sides to rest the stems against. Place the lifted bulbs in a shallow trench, then return the soil to cover them. Water in well, and keep moist if the weather is dry.

Once the foliage has died back, lift the bulbs if the ground is required for other plants. Dry them off in a warm, dry place, such as a greenhouse, and allow the old stems to shrivel before cleaning the bulbs. Pull off any dead stems and the remains of old roots before storing.

Clean up the bulbs and place small offsets from the bulbs on one side to grow on in a spare piece of ground to reach flowering size. Store all the bulbs in paper bags and keep in a cool, dry place.

LIFTING AND STORING GLADIOLI

1 At the end of the season, loosen the soil and lift gladioli corms carefully. To save and grow the cormlets around the base, take care not to pull the corms out of the ground roughly. Cut off most of the stem, leaving a stub attached to the corm.

2 Place the lifted corms in a shed or greenhouse to dry. Once the old stem has dried, usually after a week or two, break it or cut it off with secateurs (pruners), being careful not to damage the corm.

3 Remove the small cormlets from around the base of the corm. If you want to grow them, store them separately and plant out in spring; otherwise discard them. Break off the old shrivelled corm at the base of the new one, and discard.

4 Store gladiolus corms in paper bags, or in trays, in a frost-free place. Do not forget to label them.

Dealing with Pests and Diseases

In a well-managed garden, pests and diseases should not be too much of a problem. A variety of plants, a watchful eye for any infestation and good garden hygiene are the essential keynotes.

THE BENEFITS OF VARIETY

The greater the variety of plants you grow in the garden, the fewer pests and diseases you are likely to encounter, because the greatest problems come with monocultures. If you grow only roses, for example, there is lots of foods for aphids, and once they start breeding they spread very rapidly, and become almost uncontrollable. In a mixed herbaceous border, not only is the number of plants that will be attacked by aphids limited, but there are also plenty of host plants for their predators the ladybirds and hoverflies, and so a balance is struck and the gardener rarely has to interfere. The same applies with diseases such as blackspot: since not all plants will be affected, the damage will be limited.

KEEPING THE GARDEN TIDY

Clearing away dead leaves and dying material will remove the homes and food for many pests and diseases. Compost this type of material, unless it is diseased itself. Many weeds are hosts to diseases, especially fungal ones. Vigilance while weeding should prevent these diseases from spreading. If pests and diseases do gain hold, it may be necessary to apply chemical controls. Always follow the instructions on the packet.

Slugs can be one of the worst pests that the gardener is likely to meet. A healthy lupin can be gnawed to the ground overnight. You can use bait, but going out over several consecutive nights with a torch and destroying them will usually bring the situation under control.

IDENTIFYING THE PROBLEM

Aphids: The most troublesome are likely to be the common greenfly and blackfly, which will attack plants and bulbs alike.

Botrytis: Also known as grey mould, this is a widespread fungal disease. Poor garden hygiene, overcrowding or lack of air circulation are causes.

Bulb and corm rots: Various fungi and bacteria cause bulbs, corms and tubers to rot. Soaking bulbs in a fungicide solution before planting may help.

Lily beetle: The adult beetle is bright red and 6 mm (¼ in) long. The beetle and its grubs can destroy a lily by eating the leaves and flowers. These, along with snails, can be one of the worst pests that the gardener is likely to meet. Destroying them by hand is very effective.

Viruses: These can be impossible to see, so you can judge an infection only by the symptoms, which include stunted growth and distorted or unevenly coloured leaves.

1 Chemicals provide a way of controlling pests and diseases. Although more and more gardeners are trying to avoid the use of chemicals, there are times when any other solution is difficult.

2 Fungal diseases, such as mildew, seen here, are often a problem, especially in either very dry or very wet years. Asters are particularly prone to mildew but they do not seem to suffer if it goes untreated.

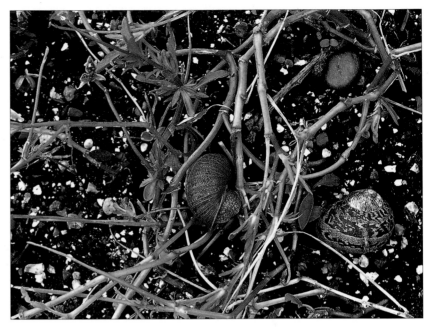

3 Butterfly and moth caterpillars can cause a lot of damage to both flowers and foliage. Usually sufficient control can be had by picking them off by hand. If necessary there are sprays and dusts that can be used.

4 Slugs and snails are two of the gardener's worst enemies. The worst time is late winter and early spring when new growth is reduced so much that plants fail to grow. Hand picking at night with the aid of a torch is one of the most effective methods of control.

5 Rabbit and other mammal damage can be heart-breaking as they will often browse a plant to the ground. Physical control by surrounding the garden with a wire netting fence is the best defence.

6 Aphids, green fly and blackfly are some of the most common insect pests. A mixed garden usually attracts enough predators to keep them under control. However when serious outbreaks occur then chemical control may be the only solution, but it must be done with care.

PRUNING AND PROPAGATION

Pruning is the one thing that gardeners worry about more than anything else and it results in many being too frightened to do any pruning, feeling that it is best to leave things well alone. While this may work with a number of plants, it is best to get into the habit of regularly checking all plants and pruning those that need it. Certainly the plants will benefit from this because they will eventually deteriorate if left to their own devices. Growing a plant from seed is one of the easiest methods of propagation as well as being satisfying, however, it can take rather a long time. Other types of propagation, including taking cuttings, layering and buying seedlings can take much less time and be just as rewarding.

Left: Papaver commutatum, Atriplex hortensis *var.* rubra *and* Coreopsis verticillata.

PRUNING TECHNIQUES

Principles of Pruning

Pruning is the one thing that gardeners worry about more than anything else. The upshot is that many are frightened to do any pruning, feeling that it is probably best to leave things alone. While this may work with some plants, it is best to get into the habit of regularly checking all shrubs and climbers, and pruning those that need it. Certainly, the plants will benefit from this and will eventually deteriorate if left to their own devices.

BASIC PRUNING

There are several basic elements to pruning and taking them one step at a time makes the process easier. The first step is to remove all dead wood. This opens up the plant and makes it easier to see what is happening. The second is to remove any diseased wood. These are easy steps as it is not difficult to decide what to remove. The third stage is more difficult but becomes easier with practice. This is to remove any weak wood from the plant and to cut off stems that cross or rub others. Finally, to keep a plant vigorous it is important to encourage new growth. The way to do this is to remove a few of the oldest stems. Up to a third of the plant can be removed at any one time. Finally, check to see if any stems need removing to give the plant an attractive shape. Use sharp secateurs (pruners) or a saw for thicker branches, and keep your pruning cuts clean.

GOOD CUTS

1 A good pruning cut is made just above a strong bud, about 3 mm (⅛ in) above the bud. It should be a slanting cut, with the higher end above the bud. The bud should generally be outward bound from the plant rather than inward; the latter will throw its shoot into the plant, crossing and rubbing against others, which should be avoided. This is an easy technique and you can practise it on any stem.

2 If the stem has buds or leaves opposite each other, make the cut horizontal, again about 3 mm (⅛ in) above the buds.

PRUNING THICKER BRANCHES

Most stems can be removed with secateurs (pruners), but thicker branches of large shrubs and rambling roses will require the use of a sharp pruning saw.

The major problem of cutting thicker stems is that they usually have a considerable weight. If cut straight through, this weight bends the stem before the cut has been completed, tearing the branch below the cut back to the main stem or trunk. The following technique avoids this. It is no longer considered necessary to paint large cuts to protect them.

1 Make a cut from the underside of the stem. Cut about half-way through or until the saw begins to bend as the weight of the stem closes the gap, pinching the saw.

2 Next, make a second cut from the upper edge of the stem, this time about 2.5 cm (1 in) away from the previous cut and further away from the main stem. The weight of the stem will then cause it to split across to the first cut so that the main part of the branch falls to the ground.

3 Make the third cut straight through the stem at the place to which you want to cut back. This should not tear the stem, because the weight has gone.

BAD CUTS

 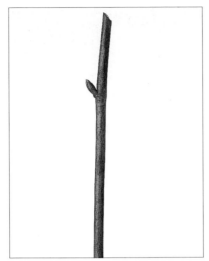  

3 Always use a sharp pair of secateurs (pruners). Blunt ones will produce a ragged or bruised cut, which is likely to introduce disease into the plant.

4 Do not cut too far above a bud. The piece of stem above the bud is likely to die back and the stem may well die back even further, causing the loss of the whole stem.

5 Do not cut too close to the bud otherwise the bud might be damaged by the secateurs (pruners) or disease might enter. Too close a cut is likely to cause the stem to die back to the next bud.

6 It is bad practice to slope the cut towards the bud as this makes the stem above the bud too long, which is likely to cause dieback. It also sheds rain on to the bud, which may cause problems.

DECIDING WHEN TO PRUNE

Perhaps the most difficult aspect of pruning is deciding when to do it. Gardeners worry that if they do it at the wrong time they might kill the plant. This is possible but unlikely. The worst that usually happens is that you cut off all the stems that will produce the year's flowers and so you miss a season. As a rule of thumb, most shrubs need to be pruned immediately after they have flowered, so that they have time to produce new mature stems by the time they need to flower again.

Above: Rosa *'Bantry Bay'* climbing up a metal obelisk. *Roses need to be dead-headed and pruned to keep them at their best. If you don't care for them properly, the plants become very straggly and flowering diminishes.*

Above: *Wisterias are grown for their magnificent flowers and are suitable for growing against walls, buildings and even trees. They also make good climbers for pergolas. They should be pruned after flowering and again in the winter. This is Japanese wisteria* (Wisteria floribunda).

Pruning Shrubs

Apart from pruning a shrub to improve its shape, you may also need to prune out potential problems, such as damage and disease. Once a year, thoroughly check whether your plant needs attention.

CUTTING OUT DEAD WOOD

Cut out all dead wood from the shrub. This can be done at pruning time or at any other time of year when you can see dead material. Cut the dead wood out where it reaches live wood, which may be where the shoot joins a main stem or at the base of the plant. If the shrub is a large, tangled one, it may be necessary to cut out the dead branches bit by bit, as the short sections may be easier to remove than one long piece, especially if the stems have thorns that catch on everything.

CUTTING OUT CROSSING STEMS

Most shrubs grow out from a central point, with their branches arching gracefully outwards. However, sometimes a shoot will grow in towards the centre of the bush, crossing other stems in its search for light on the other side of the shrub. While there is nothing intrinsically wrong with this growth pattern, it is best to remove such branches as they will soon crowd the other branches and will often chafe against them, rubbing off the bark from the stem.

CUTTING OUT DIEBACK

I Tips of stems often die back, especially those that have carried bunches of flowers. Another cause is the young growth at the tip of shoots being killed by frost. If this die-back is not cut out, it can eventually kill off the whole shoot. Even if die-back proceeds no further it is still unsightly and the bush looks much tidier without these dead shoots. Cut the shoot back into good wood, just above a strong bud.

CUTTING OUT CROSSING STEMS

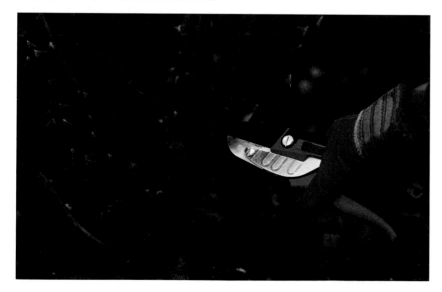

I Cut out the stems while they are still young and free from damage and disease. Using secateurs (pruners), cut the stem at its base where it joins the main branch.

CUTTING OUT DISEASED OR DAMAGED WOOD

I Cut any diseased or damaged wood back to sound wood, just above a strong bud. The wood is usually quite easy to spot. It may not be dead yet but still in the process of turning brown or black.

HARD PRUNING

1 There are a few shrubs – buddlejas are the main example – which benefit from being cut hard back each spring, much improving the foliage. Elders (*Sambucus*) and the purple smoke bush (*Cotinus*) are best treated in this way. *Rosa glauca* also responds very well to this type of pruning.

2 Cut the shoots right back almost to the ground, making the cuts just above an outward-facing bud and leaving little more than a stump. It may seem a little drastic, but the shrubs will quickly grow again in the spring. If they are not cut back, they become very leggy and do not make such attractive bushes.

3 Several plants that have attractive coloured bark in the winter are best cut to the ground in the spring.

4 So by the following winter, new attractive shoots will be displayed. The various coloured-stemmed *Rubus*, such as *R. cockburnianus* as well as some of the dogwoods (*Cornus* 'sibirica') and willows (*Salix*) are good candidates for this treatment.

DEAD-HEADING

1 Regular dead-heading will keep the shrub looking tidy and will also help promote further flowering. Roses, in particular, appreciate regular attention. Cut the flowering stems back to a bud or stem division.

Right: *The flowering on roses will always be improved if they are regularly dead-headed. This vigorous, multi-coloured rose is 'Miss Pam Ayres'.*

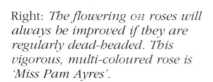

Basic Pruning for Climbers

The basics of pruning are not at all difficult, although the task of tackling a huge climber that covers half the house may seem rather daunting. Break it into three logical stages to make it more manageable.

THREE-STAGE PRUNING

The first pruning stage is to remove all dead wood. These stems are now of no use and only make the climber congested. Moreover, clearing these first will enable you to see where to prune next.

The second stage is to remove diseased and dying wood. This type of wood is usually obvious and should be taken out before it affects the rest of the plant.

The third stage is to remove some of the older wood. This has the effect of causing the plant to throw up new growth, which ensures the plant's continuing survival and keeps it vigorous, producing plenty of healthy flowers.

DISPOSAL OF WASTE

How to get rid of the mass of waste material pruned from climbing plants has always been a problem. The traditional method was to burn it but this is a waste of organic material and creates environmental problems, especially in urban areas. The best way is to shred it (avoiding diseased material). The waste is then composted for a couple of months and then returned to the beds as a valuable mulch. If you do not own a shredder then perhaps it is possible to borrow or hire one. Some local authorities run recycling schemes in which they compost all organic garden waste for reuse. The last resort is to take it to the local refuse tip. Do not dump waste in the countryside.

PRUNING OUT DISEASED WOOD

1 Remove any diseased wood, cutting it back to a point on the stem where the wood is again healthy. If the cut end shows that the wood is still diseased on the inside of the stem, cut back further still.

REMOVING OLD WOOD

1 Up to a third of the old wood should be removed, to encourage the plant to produce new growth. If possible, cut some of this out to the base; also remove some of the upper stems, cutting them back to a strong growing point.

PRUNING OUT DEAD WOOD

1 Most climbers produce a mass of dead wood that has to be removed so that the plant does not become congested. Dead wood is normally quite clearly differentiated from the live wood, by its colour and lack of flexibility.

2 Thin out the dead wood, removing it in sections, if necessary, so that the remaining stems are not damaged when it is pulled out.

TYING IN

1 Tie in the remaining stems, spreading them out rather than tying them in a tight column of stems. If possible, spread at least some of the stems horizontally: this will not only produce a better wall or trellis cover but also encourage flowering.

Right: *At their peak, roses are amongst the loveliest of climbing plants. Here the rambling* Rosa *'Excelsa' is seen climbing up a pillar.*

Pruning Climbing Roses

Roses climbing through a tree are usually left to their own devices, because they are difficult to get at; any roses climbing up a wall, trellis or pergola, however, should be regularly pruned, not only to remove dead and old wood but also to keep them vigorous and flowering well. Unpruned roses become old before their time, their flowering decreases and they look scruffy.

ONCE-FLOWERING CLIMBING ROSES

As with most woody plants, the time to prune is immediately after flowering. For once-flowering climbing roses, this normally means in midsummer.

However, if you want to see the rose's colourful hips in the autumn, leave the pruning and wait until the birds come and remove the hips or until the fruits have lost their brilliance and are no longer attractive.

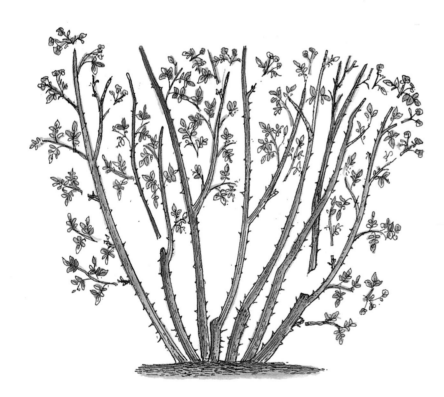

Above: *Cut out some of the older stems as soon as they have flowered, cutting back to a strong growing point, either at the base or higher up.*

1 Pruning in summer means that the plant will be in full leaf and growth. Although this may seem a daunting task to tackle, it makes it easy to see what is dead and what is alive. If possible, it is often easier to prune climbing roses by removing them from their supports and laying the stems on the ground.

2 First, remove all dead main stems and side-shoots. Cut these right back to living wood; if they are difficult to remove, take them out in sections rather than all at once. Next, remove one or two of the oldest stems. This will promote new vigorous shoots. Cut back some of the older wood growing at the top of the plant to a vigorous new shoot lower down. Do not remove more than a third of the old wood, unless you want to reduce the size of the climber drastically.

3 Tie in the remaining shoots, if they are loose. Any young shoots that come from the base will need to be regularly tied in as they grow, to prevent them from thrashing around.

4 Once secure, prune back any of the shorter side shoots to three or four buds. At the same time, cut back the tips of any new main shoots that have flowered, to a sound bud.

REPEAT-FLOWERING ROSES

There are now many roses that continue to flower throughout the summer and well into the autumn. It is obviously not desirable to prune these during the summer or you will lose the later flowers. Light pruning, restricted to removing dead flowers and any dead wood, can be carried out throughout the summer, but the main pruning is best left until the winter, when the rose is dormant. It is easier to see where to prune, too.

Below: *The abundance of flowers on* Rosa *'Alba maxima' makes it impossible to prune in summer.*

REPEAT-FLOWERING ROSES

'Agatha Christie' (pink)
'Aloha' (pink)
'Bantry Bay' (pink)
'Casino' (yellow)
'Coral Dawn' (pink)
'Danse du Feu' (red)
'Gloire de Dijon' (buff)
'Golden Showers' (yellow and cream)
'Handel' (white and pink)
'Parkdirektor Riggers' (red)
'Pink Perpétue' (pink)
'Royal Gold' (yellow)
'Schoolgirl' (orange)
'Summer Wine' (pink)

1 One advantage of pruning in the winter is that the leaves are missing, giving you a clearer picture of what you are doing. The structure of the rose, in particular, is more obvious.

2 First, remove any dead or diseased wood, cutting right back into living wood. Next, take out a few of the oldest shoots from the base, to encourage new growth for a compact shape.

3 If any flowering shoots remain on the tips of the stems, cut these out, taking the stem back to a sound bud. The side shoots can be shortened to about half their length. Tie in all loose stems.

4 In the summer, dead-head the roses as the flowers go over. This not only makes the climber tidier but promotes further flowering. With tall climbers, however, this may be impractical!

Pruning Rambling Roses

Ramblers only flower once during the summer. These flowers are formed on old wood produced during the previous season, so it is important to prune as soon as possible after flowering. This allows plenty of time for new shoots to grow, ready for next season's crop of flowers.

1 Because they are pruned in summer, the plants look congested and it is difficult to see what to prune. If possible, untie the shoots from their support and lay them out on the ground, so that you can see what you are doing. If this is not possible, remove the stems that need cutting out in sections and keep checking as you go.

Above: *Remove older stems as soon as they have flowered, cutting back to a strong growing point, either at the base or higher up.*

2 Remove any diseased, dead or dying stems at the base. This may well reduce the rambler considerably and make subsequent pruning easier.

3 Cut out to the base any wood that has flowered during the summer. This should only leave new growth. However, if there is not much new growth, leave some of the older stems intact, to flower again the following season.

4 If you have retained any older shoots, cut back their side shoots to two or three buds. Tie in all remaining shoots. If possible, tie these to horizontal supports, to encourage flowering and new growth.

BARE AT THE BASE?

Sometimes rambler roses are reluctant to produce new shoots from the base of the plant. In that case, if there are new stems arising higher up the plant, cut back the old ones to this point.

Right: Rosa 'Bobby James' is a vigorous rambling rose that needs regular pruning to keep it flowering well. Gloves should be worn as it has vicious thorns.

Pruning Clematis

Many gardeners worry about pruning clematis: the task seems complex, and is made more difficult because different clematis plants require different treatment. While this is true, the actual treatment is quite simple and soon becomes routine. If you grow a lot of clematis, keep a record of which plant needs what treatment. Alternatively, attach a label to each one, stating what type it is. This will make pruning very much easier.

Above: *There is always room to grow yet another clematis. Here the double* C. viticella *'Purpurea Plena Elegans' climbs over a wooden shed. For pruning it belongs to Group 3.*

CLEMATIS PRUNING GROUPS
There are three groups of clematis, as far as pruning is concerned. Most clematis catalogues or plant labels state what type each belongs to. However, it is possible to work it out. Small-flowered spring varieties such as *Clematis montana* belong to Group 1. Several of the early-flowering species also belong to this pruning group.

Group 2 consists of large-flowered clematis that bloom in early to midsummer, on old wood produced during the previous year.

Group 3 are the large-flowered climbing plants that bloom later in the summer on new wood produced during the spring.

PRUNING GROUPS FOR SOME OF THE MORE POPULAR CLEMATIS

C. 'Abundance'	3	C. macropetala	1
C. alpina	1	C. 'Madame Julia Correvon'	3
C. 'Barbara Jackman'	2	C. 'Marie Boisselot'	2
C. 'Bill Mackenzie'	3	C. 'Miss Bateman'	2
C. cirrhosa	1	C. montana	1
C. 'Comtesse de Bouchard'	3	C. 'Mrs Cholmondeley'	2
C. 'Daniel Deronda'	2	C. 'Nelly Moser'	2
C. 'Duchess of Albany'	3	C. 'Perle d'Azur'	3
C. 'Elsa Späth'	2	C. 'Royal Velours'	3
C. 'Ernest Markham'	2	C. 'Star of India'	2
C. 'Etoile Violette'	3	C. tangutica	3
C. 'Hagley Hybrid'	3	C. tibetana (orientalis)	3
C. 'Jackmanii'	3	C. 'The President'	2
C. 'Lasurstern'	2	C. viticella	3
C. 'Little Nell'	3	C. 'Vyvyan Pennell'	2

WHICH GROUP?
Does it flower in spring or early summer and have relatively small flowers?
Yes = It is probably Group 1.
No = Go to the next question.

Does it bloom in early or midsummer, possibly with a few flowers later, and are the flowers large?
Yes = It is probably Group 2.
No = Go to the next question.

Does it flower from mid- or late summer and into autumn?
Yes = It is probably Group 3.
No = There is an area of doubt, so consult a clematis expert or specialist nursery if you cannot find the variety listed on this page.

Pruning Group 1 Clematis

This group consists mainly of small-flowered clematis. Most flower early in the year, usually in spring, such as *C. montana*, although *C. cirrhosa* flowers in winter. This is the easiest group to deal with as you can, generally, leave them to their own devices, resorting to pruning only when they grow too big and need to be cut back.

1 Keep the climber looking healthy by removing any dead growth. This will help to reduce the bulk and weight of the climber, which can become considerable over the years.

2 If space is limited, remove some stems immediately after flowering. Cut them back to where they join a main shoot. Stray shoots that are thrashing around can also be removed.

Above: *Group 1 clematis only need pruning when they outgrow their space. Just cut out sufficient branches to reduce congestion, and take those that encroach beyond their space back to their point of origin.*

Right: *Typical of Group 1 is this* C. montana.

Pruning Group 2 Clematis

Group 2 clematis need a little more care and attention to make them flower well. If they are left alone, they become very leggy, so that all the flowering is taking place at the top of the plant, out of view. The basic pruning goal is to reduce the number of shoots while leaving in a lot of the older wood. You can do this immediately after flowering but it is more usual to wait until late winter, before the clematis comes into growth.

1 First, cut out all dead or broken wood. If this is tangled up, cut it out a little at a time, so that it does not damage the wood that is to remain.

Above: *After cutting out all the dead, damaged or weak growth, remove any wood that is making the clematis congested, cutting back to a pair of buds.*

2 Cut out all weak growths, to a strong bud. If the climber is still congested, remove some of the older stems.

3 Do not remove too much material or the flowering for the following season will be reduced. If a plant has been cut back too drastically, it will often flower much later in the season than usual, and is likely to produce smaller flowers.

4 Spread out the remaining shoots, so that the support is well covered. If left to find their own way, the shoots will grow up in a column.

Right: *Correctly pruned, Group 2 clematis, such as this* Clematis *'Niobe', will provide an abundance of flowers throughout the summer.*

Pruning Group 3 Clematis

Once you have recognized that you have one of the plants that constitute this group, the actual process of pruning is very straightforward. The flowers appear on wood that grows during the current year, so all the previous year's growth can be cut away. These make good plants to grow through early-flowering shrubs, because the shrub will have finished blooming by the time that the new growth on the clematis has begun to cover its branches.

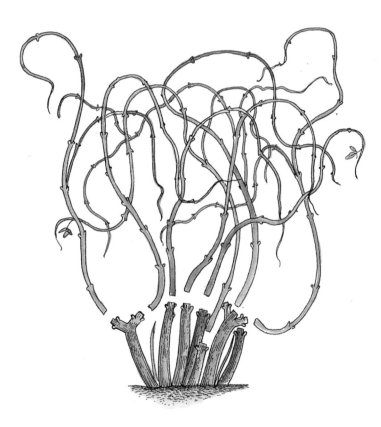

Above: *Group 3 clematis should have all the growth cut back in midwinter to the first pair of sound buds above the ground.*

1 Once Group 3 clematis become established, they produce a mass of stems at the base. If they are allowed to continue growing naturally, the flowering area gets higher and higher, leaving the base of the plant bare.

2 In mid- to late winter cut back all the shoots to within 1 m (3 ft), and preferably much less, of the ground. If the clematis is growing through a shrub, carefully untangle the stems from the shrub's branches and remove them.

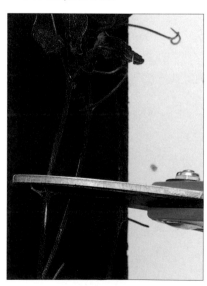

3 Cut the stems back to a sound pair of plump buds. As the wood gets older, so the cuts for subsequent years are likely to get higher, but there is always plenty of new growth from the base, which should be cut low down.

4 Once cut back, the clematis looks quite mutilated but the buds will soon produce new shoots and new growth will also appear from the base; by midsummer, the support will, once again, be covered with new growth bearing a profusion of flowers.

Pruning Wisterias

Gardeners often complain that their wisteria never flowers. One of the reasons that this might happen is that they never prune the climber and consequently all the plant's energy seems to go in producing ever-expanding, new growth rather than flowers. Gardeners often seem reluctant to prune wisteria, possibly because it is usually done in two stages, one in summer and the other in winter. However, it is not at all difficult once you know the idea behind it. For the first few years allow the wisteria to grow out to form the basic framework, removing any unwanted stems.

 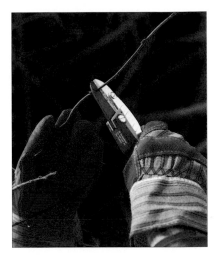

1 During the spring and early summer, the wisteria produces long, wispy new growth that looks like tendrils. Around midsummer, this new growth should be trimmed back, leaving only four leaves on each shoot. Any shoots that are required to extend the range or shape of the wisteria should be left unpruned.

2 From early to midwinter, cut back the summer-pruned shoots even further, to about half their length, leaving two to three buds on each shoot. This generally means that the previous season's growth will now be about 7.5 cm (3 in) long, thus drastically reducing the overall growth rate of the climber.

Above: *Cut back the new growth each summer to about four leaves and reduce this even further with a winter pruning.*

Right: *All the effort is worthwhile when you achieve a display as stunning as this one.*

PROPAGATION

Taking Cuttings

Raising new plants from seed is easy but takes rather a long time. The length of time between propagation and having a plant ready to go outside can be reduced by taking cuttings instead. Important as this may be, the real advantage of taking cuttings is that the resulting offspring are identical to their parent.

SEMI-RIPE AND HARDWOOD CUTTINGS

Taking cuttings is a simple procedure. A heated propagator helps but it is not essential; you can use a simple plastic bag as a cover, to create an enclosed environment. Hardy plants will root outside, but they will need a cold frame to protect them.

There are two basic types of cuttings: semi-ripe and hardwood. The semi-ripe cuttings are taken from the current year's wood. They are taken from midsummer onwards at a point when the soft tips of the shoots are beginning to harden and are no longer quite as flexible. They are often just changing colour from a light green to a darker one.

Hardwood cuttings are taken from the shrubs at the shoot's next stage, when it has become hard, ready to experience the frosts of winter. These are taken from autumn onwards.

In both cases, always choose healthy shoots that are free of disease or damage. Avoid any that are covered with insect pests. Aphids, for example, transmit viral diseases as well as weakening stems. Avoid shoots which have become drawn and spindly by growing towards the light and have a long distance between leaves. Usually, the shoots near the top of the bush are better than those towards the base, where they are starved of light. Put all cuttings in a plastic bag as soon as you take them, to stop them drying out.

The compost (soil mix) to use is a cutting compost, which can be readily purchased. However, it is easy to make your own as it consists of 50 per cent (by volume) sharp sand and 50 per cent peat or peat substitute. Instead of sand, you can use vermiculite.

The cuttings are ready to be potted on once they have rooted. Usually new growth starts on the stem, but if not carefully dig up the root ball and check for new roots.

1 Choose a stem that is not too flexible and is just turning woody where it joins last year's hard growth. Cut it just above a bud and put the whole stem into a plastic bag. Collect several stems.

2 Cut the stem below a bud and make the top cut just above a leaf 10 cm (4 in) above the base leaf. Cleanly remove the bottom leaves with a sharp knife, leaving only the top leaves.

3 Dip the base of the stem into a rooting powder or liquid. This will help the cutting to root and also protect it from disease, as the powder or liquid contains a fungicide. Tap the stem to remove the excess.

4 Make a trench in the compost (soil mix) with a small object and place the cutting in, making sure the base is in contact with the compost.

5 Firm the compost around the stem, so that there are no air pockets. Continue planting the other cuttings, making sure they are well spaced.

6 Water the compost and spray the leaves with a copper fungicide. Label the plant. If using a pot, place it in a propagator or cover with a plastic bag.

TAKING HARDWOOD CUTTINGS

In many ways, hardwood cuttings are even easier to take than semi-ripe ones, but they will take longer to root.

Once you have planted the cuttings, leave them in the ground until at least the next autumn, by which time they should have rooted. They will often produce leaves in the spring but this is not necessarily a sign that they have rooted.

Once you think they have rooted, test by digging one up. If they have, they can be transferred to pots or a nursery bed where they can be grown on to form larger plants before being moved to a permanent position.

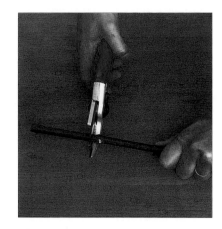

1 Cut about 30 cm (12 in) of straight, fully ripened (hard) stem from a shrub.

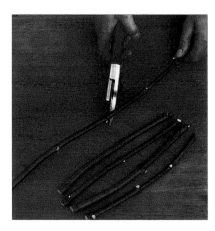

2 Trim the stem off just below a leaf joint and remove any soft tip, so that the eventual length is about 23 cm (9 in) long. Remove any leaves.

3 Although a rooting hormone is not essential, it should increase the success rate, especially with plants that are difficult to root. Moisten the bases of the cuttings in water.

4 Choose a sheltered, shady spot in the garden and dig a slit in the ground with a spade. If the soil is heavy dig out a narrow trench and fill it with either cutting compost or sharp sand.

5 Insert the cuttings in the ground, leaving the top 7 cm (3 in) or so of the stem above ground.

6 Firm the soil around the cuttings to eliminate pockets of air that would cause the cuttings to dry out. Once the cuttings have rooted, dig them up and pot them on in the normal way. This will normally be the following autumn.

SHRUBS TO TRY

These are just some shrubs that will root from hardwood cuttings:
Aucuba japonica (spotted laurel)
Buddleja (butterfly bush)
Cornus (dogwood)
Forsythia
Ligustrum
Philadelphus (mock orange)
Ribes (currant)
Rosa
Salix (willow)
Sambucus (elder)
Spiraea
Viburnum (deciduous species)

Growing from Cuttings

While using seed to increase plants is a simple procedure, it has the disadvantage that the resulting plant may not be like its parent, because not all plants will come "true" from seed. Seed-raised plants may vary in flower or leaf colour, in the size of the plant and in many other ways. When you propagate from cuttings, however, the resulting plant is identical in all ways to its parent (it is, effectively, a clone).

TAKING CUTTINGS

Taking cuttings is not a difficult procedure and nearly all climbers can easily be propagated in this way without much trouble. It is not necessary to have expensive equipment, although, if you intend to produce a lot of new plants, a heated propagator will make things much easier.

The most satisfactory method of taking cuttings is to take them from semi-ripe wood, that is, from this year's growth that is firm to the touch but still flexible and not yet hard and woody. If the shoot feels soft and floppy, it is too early to take cuttings. The best time for taking such cuttings is usually from mid- to late summer.

When taking cuttings it is vital that you always choose shoots that are healthy: they should be free from diseases and pests and not be too long between nodes (leaf joints). This usually means taking the cuttings from the top of the climber, where it receives plenty of light.

Do not take cuttings from any suckers that may rise from the base of the plant; if the climber was grafted on to a different rootstock, you might find that you have propagated another plant entirely.

CHOOSING COMPOST (SOIL MIX)

Specialist cutting compost (soil mix) can be purchased from most garden centres and nurseries. However, it is very simple to make your own. A half and half mix, by volume, of peat (or peat substitute) and sharp sand is all that is required. Alternatively, instead of sharp sand, use vermiculite.

1 Choose a healthy shoot that is not too spindly. Avoid stems that carry a flower or bud, as these are difficult to root. Cut the shoot longer than is required and trim it to size later. Put the shoot in a polythene (plastic) bag, so that it does not wilt while waiting for your attention.

2 Remove the shoot from the bag when you are ready to deal with it. Cut at an angle just below a leaf joint (node). Use a sharp knife, so that the cut is clean and not ragged.

3 Trim off the rest of the stem just above a leaf, so that the cutting is about 10 cm (4 in) long. For long-jointed climbers, this may be the next leaf joint up; for others there may be several leaves on the cutting.

4 Trim off all leaves except the upper one or pair. Cut the leaves off right against the stem, so that there are no snags. However, be careful not to damage the stem. Dip the base of the cutting into a rooting compound, either powder or liquid. This will not only promote rooting but also help protect the cutting against fungal attack.

5 Fill a 9 cm (3½ in) pot with cutting compost (soil mix) and insert the cuttings round the edge. Pushing them into the compost removes the rooting powder and damages the stems, so make a hole with a small dibber or pencil. Several cuttings can be put into one pot but do not overcrowd. Tap the pot on the bench, to settle the compost. Water gently. Label the pot.

6 If a propagator is available, place the pot in it and close the lid so that fairly high humidity and temperature are maintained. A less expensive alternative is to put the pot into a polythene (plastic) bag, with its sides held away from the leaves. Put it in a warm, light, but not sunny, position.

7 After a few weeks, the base of the cutting will callus over and roots will begin to appear. Carefully invert the pot, while supporting the compost with your other hand. Remove the pot and examine the roots. Once the roots are well developed, pot the cuttings up individually. Put the pot back in the propagator if roots are only just beginning to appear.

INTERNODAL CUTTINGS

A few plants, of which clematis is the main example, are propagated from internodal cuttings. The procedure is the same as for conventional cuttings, except that the bottom cut is through the stem, between two pairs of leaves, rather than under the bottom pair.

Right: *Your cuttings will eventually grow into hearty plants like this* Rosa *'Cedric Morris'. These rambling roses can be grown through a large tree, as long as the tree is strong enough to take all the extra weight.*

Perennial Cuttings

Increasing perennial plants by cuttings is an easy way to propagate them. If the plant to be increased is a mature specimen, it will usually mean that there is plenty of cutting material, in which case this method can be almost as productive as growing new plants from seed.

SUITABLE PERENNIALS

One of the advantages of increasing plants from cuttings is that the resulting plants are identical to the parent plant. For many plants it is, in fact, the only means of propagation, especially if your chosen plant is a sterile hybrid that does not produce seed and is impossible to divide. Some plants – the wallflower, *Erysimum cheiri* 'Harpur Crew', and many of the pinks (*Dianthus*), for example – have continued to be propagated in this way for centuries, and our existing plants are still closely related to the original parents that grew all those years ago. In effect, they still contain part of the original plant.

Not all perennial plants can be propagated from cuttings. Experienced gardeners will often know simply by looking at a plant whether it is possible or not, but the reasons for this are difficult to describe. Most encyclopedias of plants and books on propagation indicate those that can be propagated in this way, so you can consult these, or simply learn by trial and error.

Above: *Monkey flowers (*Mimulus*) are among those perennials that can be propagated by taking stem tip cuttings.*

HOW TO TAKE CUTTINGS

Most cuttings are taken in spring and summer, but many plants can be rooted at any time of the year. Penstemons are a good example of this.

The procedure for taking cuttings is straightforward. Pieces of stem are removed from the plant, trimmed up, placed in damp cutting compost (planting mix) and left in a closed environment until they have rooted. The cuttings are then potted up and treated as any other young plants. Stem cuttings can be taken either from the tip of a mature stem or from the new growth at the base of a plant, in which case they are called basal cuttings.

Cuttings should generally be about 10cm (4in) long. In most cases it is the top of the stem that is used, but in some cases – penstemons, for example – any part of the stem can be used as long as it is not too woody. Always choose shoots that are not in flower or carrying flowerbuds.

Once the cutting is removed from the plant, it should be placed in a polythene bag to keep it fresh and to prevent wilting. As soon as possible, remove the cuttings one by one from the bag and prepare them by using a sharp knife to cut through the stem just below a leaf node – that is, where the leaf joins the stem.

Most of the leaves should then be neatly trimmed off, tight to the stem, leaving just the top pair or, if they are small, two pairs. The cutting is then placed in a pot of cutting compost. It has been found that cuttings root better if they are arranged around the edge of the pot. Several cuttings can be placed in

the same pot – as many as twelve in a 9cm (3½in) pot – as long as they do not touch.

Some gardeners first dip the bottom of the cutting into a hormone rooting powder or liquid, although most perennials will root quite satisfactorily without this. An advantage of rooting compounds is that they usually contain a fungicide, which reduces the risk of rotting. Rooting compounds quickly lose their efficacy, and it is important to buy new stock every year.

PERENNIALS FROM STEM TIP CUTTINGS

Argyranthemum frutescens (marguerite)
Cestrum parqui
Clematis
Dianthus (carnations, pinks)
Diascia
Erysimum (wallflower)
Euphorbia (spurge; some)
Gazania (treasure flower)
Geranium (cranesbill; some)
Helichrysum petiolare (liquorice plant)
Lavatera (tree mallow)
Lobelia
Lythrum (purple loosestrife)
Malva (mallow)
Mimulus (monkey flower, musk)
Osteospermum
Parahebe perfoliata
Pelargonium
Penstemon
Phygelius
Salvia (sage)
Sphaeralcea (globe mallow)
Stachys coccinea
Trifolium pratense (red clover)
Verbena
Viola
Vinca (periwinkle)

TAKING STEM TIP CUTTINGS

1 Take cuttings from the tips of the stems and put them in a polythene bag. The length of the cuttings will vary, depending on the subject, but take about 10cm (4in).

2 Trim the cuttings to just below a leaf joint, and then remove most of the leaves and side-shoots, leaving just two at the top.

3 Place up to twelve cuttings in a pot of cutting compost (planting mix) or a 50:50 mixture of sharp sand and peat or peat substitute.

4 Water well, and cover the pot with the cut-off base of a soft-drinks bottle. This makes a perfect substitute for a propagator.

5 A heated propagator will speed up the rooting process. Several containers can be placed in the same unit.

AFTERCARE

Once the cuttings have been inserted into the compost (soil mix), label and water the pot, which should then be placed in a propagator or cold frame. A heated propagator, especially one that is heated from the bottom, will speed up the rooting process but it is by no means essential – any closed environment will suffice: you could simply use a polythene bag, as long as the cuttings do not touch the sides.

Leave the cuttings in the propagator until they have rooted. This will be evident when roots appear at the drainage holes at the bottom of the pot. At this stage, pot up the cuttings individually and grow them on.

BASAL CUTTINGS

These cuttings are struck in exactly the same way as stem tip cuttings except they are taken from the new growth at the base of the plant rather than from a mature stem. Although basal cuttings are often taken in the spring, when the plant first gets into growth, they can also be taken at other times of the year, simply by shearing over the plant. This removes all the older growth and encourages new shoots to start from the base. This new growth provides the material for the cuttings.

Taking basal cuttings is a useful method for increasing most asters, as well as violas, anthemis and nepetas. Other perennials that can be increased in this way are achilleas, phlox and dahlias.

TAKING BASAL CUTTINGS

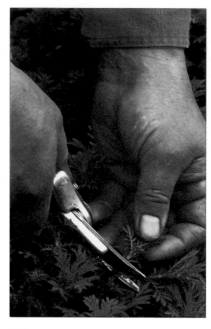

1 Take short cuttings from the new growth at the base of the plant. Place the cuttings in a polythene bag until they are required.

2 Trim the base of the cuttings. Cut through the stem just below a leaf joint and then remove all the leaves, except for a few at the top.

Above: *Lupins (*Lupinus*), with their racemes of pea-like flowers, can be propagated by taking basal cuttings.*

3 Place the cuttings in a pot of cutting compost (planting mix) made up of 50:50 sharp sand and peat or peat substitute. You can grow up to twelve in a pot.

4 Label the pot so that you will remember what the plants are, as they may all look the same. Also include the date on which you took the cuttings.

5 Water the pot and place it in a propagator. You can use a polythene bag, but ensure that no leaves are touching the polythene. Seal with an elastic band.

6 When the roots of the cuttings appear at the drainage holes of the pot, gently remove the contents.

7 Although this well-rooted cutting is shown here on the hand, it is best to avoid touching young roots if possible.

8 Pot up the rooted cuttings in individual pots, using a good quality potting compost. Keep covered for a few days and then harden off.

PERENNIALS FROM BASAL CUTTINGS

Achillea (yarrow)
Anthemis
Artemisia (wormwood)
Aster (Michaelmas daisy)
Campanula (bellflower)
Chrysanthemum
Crambe
Dahlia
Delphinium
Diascia
Epilobium (willowherb)
Gaillardia (blanket flower)
Helenium (sneezeweed)
Knautia
Lupinus (lupin)
Lychnis (catchfly)

Lythrum (purple loosestrife)
Macleaya (plume poppy)
Mentha (mint)
Monarda (bergamot)
Nepeta (catmint)
Perovskia (Russian sage)
Phlox
Platycodon (balloon flower)
Salvia (sage)
Scabiosa (scabious, pincushion flower)
Sedum (stonecrop)
Senecio (some)
Solidago (golden rod)
Verbena
Viola

Root Cuttings

As anyone who has accidentally left a section of root in the ground from a dandelion or dock while weeding will know only too well, it is possible to grow some plants from a small piece of root. This is not a large group of plants, but for some, such as named pasqueflowers (*Pulsatilla*) and oriental poppies (*Papaver orientale*), it is the only satisfactory method of reproduction.

PERENNIALS FOR INCREASING BY ROOT CUTTINGS

Acanthus (bear's breeches)
Anchusa (alkanet)
Anemone × *hybrida*
  (Japanese anemone)
Campanula
  (bellflower; some)
Catananche (cupid's dart,
  blue cupidone)
Echinops (globe thistle)
Eryngium (sea holly)
Gaillardia (blanket flower)
Geranium (cranesbill; some)
Gypsophila (baby's breath)
Limonium (sea lavender)
Macleaya (plume
  poppy)

Mertensia
Morisia monanthos
Ostrowskia magnifica
  (giant bellflower)
Papaver orientale
  (oriental poppy)
Phlox
Primula denticulata
  (drumstick primula)
Pulsatilla (pasqueflower)
Romneya (Californian
  poppy)
Stokesia laevis
Symphytum (comfrey)
Trollius (globeflower)
Verbascum (mullein)

SUITABLE PLANTS

Because it is a vegetative method of propagation, the plants grown from root cuttings will be identical to the parent. The plants from which such cuttings are taken are generally those with thick, fleshy roots, especially those with taproots. Often there is no other way of propagating these plants, because division is impossible and stem cuttings do not work. Seed can often be taken, but there is no guarantee that the plants will resemble the parent.

The best time to take root cuttings is during the plant's dormant period, which normally means the winter, and because growth often starts below ground well before the end of winter, the usual time for taking such cuttings is early winter.

Usually the plant to be propagated is dug up and the roots detached, but it is possible to dig down the side of a plant and remove one or two roots, without disturbing the whole plant. This is the safest way of dealing with a precious plant. Remove a root by cutting directly across it at right angles. Then trim the lower end with a slanting cut at about 45 degrees so that it is about 5cm (2in) long. The purpose of making these two distinct cuts is to make it obvious which is the top and which is the bottom of the cutting. This is important because there may be no distinguishing marks, and it is all too easy to plant them upside down by accident.

Fill a pot with cutting compost (planting mix) and firm it down by tapping it on a bench or table. Make a vertical hole with a pencil or piece of dowel and slip the cutting into it, making certain that the horizontal cut is at the top, which should be just below the surface of the compost. Several roots can be placed in one pot.

Water and set the pot in a cold frame for the winter. With the coming of spring, shoots should appear above the compost and closer examination should reveal new roots beginning to appear on the cutting. Once you are sure that there are roots, pot them up in individual pots and treat as any new young plant.

Above: *The elegant* Acanthus spinosus *is among those perennials that can be propagated by taking root cuttings. The pale mauve and white flowers appear in summer.*

Above: *Primulas, in this case a candelabra primula, can be increased by taking root cuttings.*

TAKING ROOT CUTTINGS

1 Carefully dig the plant from the ground, ensuring that the thicker roots come out intact.

2 Wash the soil from the roots and then remove one or more of the thicker ones.

3 Cut the roots into 5–8cm (2–3in) lengths with a horizontal cut at the top and a slanting cut at the bottom.

4 Fill the pot with a cutting compost (planting mix) and insert the cuttings vertically with the horizontal cut at the top, so that they are just level with the surface.

5 Cover the compost and the top of the cuttings with a layer of fine grit. Water and place in a cold frame.

Layering Shrubs

Layering is a good way of producing the odd few extra plants without a propagator. It is a useful method of producing one or two plants from a bush that somebody might want, without all the bother of what might be termed "formal" propagation. It is not a difficult technique and, after the initial work, nothing has to be done until the new plant is ready for transplanting – and it does not require any special equipment.

FOLLOWING NATURE

Basically, layering is simply persuading the plant to do what it often does in the wild (and in the garden, for that matter) and that is to put down roots where a branch or stem touches the ground. Encourage this by burying the stem and holding it in position with a peg or stone, so that the wind does not move it and sever any roots that are forming. It is as simple as that. Frequently, you will find that nature has already done it for you and a search around the base of many shrubs will reveal one or more layers that have already rooted on their own.

While layering might sound a casual way of propagating, it is a good one to try if you have difficulty in rooting cuttings. Being connected to the parent plant, the shoot still has a supply of nutrients and is, therefore, still very much alive, whereas a cutting may well have used up all its reserves and died before it has had a chance to put down roots. A layer is also far less prone to being killed off by a fungal disease.

DIVISION

Shrubs suitable for division produce multiple stems from below the ground or increase by suckering or running (self-layering). At any time between autumn and early spring, dig up one of the suckers or a portion of the shrub, severing it from the parent plant with secateurs (pruners) or a sharp knife and replant or pot up the divided portion. Suitable shrubs include *Arctostaphylos*, *Calluna*, *Clerodendrum bungei*, *Cornus alba*, *C. canadensis*, *Erica*, *Gaultheria*, *Holodiscolor*, *Kerria*, *Leucothoe*, *Mahonia*, *Nandina*, *Pachysandra*, *Rubus*, *Sarcococca* and *Sorbus reducta*.

1 Choose a stem that will reach the ground without breaking and prepare the ground beneath it. In most cases, the native soil will be satisfactory but if it is heavy clay add some potting compost (potting soil) to improve its texture.

2 Trim off any side-shoots or leaves. Dig a shallow hole and bend the shoot down into it.

3 To help hold the shoot in place, peg it down with a piece of bent wire.

4 Fill in the hole and cover it with a stone. In many cases, the stone will be sufficient to hold the layer in place and a peg will not be required. The stone will also help to keep the area beneath it moist.

5 It may take several months, or even years, for shrubs that are hard to propagate to layer but, eventually, new shoots will appear and the layer will have rooted. Sever it from its parent and pot it up into a container.

IMPROVING ROOTING

Although it is not essential, rooting can be improved with difficult subjects by making a slit in the underside of the stem at a point where it will be below ground. This slit can be propped open with a thin sliver of wood or a piece of grit. This cut interrupts the passage of hormones along the stem and they accumulate there, helping to promote more rapid rooting.

If several plants are required, it is quite feasible to make several layers on the same shoot, allowing the stem to come above the surface between each layer. This is known as "serpentine layering".

6 If the roots are well developed, transfer the layer directly to its new site.

Above: *Rhododendrons frequently self-layer in the wild and may also do so in the garden, but the prudent gardener always deliberately makes a few layers just in case a visiting friend takes a liking to one of the varieties that he grows.*

Layering Climbers

Layering is a simple technique, useful for propagating plants that are difficult to root from cuttings. It can be a slow process: occasionally, some plants can take several years to root. If one or two layers can be laid down at regular intervals, however, you should have a continuous supply of new plants at your disposal.

TIMING LAYERING

Layering can be carried out at any time of year. The time taken for roots to appear on the chosen stem depends on various factors and varies considerably from one type of plant to another. Usually, growth appearing from the area of the layer indicates that it has rooted and is ready for transplanting to another position.

ACHIEVING SUCCESS

One way of increasing the success rate with layering is to make a short slit in the underside of the stem at its lowest point. This checks the flow of the sap at this point and helps to promote rooting. Alternatively, a notch can be cut or some of the bark removed. Sometimes, just the act of forcing the stem down into a curve will wound the bark enough.

1 Make a shallow depression in the soil and place the selected stem in it. If the soil is in poor condition, remove some of it and replace it with potting compost (soil mix).

2 Use a metal pin or a piece of bent wire to hold the stem in place, if necessary, so that it cannot move in the wind.

3 Cover the stem with good soil or potting compost, and water it.

4 If you haven't pinned the stem down, place a stone on the soil above the stem, to hold it in position.

5 Once growth starts – or the stem feels as if it is firmly rooted when gently pulled – cut it away from the parent plant, ensuring that the cut is on the parent-plant side. Dig up the new plant and transfer it to a pot filled with potting compost. Alternatively, replant it elsewhere in the garden.

6 An alternative method is to insert the layer directly into a pot of compost, which is buried in the ground. Once the stem has rooted, sever it from the parent as above and dig up the whole pot. This is a good technique for making tip layers, as with this fruit-bearing tayberry. Tip layers are made by inserting the tip of a stem, rather than a central section, in the ground, until it roots; it is a suitable propagation technique for fruiting climbers, such as blackberries.

Right: *Roses are just one of the types of climber that can be propagated by layering.*

Dividing perennials

The division of perennial plants is one of the easiest and most frequently used methods of propagation. It is done not only to produce new plants, but also as a means of keeping existing plants healthy and free from congestion. The basic idea behind division is that the plants involved do not have a single root, but a mass of roots emerging from all parts of the plant that touch the soil or are actually in the soil. A new plant can be formed simply by breaking a part of the plant away with some roots attached.

SUITABLE CANDIDATES

A large number of perennials can be increased through division. Most of the clump- or mat-forming plants are easy to divide. A plant can usually be divided if it consists of several "noses" or growing points. Division is another vegetative method of propagation, and each of the divisions will resemble the parent plant.

WHEN AND HOW TO DIVIDE

The best time for dividing most plants is just as they are coming into growth, usually in spring. Some, especially those with shallow, fibrous roots like asters, can be divided at any time as long as they are kept moist during dry weather, but even these are best dealt with in spring.

A suitable time is when you are busy with the spring tidy-up. Any old or congested plants can then be dug up, divided and replanted. This is, in fact, an essential part of the maintenance of many herbaceous plants, which would otherwise die out in the centre of the clump and might soon die out altogether.

Dig up the clump to be divided and work on it in the border, if it is a simple division, or in a potting shed, greenhouse, or at least on a table, if the plant is to be propagated. You will need the young growth around the outside of the clump. The centre is usually old and congested, and should be thrown away.

The simplest way of dividing the clump, especially for tougher plants like asters, is to place it on the ground and insert two forks back to back. When the forks are levered apart, the roots are pulled with it, and you will have two plants. Repeat this process until the plant is in small pieces. This is, however, a rather crude method, and the plant can be damaged, allowing in disease.

Left: *Hellebores can be increased through division.*

PERENNIALS THAT CAN BE DIVIDED

Acanthus (bear's breeches)
Achillea (yarrow)
Aconitum (monkshood; this plant is poisonous)
Adenophora (gland bellflower)
Agapanthus (African lily)
Anaphalis (pearl everlasting)
Anemone
Anthemis
Artemisia (wormwood)
Aster (Michaelmas daisy)
Astilbe
Astrantia (masterwort)
Bergenia (elephant's ears)
Campanula (bellflower; some)
Convallaria (lily-of-the-valley)
Coreopsis (tickseed)
Crambe
Delphinium
Epilobium (willowherb)
Epimedium
Euphorbia (spurge; some)
Galega (goat's rue)
Geranium (cranesbill; some)
Helenium (sneezeweed)
Helianthus (sunflower)
Helleborus (hellebore)
Hemerocallis (daylily)
Heuchera (coral bells)
Hosta
Hylomecon japonica
Inula
Iris
Kniphofia (red-hot poker)
Lamium (dead nettle)
Liatris (gay feathers)
Ligularia (leopard plant)
Lobelia
Lychnis (catchfly)
Lysimachia (yellow loosestrife)

Lythrum (purple loosestrife)
Meconopsis (blue poppy)
Mentha (mint)
Monarda (bergamot)
Nepeta (catmint)
Ophiopogon
Paeonia (peony)
Persicaria (knotweed)
Phlomis
Phormium tenax (New Zealand flax)
Physostegia (obedient plant)
Polemonium (Jacob's ladder)
Polygonatum (Solomon's seal)
Potentilla (cinquefoil)
Primula
Pulmonaria (lungwort)
Ranunculus (buttercup, crowfoot)
Ranzania
Rheum (ornamental rhubarb)
Rudbeckia (coneflower)
Salvia (sage; some)
Saponaria (soapwort)
Scabiosa (scabious, pincushion flower)
Schizostylis coccinea (Kaffir lily)
Sedum (stonecrop)
Sidalcea (prairie mallow)
Smilacina
Solidago (golden rod)
Stachys
Symphytum (comfrey)
Tanacetum
Thalictrum (meadow rue)
Tradescantia
Trollius (globeflower)
Uvularia (merrybells)
Vancouveria
Vernonia (ironweed)
Veronica (speedwell)

SIMPLE DIVISION

1 Water the plant to be divided during the previous day. Dig up a clump of the plant, in this case the Michaelmas daisy, *Aster novi-belgii*.

2 Insert two forks back-to-back into the plant and lever apart by pushing the handles together. Keep on dividing until the pieces are of the required size.

3 The pieces of the plant can be replaced in the bed, but dig over the soil first, removing any weeds and adding some well-rotted organic material.

4 Alternatively, small pieces of the plant can be potted up individually. After watering, place these in a closed cold frame for a few days, before hardening off.

DIVISION BY HAND

A better method is to divide the plant with your fingers. Hold the plant in both hands and shake it so that the earth begins to fall off. At the same time, gently pull the plant apart. Many plants – primulas and sisyrinchiums, for example – seem to fall apart in your hands.

If your soil is heavy and sticky, it will not fall off easily, or, if the plants have very tangled roots, it can be difficult to separate them. However, if you hold the plant under water and manipulate it in the same way, a surprising number of plants will come apart quite easily, without damaging the roots.

Some plants will not separate easily and will need to be cut. Wash off all the soil so that the growing points can be seen and then cut cleanly through the main root that is holding them together. This limits the damage to the plant. Cutting a plant into pieces with a spade will work, but you are likely to cut through so many roots that wounds are left through which infection can take hold.

Larger divisions can be replanted directly back in the soil as long as the weather is not too hot and dry; dull, damp weather is ideal. Firm them in and keep watered until they become established. Before replanting, it is a good idea to remove any weeds and to rejuvenate the soil by digging in some compost.

When a plant is divided into smaller pieces it is best to re-establish the plant by growing it on in a pot before planting out. This is important if you want to sell or give away the plants. Once you have made the division, pot it up into an appropriately sized pot, using a good quality potting compost (soil mix).

Label and water the pot and then place it in an enclosed environment such as a shady cold frame or greenhouse. Make sure that you do not place the pots in direct sunlight. Water and grow the plants on until they are established, when they can be hardened off and then planted out or sold.

DIVIDING BY HAND

1 Dig up a section of the plant, large enough to provide the quantity of material that you require.

2 Hold the plant firmly at the base and shake it vigorously so that the soil falls off and the roots are exposed.

3 Gently pull the plant into individual pieces, simply by manipulating it with your hands. Many plants, such as this sisyrinchium, will come apart very easily.

4 The pieces should now be potted up individually using a good compost (soil mix). Place in a shaded cold frame for a few days and then harden off.

Above: *Some geraniums can be increased through division.*

DIVIDING UNDER WATER

1 Many plants, such as these kniphofias, have very tangled roots or are growing in heavy soils that will not easily fall away.

2 Shake the plants in a bucket of water so that the soil is washed from the roots. Wash with a hosepipe if the soil is very difficult to remove.

3 Once the soil is washed away, most plants break up surprisingly easily into individual sections, each with a growing point.

4 Some plants do not come apart very easily. If this is the case, cut the sections apart with a sharp knife, making certain that each section has a bud.

5 Once the plants have been cleaned and divided, they can be potted up individually and then kept in a shaded frame until they have recovered.

Propagating Bulbs

It is usually much easier – and certainly a lot quicker – to buy flowering-sized bulbs than to attempt to propagate your own, but propagation can be fun, and raising your own plants can give a great sense of achievement.

ADVICE ON PROPAGATION

Bulbs are wonderful self-propagators. In just one year a rhizome can develop into a mass of rhizomes, which you can divide up and replant to form separate plants. Other bulbs have flowers that produce generous amounts of seed from which you can grow new plants. In fact, some, such as bluebells, seed far too prolifically for most gardeners: a small patch of bluebells can take over a border. Established tubers and bulbs can be divided into smaller sections. Some bulbs, in particular dahlias and begonias, can be raised from cuttings.

DIVIDING TUBERS

Tuberous plants grow to quite large proportions, and produce generous quantities of seeds and shoots. Tubers can be divided provided each piece has an "eye" (growth bud or shoot). Dahlia tubers that form a crown will not grow if individual tubers are separated without an attached growth bud. If the group is divided with a sharp knife it is important to ensure that each has a piece of main stem and a growth bud attached.

Begonia and gloxinia tubers can be treated in the same way. Divide the tubers in late winter or early spring.

DIVIDING CLUMPS

Dividing a clump of established bulbs gives you more flowering-sized plants instantly, and for free, and propagation does not come easier than that. It is immensely satisfying to dig up a bulb you planted a year or two ago and discover that it has now formed a clump of four or five bulbs. The best time to divide established clumps is after the leaves have died back, or after they have flowered if they have persistent leaves.

Lift the clump with a fork, taking care not to damage it, and shake off most of the soil. Pull the clump apart into separate bulbs. Replant each bulb at their original depth, arranging them fairly close together if you have a lot and want quick impact, or spacing them out more to allow for future growth.

LILY SCALES

Lilies have yet another way of propagating themselves. They produce seed and their bulbs can be divided, but they also grow bulbils at leaf axils up their stems. These eventually fall off and root into the soil, where they grow into new plants. If possible, remove them from the stem and plant in separate pots. This method will give you more plants than division. It is also quicker than raising seedlings (and there is no worry about whether they will be like their parents).

DIVIDING RHIZOMES

Plants with rhizomes are best divided when the leaves die down, or after flowering if the foliage is persistent.

Lift the clump with a fork and shake off any surplus soil. Tease out the rhizomes, and cut into smaller sections, then replant at their original depth. Rhizomes usually grow horizontally, but if you do plant them vertically they will probably still grow.

DIVIDING A BEGONIA

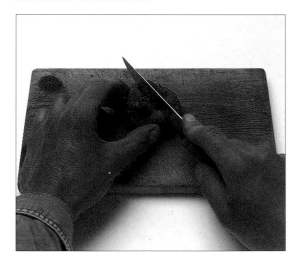

1 Cut the tuber with a sharp knife, making sure each piece has a bud. These are easier to detect when the tubers are about to start into growth.

2 Dip the cut surface into a fungicide to reduce the risk of the tuber rotting. A sulphur dust is suitable, though other fungicides can be used.

3 Pot up the pieces of tuber as you would normally, but keep an eye on them to ensure a fungal infection does not become established.

CUTTINGS

Dahlias and begonias are among the few bulbous plants that can be raised from cuttings. This will give more plants than propagating by dividing the tuber.

Lay the tubers in deep trays of potting soil in a greenhouse in late winter. When the new shoots are a couple of inches long, take cuttings to root in the usual way.

OFFSETS

A large number of true bulbs produce offsets (small bulbs around the base of the old one). These will eventually separate from the parent bulbs, but you can remove them while small and grow them in a spare piece of ground until they reach flowering size. They are best removed and replanted when the leaves die down.

After flowering, corms, such as gladioli and crocosmia, die and a new one will form on top of the old one. Sometimes a large number of cormlets are produced around the base of the old corm. If detached and grown for a couple of years, they will reach flowering size and can then be planted in the border.

BULBS FROM SEEDS

Raising seedlings will provide a large number of plants cheaply, but it is usually slow. This is a useful method if you require a large number of bulbs at little cost, perhaps for naturalizing. Since hybrids and named varieties are unlikely to produce plants the same as their parents, it is best to restrict seed-sowing to species. If you definitely want your new plant to be exactly the same as the parent, choose division rather than growing from seed.

If you save your own seed, sow as soon as possible, but be prepared to wait for germination. Some bulbs may be slow to germinate. If possible, keep the pots or trays in a cold frame, but do not forget to water them.

When large enough, grow the seedlings in a spare piece of ground for a couple of years, then move to their permanent flowering positions.

Above: *Start tuberous begonias into growth in trays, then remove the shoot with a bit of the tuber attached. Pot up.*

Above: *Seeds can be sown in trays or pots, but be prepared to be patient. Keep them in a cold frame to germinate.*

Above: *Small bulb offsets are often produced around the base of a mature bulb (here a muscari). Simply detach and grow on.*

Right: *Bluebells are among the plants that can be raised easily from seed, and in fact they self-seed freely. Seed is an economic way to raise large numbers of plants.*

SHRUBS

Shrubs have a place in any garden and it is, in fact, impossible to imagine a garden without them. They provide so much: colour, shape, bulk, a habitat for wildlife, screens from the neighbours, dividers and even 'camps' for children to play in. Flowering shrubs provide sudden bursts of colour. With the notable exception of roses, most shrubs only have a brief flowering period but while they are in bloom they are usually glorious. In many cases, the visual power of the flowers is enhanced by a wonderful fragrance which wafts throughout the whole garden. There are flowering shrubs for every month of the year, including the depths of winter. Some can simply be enjoyed in the garden, while others may be cut to provide material for bunches of flowers for indoors or to give away.

Left: *This* Cotinus coggygria *'Royal Purple' is blessed with strikingly handsome, dark purplish-red leaves.*

DESIGNING A BORDER

Drawing a Border Plan

There are several ways of designing a border. The majority of gardeners undoubtedly go for the hit-and-miss approach, simply putting in plants as they acquire them. Then, if they feel inclined, they may move them around a bit to improve the scheme. Many good gardens have been created in this way but a more methodical approach tends to produce better results from the outset. However, do not be fooled: no method produces the best results first time. Gardening is always about adjustment, moving plants here and there to create a better picture or to change the emphasis or mood.

MAKING A SKETCH

The most methodical approach to designing a border is to draw up a plan and to work from this. Making a plan is one of the many enjoyable parts of gardening. It involves choosing the plants that you want to grow, sorting them into some form of pattern and committing this to paper, so that you can follow it through. A further refinement is to produce a drawing of what the border will roughly look like at different stages of the year. You do not have to be an artist to do this; it is for your own satisfaction and, since no one else need see it, the drawing can be quite crude!

The plan itself should, preferably, be drawn up on squared paper (graph). This will help considerably in plotting the size and relationship of plants. The sketches can be on any type of paper, including the back of an envelope, if you can't find anything else at the time.

Decide whether you are going to treat the garden as a whole or whether you are going to concentrate on a single border. This border will need to be accurately measured if it is already in existence or you must firmly decide on its intended shape and dimensions.

Draw up a list of the plants that you want to grow, jotting details alongside as to their colour, flowering period, eventual height and spread and their shape.

Plot the plants on the plan, making sure you show them in their final spread, not the size they are in their pots. Bear in mind details such as relative heights, foliage and flower colour. These can be further explored by making an elevation sketch of the border as seen from the front. It can be fun to colour this in with pencils or watercolours, to show roughly what it will look like in the different seasons.

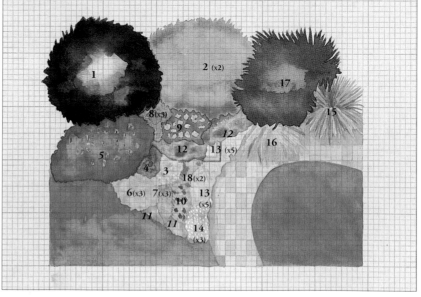

Key

1. *Cotinus coggyria* 'Royal Purple'
2. *Weigela florida* 'Florida Variegata'
3. *Perovskia atriplicifolia* 'Blue Spire'
4. *Allium chrisophii*
5. *Daphne x burkwoodii* 'Somerset'
6. *Sedum spectabile* 'September Glow'

7. *Eryngium giganteum*
8. *Digitalis purpurea*
9. *Rosa* 'Wenlock Castle'
10. *Papaver somniferum*
11. *Astrantia major*
12. *Salvia forsskaolii*

13. *Stachys byzantina*
14. *Lychnis coronaria* 'Alba'
15. *Yucca gloriosa* 'Variegata'
16. *Phormium cookianum*
17. *Berberis thunbergii* 'Rose Glow'
18. *Dictamnus albus purpureus*

Above: *It will take a few years before your plans and sketches develop into the established border you would like to see.*

Designing with Shrubs

Of all aspects of gardening, designing a garden or border is probably one of the most exciting and, at the same time, one of the most difficult. It requires the ability to see things that are not yet there and to assemble whole groups of different plants in the mind's eye.

THE BASIC ELEMENTS

Most people have an awareness of the basic elements of garden design from other disciplines; most of us, for example, are adept at choosing what clothes to wear. We know what colours go together and what suits our shape and height. We are aware that certain fabrics add a touch of luxury to an outfit and that certain colours create a bright effect, while others produce a more subtle image. Similarly, most people are at least involved in decorating their home, where again the choice of colours, textures and finishes have become almost second nature over the years.

PERSONAL TASTE

The same principles we apply to choosing clothes and items for the home are used when designing in the garden, with many of the choices coming from an innate feeling for what the gardener likes and dislikes. This means that, like clothing, gardens are personal, with the fortunate result that each garden is different from the next. By all means be inspired by ideas seen in other gardens, but do not slavishly imitate another garden: the chances are that it will not work in your situation – the climate might be slightly different or the soil might be wrong. There are no definite rules with regards to design; there is no ultimate garden. However, there are a few guidelines that the experience of many centuries of gardening have produced, and it is worth bearing these in mind.

THE SHAPE OF THE BORDER

A border can be any shape, to suit the garden. Curved edges tend to create a more informal, relaxed feeling, while straight edges are more formal. The one point to remember is that the border should not be too narrow. Shrubs look better in a border where they have room to spread without being too crowded. A border that is only wide enough to take one shrub at a time has a habit of looking more like a hedge than a border. A wider border also allows the gardener to build up a structure of planting, which is more visually satisfying.

Left: *An attractive border filled with a mixture of shrubs and herbaceous plants designed to provide interest over a long period of time. Shrubs in flower include the blue* Ceanothus, *white* Olearia, *purple* Lavandula stoechas *and the white* Prostanthera cuneata, *with a purple rhododendron in the background.*

PART OF THE SCHEME

Shrubs need not be confined to borders – they can become part of the overall scheme of the garden. This is particularly important where the garden is small and there is little room for formal borders. Shrubs can be mixed with other plants or simply used in isolation, as focal points that draw the eye. They can be taken out of the ground and used in pots or other containers, or grown against walls and fences. Besides being part of the design, they can have a sense of purpose, perhaps to screen a dustbin (trash can) or to create a perfumed area near where people sit in the evening.

HEIGHT AND SHAPE

Shrubs have a lot to offer the designer as there is such a wide choice of attributes that can be applied to them. Shrubs come in all sorts of shapes and sizes, from tiny dwarf ones to those that are difficult to distinguish from trees. The general principle of design is to put the tallest at the back and smallest at the front. This must not be rigidly adhered to or the the border will begin to look like choir stalls, all regularly tiered. Bring a few of the taller ones forward and place some of the shorter ones in gaps between bigger ones. This makes the border much more interesting and prevents the viewer from taking in the whole border at a glance.

The different shapes of the plants also add variety. Some are tall and thin, others short and spreading. The latter are particularly useful as ground cover and can be woven in and out of other shrubs as if they were "poured" there. Heathers are especially useful for this.

Above: *In this small garden, shrubs are not only used to make an interesting background of different textures, shapes and colours, but are also planted in containers to break up the foreground. To complete the picture, formal hedges hold the whole scheme together.*

Right: *This attractive border builds up beautifully from the front but, at the same time, is not regimented as the heights vary along its length. It demonstrates well the effectiveness of differently-shaped shrubs and other plants while, at the same time, illustrating the importance of colour and leaf shapes.*

Using Colour in the Border

Colour is an extremely important aspect of shrub gardening, perhaps more so than other areas because shrubs not only offer a large range of flower colours but also a vast range of foliage colour and texture.

MIXING COLOURS

Colour is the most tricky thing to get right in the garden. It is essential to spend time looking at other gardens and looking at pictures in books and magazines, to see how colours are best handled. It is not just a question of saying that reds mix well with purples: some do, others do not. Orange-reds and blue-reds are quite different from each other and cannot all be used in the same way.

A good garden will combine all the colours in a variety of ways in all areas. Sticking to just one style, especially in a large garden, can become boring. In a small garden, trying to mix too many different colour schemes has the reverse effect and may become uncomfortable.

Using shrubs gives colour in both leaves and flowers. When planning, it is important that the foliage of the various plants blends well together as they are generally around for a long time – all year, in fact, if they are evergreen. Try not to use too many different colours of foliage together and avoid too many variegated shrubs in one place as this can look too "busy". The colour of nearby flowering plants can also enhance the foliage.

Colours can also be affected by the texture of the leaves. A shiny green leaf can light up a dull area almost as brilliantly as a gold leaf while a soft, hairy foliage adds a sense of luxury.

Right: *The sharp contrast between the silver leaves of the* Elaeagnus *'Quicksilver' and the purple of the flowers of* Erysimum *'Bowles Mauve' makes a beautiful, if startling, combination.*

Below: *Here, the purple flowers of* Lavandula stoechas pedunculata *make a much softer contrast to the purple-leaved sage* Salvia officinalis *'Purpurascens'.*

Left: *The bright red stems of* Cornus alba *'Sibirica' add a great deal of interest to the winter scene, especially if sited so that the low sun strikes them.*

Right: *A dwarf willow,* Salix repens, *grows with the ground-hugging* Lithodora diffusa. *The contrast in the flowers makes this an exciting combination in the spring and, for the rest of the year, the different foliage shapes make them an interesting ground cover.*

COLOURFUL STEMS

It is not only the leaves and flowers of shrubs that have colour: stems, too, can provide it. This is particularly true in the winter, when the leaves are off most shrubs and there is little to lighten the grey scene. White, yellow, green, red and black stems then come into their own. Plants grown for their winter stems are often uninteresting for the rest of the year and so should be planted where they will not be noticed in summer but will stand out in winter.

Right: *It is possible to jazz up the appearance of the garden with bright colour combinations, such as this azalea and alyssum,* Aurinia saxatilis. *The dazzling picture they create is wonderful but, fortunately, neither plant lasts in flower too long, otherwise the effect would become tiresome.*

Mixing Shrubs

Shrub borders or shrubberies have died out as gardens have become smaller. In many ways, the border devoted to only shrubs would be a labour-saving form of gardening, but being able to mix in a few other plants helps to make it more interesting.

GROWING SHRUBS WITH PERENNIALS AND ANNUALS

As well as being more interesting from a visual point of view, mixing shrubs and other plants creates a greater variety of different habitats in the garden for a greater range of plants. For example, there are many herbaceous plants, many coming from wooded or hedgerow habitats in the wild, that need a shady position in which to grow. Where better than under shrubs? Many of these, such as the wood anemone, *Anemone nemorosa*, appear, flower and die back in early spring before the leaves appear on the shrubs, thus taking up a space that would be unavailable later in the season once the foliage has obscured the ground beneath the shrub.

Herbaceous plants can also be used to enliven a scene where all the shrubs have already finished flowering. For example, if you have a number of rhododendrons, most will have finished flowering by early summer and will be comparatively plain for the rest of the year. Plant a few herbaceous plants between them and retain interest for the rest of the year.

Herbaceous plants also extend the range of design possibilities. For example, it might not be possible to find a shrub of the right height that blooms at the right time with the right-coloured flowers. One of the thousands of hardy perennials may offer the perfect solution. Similarly, the combination of textures and shapes might not be available in shrubs, so look to see if there are herbaceous or annual plants that will help solve the problem.

In the early stages of the establishment of a shrub border or a mixed border, the shrubs are not likely to fill their allotted space. To make the border look attractive in the meantime, plant annuals or perennials in the gaps. These can be removed as the shrubs expand. As well as improving the appearance of the border, the plants will also act as a living mulch and help to keep weeds at bay.

WOODLAND PLANTS FOR GROWING UNDER SHRUBS

Anemone nemorosa (wood anemone)
Brunnera macrophylla
Campanula latifolia
Convallaria majalis (lily-of-the-valley)
Cyclamen hederifolium
Eranthis hyemalis
Euphorbia amygdaloides robbiae (wood spurge)
Galanthus (snowdrop)
Geranium
Helleborus (Christmas rose)
Polygonatum
Primula

Above: *This* Lychnis chalcedonica *adds the final touch to a good combination of foliage. Without it, the grouping might seem dull compared with other parts of the garden in the summer.*

Above: *The geranium in the foreground is the right height and colour to match the roses and the ceanothus behind. It would be hard to find a shrub to fit in with this combination.*

Left: *Sometimes, one startling combination acts as a focal point and draws the eye straight to it. This combination of the blue flowers of a ceanothus and the silver bark of the eucalyptus is extraordinarily beautiful. There are many such combinations that the gardener can seek and this is one of the things that makes gardening so satisfying and even, at times, exhilarating.*

Above: *A good combination of textures, shapes and colours is achieved here with the cardoon (Cynara cardunculus) providing interesting colour and structure, while the* Salvia sclarea *in the front provides the subtle flower colour.*

CHOOSING SHRUBS

Hedges

Few gardens are without a hedge of some sort. They are used as a defensive barrier around the garden as well as having a more decorative purpose within. The defensive role is to maintain privacy both from intruders and prying eyes (and, increasingly, against noise pollution). This type of hedge is thick and impenetrable, often armed with thorns to discourage animals and humans pushing through. Hedges also have less sinister functions, more directly related to gardening. One is the important role of acting as a windbreak to help protect plants. Another is to act as a foil for what is planted in front of it. Yew hedges, for example, act as a perfect backdrop to herbaceous and other types of border.

Above: *A formal beech hedge (*Fagus sylvatica*) makes a neat and tidy boundary to any garden. Beech, yew (*Taxus baccata*) and hornbeam (*Carpinus betulus*) also make good formal hedges as long as they are kept neat. They are all slow growing and need less attention than many others.*

USING HEDGES

Hedges are widely used within the garden, where they are perhaps better described as screens or frames. Screens are used to divide up the garden, hiding one area from view until you enter it. In some cases, the hedges are kept so low that they can hardly be called hedges; they are more like decorative edging to a border. Box reigns supreme for this kind of hedge. Others are informal hedges, in which the plants are allowed to grow in a less restricted way, unclipped, so they are able to flower, adding to their attraction. Roses and lavender are two popular plants for using like this.

We all want hedges that grow up as quickly as possible and usually end up buying one of the fastest growers. However, bear in mind that once grown to the intended height, these fast growers do not stop, they just keep growing at the same pace. This means that they need constant clipping to keep them under control. A slower growing hedge may take longer to mature, but once it does, its stately pace means that it needs far less attention. In spite of its slow-growing reputation, in properly prepared ground, yew will produce a good hedge, 1.5–2 m (5–6 ft) high in about 5 to 6 years from planting.

Right: *Although often much maligned, leyland cypress (*x Cupressocyparis leylandii*) makes a good hedge. The secret is to keep it under control and to clip it regularly. Here, although soon due a trim, it still looks attractive, as the new growth makes a swirling movement across the face of the hedge.*

Above: *This tapestry hedge is made up of alternate stripes of blue and gold conifers. Here, the bands have been kept distinct but, if deciduous shrubs are used, the edges often blend together, which gives a softer appearance.*

Above: A *country hedge makes an attractive screen around the garden. This one is a mixture of shrubs, all or most of them being native trees: there is box* (Buxus sempervirens)*, hawthorn* (Crataegus monogyna)*, hazel* (Corylus avellana) *and holly* (Ilex aquifolium)*. The only problem with this type of hedge is that the growth rates are all different so it can become ragged looking, but then country hedges always are!*

Above: *Informal hedges of lavender border a narrow path. The joy of such hedges is not only the sight of them but the fact that, as you brush along them, they give off the most delicious scent. Such hedges fit into a wide variety of different situations within a garden.*

Left: *An informal flowering hedge is formed by this firethorn* (Pyracantha)*. The flowers make it an attractive feature while the powerful thorns give it a practical value as an impenetrable barrier. Flowering hedges should not be clipped as frequently as more formal varieties and trimming should be left until flowering is over.*

Maintaining a Hedge

Planting a hedge in most respects is like planting any shrub. Prepare the ground thoroughly as the hedge is likely to stay in place for many years, possibly centuries.

INGREDIENTS FOR A HEALTHY HEDGE

Add plenty of organic material to the soil, both for feeding the hedge and for moisture retention. If the ground lies wet, either add drainage material or put in drains. Plant the hedge between autumn and early spring. For a thick hedge plant the shrubs in two parallel rows, staggering the plants in each. Water as soon as it is planted and keep the ground covered in mulch. Use a netting windbreak to protect the hedge if it is in an exposed position.

CLIPPING HEDGES

If a hedge is neglected, it soon loses a lot of its beauty. Regular trimming soon helps to restore this but it is also necessary for other reasons. If the hedge is left for too long, it may be difficult to bring it back to its original condition. Most can be restored eventually but this can take several years. A garden can be smartened up simply by cutting its hedges. Untrimmed hedges look ragged and untidy. Some types of hedging material need more frequent trimming than others, to keep them looking neat.

1 Cutting a hedge also includes clearing up the trimmings afterwards. One way of coping with this task is to lay down a cloth or plastic sheet under the area you are clipping and to move it along as you go.

2 When using shears, try to keep the blades flat against the plane of the hedge as this will give an even cut. If you jab the shears forward with a stabbing motion, the result is likely to be uneven.

WHEN TO CLIP HEDGES

Buxus (box)	late spring and late summer
Carpinus betulus (hornbeam)	mid/late summer
Chamaecyparis lawsoniana (Lawson's cypress)	late spring and late summer
Crataegus (hawthorn)	early summer and early autumn
x Cupressocyparis leylandii (leyland cypress)	late spring, midsummer or late spring, early autumn
Fagus sylvatica (beech)	mid/late summer
Ilex (holly)	late summer
Lavandula (lavender)	spring or early autumn
Ligustrum (privet)	late spring, midsummer and early autumn
Lonicera nitida (box-leaf honeysuckle)	late spring, midsummer and early autumn
Prunus laurocerasus (laurel)	mid-spring and late summer
Prunus lusitanica (Portuguese laurel)	mid-spring and late summer
Thuja plicata (thuja)	late spring and early autumn
Taxus (yew)	mid/late summer

3 A formal hedge looks best if it is given a regular cut. The top, in particular, should be completely flat. This can be best achieved by using poles at the ends or intervals along the hedges, with strings tautly stretched between them. These can be used as a guide. Take care not to cut the strings! If you have room to store it, make a template out of cardboard in the desired shape of the hedge so that the shape of the hedge is the same each time you cut it.

4 Keep the blades flat when you cut the top of a hedge. If it is a tall hedge, you will need to use steps rather than trying to reach up at an angle.

5 Power trimmers are much faster than hand shears and, in consequence, things can go wrong faster as well, so concentrate on what you are doing and have a rest if your arms feel tired. Wear adequate protective gear and take the appropriate precautions if you are using an electrically operated tool. Petrol- (gasolene-) driven clippers are more versatile, in that you are not limited by the length of the cord or by the charge of the battery, but they are much heavier than the electrically-powered equivalent.

6 Some conifers are relatively slow growing and only produce a few stray stems that can be cut off with secateurs (pruners) to neaten them. Secateurs should also be used for large-leaved shrubs, such as laurel (*Prunus laurocerasus*). This avoids leaves being cut in half by mechanical or hand shears, which always looks a bit of a mess.

Above: *A well-shaped hedge should be wider at the bottom than it is at the top. This allows the lower leaves to receive plenty of light and thus prevents the bottom branches from drying out.*

Ground Cover

One of the most valuable uses of shrubs is as ground cover. Ground cover is what its name implies, planting that covers the ground so that no bare earth shows. While there are obvious visual attractions in doing this, the main benefit is that ground cover prevents new weeds from germinating and therefore reduces the amount of maintenance required.

PLANTS FOR COVER

In the main, ground-covering plants are low-growing, but there is no reason why they should not be quite large as long as they do the job. Large rhododendron bushes form a perfect ground cover, for example, as nothing can grow under them.

Some ground-covering plants have flowers to enhance their appearance – heather (*Erica* and *Calluna*) and *Hypericum calycinum*, for example – while others depend on their attractive foliage – ivy (*Hedera*) and euonymus are examples.

Ground cover will not stop established weeds from coming through; it does inhibit the introduction of new weeds by creating a shade that is too dense for the seed to germinate and that starves any seedlings that do manage to appear.

SHRUBS SUITABLE FOR PLANTING AS GROUND COVER

Acaena
Arctostaphylos uva-ursi
Berberis
Calluna vulgaris (heather)
Cistus (rock rose)
Cotoneaster
Erica (heather)
Euonymus fortunei
Hebe pinguifolia 'Pagei'
Hedera (ivy)
Hypericum calycinum
Juniperus communis 'Prostrata'
Juniperus sabina tamariscifolia
Juniperus squamata 'Blue Carpet'
Lithodora diffusa
Pachysandra terminalis
Potentilla fruticosa
Salix repens
Stephandra incisa
Vinca minor (periwinkle)

Above: *A solid block of gold shimmers above the soil. The evergreen* Euonymus fortunei *'Emerald 'n' Gold' makes a perfect ground cover plant because it is colourful and dense.*

Right: *Prostrate conifers perform well. One plant can cover a large area and the texture and colour of the foliage makes it a welcome feature. They have the advantage of being evergreen and thus provide good cover all year round.*

Above: *The periwinkles, especially* Vinca minor, *make good ground cover. They are evergreen and will thrive in quite dense shade. However, if you want them to flower well it is better that they are planted more in the open.*

Above: *In the rock garden, the ground-hugging* Salix repens *rapidly covers a lot of territory. It can be a bit of a thug and needs to be cut back from time to time, to prevent it from spreading too far.*

Above: Lithodora diffusa *is one of those plants that straddles the divide between hardy perennials and shrubs, because it is classed as a subshrub. It provides a very dense ground cover for the rock garden and, in the early spring, makes a wonderful carpet of blue.*

Right: *By late summer and into autumn, much ground cover is looking a bit tired and jaded. However,* Ceratostigma plumbaginoides *is still flowering and presents a good choice of plant for providing colour at this time of year.*

Planting Ground Cover

The benefits of ground cover only occur if the ground has been thoroughly prepared. Any perennial weeds left in the soil when the shrubs are planted will soon come up through the cover as it will not control existing weeds, it will only prevent new ones germinating.

TENDING GROUND COVER

Once planted, the space between the shrubs should be constantly tended until the plants have grown together, and from then on they truly create ground cover. Take care when planning ground cover as it is not something you want to replant too often.

Although one of the aims of using ground cover is to reduce maintenance by cutting out weeding, it still requires some attention and may need trimming once a year. Ivy, for example, looks much better if it is sheared in the late winter or early spring and hypericum should be cut back after flowering.

1 It is important to remove any weeds from the soil where you are going to grow ground cover, otherwise the weeds will grow through the shrubs which will make them very difficult to eradicate.

2 Thoroughly prepare the soil in the same way as you would for any other type of shrub. Dig in plenty of well rotted organic material.

3 Position the plants in their pots so that you get the best possible layout, estimating how far each plant will spread. The aim is to cover all the bare earth eventually.

4 Dig holes and plant the shrubs. Firm them in so that there are no air pockets around the plants and then water the shrubs well.

5 The gaps between the plants may take a year or more to close up. In the meantime, plant annuals, perennials or other shrubs to act as temporary ground cover while the main plants spread. Arrange the "fillers" in their pots first, so you can create the most effective planting.

Right: *When you are satisfied with the arrangement you have, plant the fillers and water them in. Remove them when the main ground cover takes over.*

MAINTAINING GROUND COVER

1 Ground cover is often neglected and, because it is a low, permanent planting, it tends to collect all kinds of litter and rubbish. Take time to regularly clean through all your ground cover, removing any litter that is lurking between the leaves.

2 Most ground cover benefits from being trimmed back at least once a year. Here, the periwinkle *Vinca minor* is given a much-needed trim.

3 Regular trimming means that the ground cover grows at a more even rate, with fewer straggly stems. It looks tidier and healthier.

GROUND COVER PLANTS FOR SHADY AREAS
Acuba
Cassiope
Cornus canadensis (dogwood)
Euonymus
Gaultheria
Hedera (ivy)
Lonicera pileata
Pachysandra
Rhododendron
Sarcococca
Vaccinium
Vinca minor (periwinkle)

Dwarf Shrubs

In the small garden and the rock garden, dwarf shrubs are much more in keeping with the scale of things than large plants. Being small, they also have the advantage that you can grow more varieties in the same space.

USING DWARF SHRUBS

Size apart, dwarf shrubs are no different from the larger ones and are treated in exactly the same way. They can be used by themselves in rock gardens or separate beds. Or they can be mixed in with taller shrubs, perhaps in front of them or even under them. Many dwarf shrubs make very good ground cover plants. They can also be used in pots and other containers, either in groups or as specimen plants.

ROCK GARDEN SHRUBS

The really small dwarf shrubs are usually grown in the rock garden and even in troughs. Many are not much more than a few centimetres high. Like their larger brethren, they are equally grown for their foliage and flowers. Some are perfect miniatures of larger plants. *Juniperus communis* 'Compressa', for example, could be a large conifer seen through the reverse end of a telescope.

Above: *For those who like bright colours, nothing could fit the bill better than* Genista lydia. *In spring, it is absolutely covered with a mound of bright, gold-coloured, pea-like flowers. It looks good tumbling over rocks or a wall but can be used anywhere. It requires very little attention.*

Above: *Most ceanothus are large shrubs, often needing wall protection to bring them through the winter.* C. *'Pin Cushion' is a miniature version for the rock garden. It still retains both the good foliage and the blue flowers that attract so many gardeners to this group of plants and has the advantage that it needs little attention.*

Above: *As well as the more common dwarf shrubs, there are many varieties that will appeal to those who may want to start a collection of unusual shrubs:* x Halimiocistus revolii *is one example. This beautiful plant spreads to form a mat of dark green leaves, dotted with white flowers in midsummer. It likes a well-drained soil but needs little attention.*

Above: *The rock rose* (Helianthemum*) is one of the great joys of dwarf shrubs. There are many different varieties, with a wide range of colours, some bright while others are more subtle. The colour of their foliage also varies, from silver to bright green. Rock roses are suitable for the rock garden, raised beds or mixed borders. They spread to make large sheets, but rarely get tall. They need to be sheared over after flowering, to prevent them from becoming too sprawling.*

Above: *There are a number of dwarf willows of which this,* Salix helvetica, *is one of the best. It forms a compact shrub with very good silver foliage. It can be used in a rock garden or wherever dwarf shrubs are required. It looks especially good with geraniums –* G. sanguineum, *for example – growing through it. This willow needs very little attention.*

Left: *The group of dwarf conifers growing in this rock garden is* Juniperus communis *'Compressa'. This is one of the very best varieties of dwarf conifer, because it never grows very high, usually not more than 45 cm (18 in), and it takes many years to reach that height. Their slow growth rate means they are useful for alpine troughs and they have the advantage that they need very little attention.*

Above: *Using a few dwarf shrubs and conifers in a trough or sink adds to the height of the planting, giving it more structure and interest than if it were simply filled with low-growing alpine plants.*

Planting a Gravel Bed

Most dwarf rock garden plants need a well-drained soil with plenty of grit or sharp sand added to it. Plant between autumn and spring, as long as it is not too wet or cold. They look best grown with other alpine plants, set amongst rocks or in gravel beds. The miniature landscape of the trough can be designed in the same way.

1 Prepare the ground for planting. Dig the ground to allow about 5 cm (2 in) of gravel. Level the ground and lay heavy-duty black plastic or a mulching sheet over the area, overlapping strips by about 5 cm (2 in).

2 Tip the gravel on top of the plastic and level it off with a rake.

3 Draw the gravel back from the planting area and make a slit in the plastic. Plant in the normal way.

4 Firm in the plants and pull back the plastic, then cover again with gravel.

Right: *A rock garden with dwarf and slow-growing shrubs.*

DWARF SHRUBS FOR THE ROCK GARDEN

Aethionema
Berberis (dwarf forms)
Ceanothus prostratus
Chamaecyparis obtusa
  (and various 'Nana' forms)
Convolvulus cneorum
Convolvulus sabatius
Daphne
Dryas octopetala
Erica (heather)
Euonymus nana
Euryops acreus
Fuchsia procumbens
Genista lydia
x *Halimiocistus revolii*
Hebe (many dwarf forms)
Helianthemum (most forms)

Hypericum (many dwarf
  forms)
Juniperus communis
  'Compressa'
Leptospermum scoparium
  'Nanum'
Lithodora diffusa
Lonicera pyrenaica
Micromeria corsica
Ononis
Salix helvetica
Salix repens (and several
  other forms)
Sorbus reducta
Teucrium (various dwarf forms)
Thymus (many forms)
Verbascum 'Letitia'

WOODLAND BEDS

As well as a rock garden built in the sun, with free-draining material, many rock gardeners also have what is traditionally known as a woodland or peat bed, although other materials besides peat are now used for planting. The beds are positioned in part shade, where they catch dappled sunlight or sun only at the end of the day. Here, in a woodland-type soil, a wide range of plants that like damp, shady conditions can be grown. Amongst these are many dwarf shrubs, perhaps the most popular being the dwarf rhododendrons.

The soil here is usually a mixture of leaf mould and good garden soil. In the past, quantities of peat were also used, although a peat substitute, such as coir, is now commonly used instead. The soil is usually acidic in nature, suiting many of the plants that grow in woodland conditions. The peat, or peat substitute, gives it the right pH balance, although it is possible to make soil more acid by adding rotted pine needles to it.

DWARF SHRUBS FOR A WOODLAND BED

Andromeda
Arctostaphylos
Cassiope
Daphne
Erica (heather)
Gaultheria
Kalmia
Kalmiopsis
Pernyetta
Phyllodoce
Rhododendron (many dwarf forms)
Vaccinium

Above: *Daphnes are excellent dwarf shrubs to use in the garden. They all have deliciously scented flowers and many, such as this* D. tangutica, *are evergreen. They have the advantage that they very rarely need any pruning, just the removal of dead wood should any occur. They can be used in rock gardens or elsewhere.*

Top right: *Heathers make good all-year-round plants and appreciate the acid nature of a woodland bed.*

Right: *A colourful woodland bed can be made up of heathers and conifers. This kind of bed is low maintenance, although the heathers stay tighter and more compact if they are sheared over once a year.*

Evergreens

The great feature of evergreens is the fact that they hold on to their leaves throughout the winter. They can be used as a permanent part of the structure of any border or garden. This has advantages and disadvantages. The advantage is that throughout the year there is always something in leaf to look at; on the other hand, unless carefully sited, evergreens can become a bit dull, so plan your planting with care.

WORK-FREE GARDENING

In many respects, evergreen shrubs form the backbone of a work-free garden, because they need very little attention unless they are used as hedging, where they need regular clipping. Although they do not drop their leaves in autumn, as deciduous bushes do, they still nonetheless shed leaves. This is usually done continuously through the year.

Many evergreens have dark green leaves, which can make the scene in which they are used a bit sombre but this effect can be brightened with the use of plants with variegated leaves. Because evergreen leaves have to last a long time, many are tough and leathery, with a shiny surface. This shine also helps to brighten up dull spots, reflecting the light back towards the viewer.

Evergreens are no more difficult to grow than other shrubs; indeed they are easier because they need less maintenance.

Above: *Conifers can become boring and so familiar that you do not even see them. However, there are some that provide a wonderful selection of shapes and textures. This juniper produces an attractive "sea of waves" effect that can never become boring.*

Left: *Privet is a good evergreen shrub although in its common form it is better known as a hedging plant. This is* Ligustrum lucidum *'Excelsum Superbum'. In the open the variegation is golden but in shade it becomes a yellowish green.*

Left: *Choisya is a good evergreen. The leaves are shiny and catch the sun and it produces masses of white flowers in spring and often again later in the year. These perfume the air for a good distance around. This form with golden foliage is C. ternata 'Sundance'.*

Above: *One tends to think of evergreens as being dull green and without flowers, but there are many that put on a magnificent display of flowers each year. Rhododendrons are a good example of this.*

Below: *This Pieris japonica is an evergreen that will grace any garden, as long as the area is not prone to late frosts. The foliage alters its colour as it matures, providing a constantly changing picture. This is enhanced by long plumes of white flowers.*

Above: *Many of the hebes are evergreen. This one, H. cupressoides, belongs to the whipcord group; it has very small leaves pressed tightly against its stems and, when out of flower, it could easily be mistaken for a conifer.*

Shrubs with Coloured Foliage

Most foliage is green, but the discerning gardener will soon notice that the number of different greens is almost infinite. A lot can be done by careful arrangement of these various greens, but even more can be achieved by incorporating into the garden the large number of shrubs that have foliage in other colours besides green.

VARYING SHADES OF GREEN

Leaves need green chlorophyll to function, so leaves are never completely devoid of green, another colour may just dominate. For example, yellow foliage still has a green tinge to it and purple likewise. Scrape back the hairs that make a leaf look silver or grey and, again, there will be green. When grown out of the sun, particularly later in the season, this green becomes more apparent. Occasionally, stems bearing paper-white leaves appear on some shrubs. It would be wonderful if one could propagate these by taking cuttings but, unfortunately, their total lack of chlorophyll means they will not grow.

MAINTAINING THE COLOUR

Purple leaves need the sun to retain their colour. Silver-leaved plants must always be grown in the sun; they will not survive for long in shade. Golden and yellow foliage often need a dappled shade – too much sun and the leaves are scorched. However, too much shade and the leaves turn greener, so the balance is a delicate one. The thing to avoid is midday sun.

Growing coloured-leaved shrubs is no different from any other shrub. They need the same pruning, except that if a reversion occurs, this must be cut out.

As well as shrubs with single-coloured foliage, there are shrubs with foliage in two or more colours, known as "variegated" foliage, and shrubs which are planted for their autumn foliage – just two other interesting aspects of the coloration of shrubs.

SILVER FOLIAGE

Caryopteris x clandonensis
Convolvulus cneorum
Elaeagnus 'Quicksilver'
Hebe pinguifolia 'Pagei'
Hippophaë rhamnoides
Lavandula angustifolia
Pyrus salicifolia 'Pendula'
Rosa glauca
Salix lanata
Santolina chamaecyparis
Santolina pinnata neapolitana

BETTER FOLIAGE

Coppicing or pollarding some coloured-leaved shrubs improves the quality of the leaves. It produces bigger and often richer-coloured foliage. Cut the plants back in the early spring, before growth begins. They will quickly regain their original size but the foliage will be bigger and better. *Sambucus* (elder), *Cotinus* (smoke tree) and *Rosa glauca* all benefit from this.

Above: Rosa glauca *has the most wonderful glaucous (grey- or blue-green) foliage with a purple-blue tint which contrasts well with the pink and white flowers. The foliage is improved by coppicing.*

POLLARDING

1 Cut back the stems to very short stubs, leaving perhaps one or two buds on each stem to grow. The treatment looks a bit drastic, but a mass of new shoots will be produced during the summer, with colourful stems in winter.

2 A head of brightly-coloured branches will stem from the base in the winter as on this *Salix alba vitellina* 'Britzensis'.

Left: *Silver foliage is very desirable. All silver plants need a sunny position and a well drained soil, this cotton lavender,* Santolina chamaecyparis *being no exception. Shear the plant over in the spring, just as new growth begins, to keep it compact. Many gardeners also prefer to cut off the flowering stems, because they find the sharp yellow flowers too harsh.*

Below: *This shrub grows in areas that are too dry to grow many other plants. It has had many names over the years and is now called* Brachyglottis *(Dunedin Group) 'Sunshine'.*

Above: *The silver leaves of plants can often set off the colour of their flowers beautifully. Here, the silvery-grey leaves of* Helianthemum *'Wisley Pink' are a perfect foil for its pink flowers. Shear over the plant after flowering, to keep it from becoming straggly.*

Above: *A favourite silver-leaved shrub is* Elaeagnus *'Quicksilver' which in the sunshine looks like burnished pewter. During the spring, the leaves are supplemented by masses of small, pale primrose-yellow flowers which as well as being attractive have a delicious scent that wafts all over the garden.*

Shrubs with Purple Foliage

Purple foliage is a very useful component when designing a garden. It forms a pleasant alternative to the normal green, without being quite as stark in contrast as silver, yellow or one of the variegated foliages.

A PLEASANT CONTRAST

Purple is ideal as a main background colour or in combination with other plants as it goes with most other colours. It works well, in particular, as a background to various coloured flowers, so can be used with herbaceous or annual plants.

The one big drawback with purple foliage is that it can look very heavy and leaden if used in too great a quantity. A few shrubs will work better than too many. But purple can look superb if placed where the evening sunlight comes from behind the shrub so that the leaves are backlit. They then positively glow with colour and no other shrub can match them.

PURPLE-LEAVED SHRUBS

Acer palmatum
'Atropurpureum'
Berberis thunbergii
'Atropurpurea'
Berberis thunbergii
'Bagatelle'
Cordyline australis
'Atropurpurea'
Corylus maxima 'Purpurea'
Cotinus coggygria 'Royal Purple'
Fagus sylvatica 'Riversii'
Prunus cerasifera 'Nigra'
Salvia officinalis
'Purpurascens'
Weigela florida 'Foliis Purpurea'

Above: *A really rich purple is to be seen on* Prunus x cistena. *This is beautifully enhanced in the spring by numerous pink flowers with purple centres. The total effect can be stunning.*

Left: *This* Cercis canadensis *'Forest Pansy' has purple foliage, exquisitely flushed with green and greenish blue. The heart-shaped leaves add to the attraction of this bush. In the autumn, the leaves take on a bright scarlet hue.*

Left: *The hazels (Corylus) have several purple forms to offer. They generally have large, imposing leaves. However, if they are in too shady a place they are liable to turn green.*

Right: *Another very good series of purples are the various smoke bushes, Cotinus. They look especially effective when they are planted so that the evening sun shines through the leaves. Cutting this shrub back hard in the spring produces much larger leaves the following year.*

Above: *In some shrubs, the colour is in the young leaves and once they begin to mature, they revert to their original colour. Although in some ways this is disappointing, in others, as here with this purple sage, the effect can be stunning.*

Above: *A good source of purple foliage is* Berberis thunbergii *'Atropurpurea' in its various forms, including a dwarf one. In the autumn, the leaves colour-up beautifully and the shrub has the added attraction of red berries.*

Shrubs with Variegated Foliage

There has been a steady increase of interest in variegated shrubs and today they can be seen in one form or another in most gardens. This increase of interest is most welcome, because it has stimulated the search for more types of variegated plants and now there are many more from which to choose.

TYPES OF VARIEGATION

There are many different types of variegation. First there is the aspect of colour. Most variegations in shrubs are gold, followed very closely by cream and white. These have the effect of lightening any group of plants they are planted with. They are particularly useful in shade or in a dark corner, because they shine out, creating interest where it is often difficult to do so. Other colours include different shades of green. Again, these have a lightening effect. On the other hand, variegation that involves purples often introduces a more sombre mood. Sometimes, there are more than two colours in a variegation and this leads to a sense of gaiety, even if combined with sombre colours.

When looked at closely there are several different patterns of variegation. From a distance the differences blur and the leaves just register as variegated, but if you get closer you can see how the variegation can alter the appearance of the leaves. In some cases, it is the edges of the leaves that are variegated, sometimes as a ribbon and in others as an irregular margin, perhaps penetrating almost to the centre of the leaves. Another common type is where the centre of the leaves are variegated. Sometimes this is an irregular patch in the centre and in others the variegation follows the veins of the leaf. Yet a third form of variegation is where the leaves are splashed with an alternative colour, as though paint has been flicked onto their surface. A final type is where the variegation appears as long parallel strips down the leaves.

All these are attractive and it is worth looking out for and collecting at least one of each type. The more one looks at this group of plants, the more fascinating they become.

SILVER AND WHITE VARIEGATION

Cornus alternifolia 'Argentea'
Cornus alba 'Elegantissima'
Cornus controversa 'Variegata'
Euonymus fortunei 'Emerald Gaiety'
Euonymus fortunei 'Silver Queen'
Euonymus fortunei 'Variegatus'
Euonymus japonicus 'Macrophyllus Albus'
Fuchsia magellanica 'Variegata'
Prunus lusitanica 'Variegata'
Rhamnus alaternus 'Argenteovariegata'
Vinca minor 'Argenteovariegata'

Above: *The variegated* Weigela florida *'Albomarginata' is seen here against a spiraea. The white-striped leaves blend well with the white flowers of the spiraea in spring, and in summer the interest is continued because the weigela produces pink flowers.*

Below: Cornus mas *'Aureoelegantissima' creates a very different effect here, by being planted next to a different type of plant. Here the colours are more muted and do not provide such a contrast as they do against the leaves of the* Geranium x oxonianum.

Above: *One of the most popular of variegated plants,* Cornus mas *'Aureoelegantissima', is shown here with* Geranium x oxonianum *growing through it. This is an easy plant to grow and its subtle coloration means it can grow in a wide variety of situations.*

Left: Rhamnus alaternus *'Argenteovariegata', as its name implies, has a silver variegation. This is present as stripes down the margins of the leaves and sets the whole shrub shimmering. It can grow into quite a large shrub, up to 3.5–4.5 m (12–15 ft) high.*

CUTTING OUT REVERSION IN SHRUBS

Variegation is an abnormality that comes about in a number of different ways. Frequently, the process is reversed and the variegated leaves revert to their original green form. These green-leaved stems are more vigorous than the variegated ones, because they contain more chlorophyll for photosynthesis and thus produce more food. If these vigorous shoots are left, they will soon dominate the shrub and it may eventually all revert to green. The way to prevent this is to cut out the shoots as soon as they are seen.

Above: *Green-leaved shoots have appeared in this* Spiraea japonica *'Goldflame'. If left, they may take over the whole plant. The remedy is simple. Remove the affected shoots back to that part of the stem or shoot where the reversion begins.*

Shrubs with Variegated Foliage 2

USING VARIEGATED PLANTS

Variegated plants should be used with discretion. They can become too "busy": if several are planted together they tend to clash. Reserve them to use as accent plants, to draw the eye. Also use them to leaven a scene, brightening it up a bit.

On the whole, variegated shrubs are no different in terms of planting and subsequent maintenance to any other plants, although you may need to consider how much sunlight they can tolerate.

Although many variegated shrubs will tolerate full sun, many others prefer to be away from the hot midday sun, in a light, dappled shade. Always check the planting instructions when you buy a new shrub, to see what situation it requires.

Above: *Several of the herbs, such as thyme, rosemary and sage, can be variegated. Here, the sage* Salvia officinalis *is shown in the yellow and green form 'Icterina'. As well as providing a visual attraction throughout the year, these evergreen variegated forms of herbs are also always available for use in the kitchen.*

Above: *This elder,* Sambucus racemosa *'Plumosa Aurea', is not, strictly speaking, a variegated plant, but the variation from the young brown growth to the golden mature leaves gives the overall impression of a variegated shrub. In order to keep this effect, prune the elder almost to the ground each spring.*

YELLOW AND GOLD VARIATIONS

Abutilon metapotamicum
    'Variegatum'
Aucuba japonica 'Picturata'
Aucuba japonica 'Mr Goldstrike'
Aucuba japonica 'Crotonifolia'
Caryopteris x clandonensis
    'Worcester Gold'
Cornus alba 'Spaethii'
Daphne x burkwoodii
    'Somerset Gold Edge'
Euonymus fortunei 'Sunshine'
Euonymus fortunei 'Gold Spot'
Euonymus japonicus
    'Aureopictus'
Ilex aquifolium 'Golden
    Milkboy' (centre)
Ilex aquifolium 'Aurifodina'
    (edge/centre)
Ilex x altaclerensis 'Golden
    King' (edge)
Ilex aquifolium 'Crispa
Aureopicta' (centre)
Ilex x altaclerensis
    'Lawsoniana' (centre)
Ligustrum ovalifolium 'Aureum'
Osmanthus heterophyllus
    'Goshiki'
Sambucus nigra
    'Aureomarginata'

Above: *There are many variegated evergreens that can add a great deal of interest to what could otherwise be a collection of plain, dark green shrubs. The hollies, in particular, provide a good selection. This one is* Ilex x altaclerensis 'Lawsoniana'. *Its green berries have yet to change to their winter colour of red.*

Above right: Berberis thunbergii *'Rose Glow' is a beautifully variegated shrub, its purple leaves splashed with pink. It is eye-catching and fits in well with purple schemes. Avoid using it with yellows.*

Right: *An exotic variegation is seen on this* Abutilon megapont-amicum *'Variegatum', with its green leaves splashed with gold. It has the added attraction of red and yellow flowers that appear in the latter half of the summer and continue into the autumn. It is on the tender side and in colder areas should be grown in pots and moved inside for the winter.*

Shrubs with Fragrant Foliage

There are a surprising number of shrubs with fragrant foliage. Some fragrances might not be immediately apparent, because they need some stimulant to produce it. Rosemary, for example, does not fill the air with its perfume until it is touched. Some of the rock roses (*Cistus*) produce a wonderfully aromatic scent after they have been washed with rain. Similarly, the sweet-briar rose (*Rosa rubiginosa*) and its hybrids, such as 'Lady Penzance', produce a delightfully fresh scent after rain.

WHERE TO PLANT

It is a good idea to plant shrubs with aromatic foliage near where you walk, so that when you brush against them they give out a delicious aroma. Few gardeners can resist running their fingers through rosemary foliage as they pass, and a lavender path is a pleasure to walk along, because the soothing smells of the herb are gently released along the path as you go.

For hot, dry gardens, *Camphorosma monspeliaca* is one of the best plants to grow, because it smells of camphor when the new shoots are touched. Thyme planted in the ground may be too low to touch with the hands, but it releases its fine fragrance if it is walked on

in paving. Many conifers have a pleasant, resinous smell when they are rubbed. Juniper, in particular, is good.

But, of course, not all smells are pleasant. *Clerodendron bungei* has sweetly-scented flowers, but its leaves smell revolting if they are crushed. Many people dislike the sharp smell of the foliage of broom (*Cytisus*) and elder (*Sambucus*).

Above right: *While it is sensible to plant thyme used for the kitchen in a more hygienic position, it does make a wonderful herb for planting between paving stones because when crushed by the feet it produces a delicious fragrance – and trampling on it does not seem to harm the plant. Beware doing so in bare feet though, because there may well be bees on the thyme.*

Right: Prostanthera cuneata *is an evergreen shrub that has leaves with a curious aromatic scent that is very appealing. In spring, and again in the summer, white, scented flowers are produced, which look very attractive against the dark foliage.*

SHRUBS WITH FRAGRANT FOLIAGE

Aloysia triphylla
Laurus nobilis (bay)
Lavandula (lavender)
Myrica
Myrtus communis (myrtle)
Perovskia
Rosmarinus (rosemary)
Salvia officinalis (sage)
Santolina

Above: *One of the most beguiling of garden scents is that of rosemary, another culinary herb. If given a sunny well-drained site, this shrub will go on growing for many years, until its trunk is completely gnarled and ancient looking.*

Above: *Culinary herbs are a great source of scented foliage. Sage, for example, has a dry sort of herby smell, which will usually evoke in the passer-by thoughts of delicious stuffing mixtures. This is an evergreen and provides fragrance all year round.*

Right: Hebe cupressoides, *like so many plants, has a smell that is characteristically its own. It is a resinous type of fragrance that is reminiscent of the cypresses after which it is named.*

Shrubs with Fragrant Flowers

It is always worthwhile to include at least a few shrubs in the garden that have fragrant flowers. Unlike foliage scents, which generally need to be stimulated by touch, flower fragrances are usually produced unaided, and flowers will often fill the whole garden with their scent. This is particularly noticeable on a warm evening.

SOOTHING SCENTS

A good position for fragrant shrubs is next to a place where you sit and relax, especially after the day's work. The soft fragrance from the shrubs helps to soothe tiredness if put next to a seat or perhaps near an arbour or patio where you sit and eat. Psychologically, it can help to plant a shrub that has evening fragrance near the front gate or where you get out of the car, so that you are welcomed home by characteristically soothing scents. Choose an evening-scented shrub so that you do not get the scent on your way out in the morning, or you might not get to work at all! Another good position for a fragrant shrub is near a window or door that is often open, so the scents drift into the house.

As with foliage scents, some flowers smell unpleasant. Many dislike the smell of privet flowers, while the scent from *Cestrum parqui* is foetid in the day but sweet in the evening and at night.

One way to store summer fragrances is to turn some of the flowers into *potpourri*. Roses, in particular, are good for this.

In the winter, a surprising number of winter-flowering shrubs have very strong scents that attract insects from far away. Always try to include a few of these, such as the winter honeysuckles, in the garden.

FRAGRANT FLOWERS

Azara
Berberis x stenophylla
Clethra
Corylopsis
Daphne
Elaeagnus
Hamamelis (witch hazel)
Itea
Magnolia
Mahonia
Myrtus (myrtle)
Osmanthus
Philadelphus (mock orange)
Rhododendron luteum
Sarcococca (sweet box)
Skimmia

Above right: *Daphnes are a good genus of plants for fragrance, because they nearly all have a very strong, sweet scent.* Daphne x burkwoodii *is one of the largest of the genus, seen here in its variety 'Somerset'. When in full flower in the spring, it will perfume a large area.*

Right: *The Mexican orange-blossom,* Choisya ternata, *is another sweet-smelling shrub. It flowers in the spring and then sporadically again through the summer. The delightful flowers contrast with the glossy foliage.*

Above: *Not everybody likes the smell of elder flowers, and even fewer people like the smell of elder leaves, but the flowers do have a musky scent that is popular with many country people.*

Left: *Many flowers produce a sweet scent in the spring and early summer and this* Viburnum x juddii *and its close relatives are always amongst the best examples. It produces domes of pale pink flowers with a delicious perfume that spreads over quite a wide area.*

Above: Philadelphus *(mock orange) is one of the most popular of fragrant shrubs. The combination of the pure white flowers (sometimes tinged purple in the centre) and the sweet perfume seems to remind many people of purity and innocence. They flower after many of the other sweet-smelling flowers are over.*

Above: *The most popular perfumed shrub of all must surely be the rose. One of the advantages of many modern varieties of rose is that they continue to flower and produce their scent over a long period, often all the summer and well into the autumn. 'Zéphirine Drouhin' has a wonderful scent and is repeat-flowering. It can be grown either as a bush or as a climber and has the added advantage of being thornless.*

Shrubs with Berries and Fruit

It is not just the leaves and flowers that make a shrub worth growing. Flowering usually produces some form of seed, which is often carried in an attractive casing of fruit or berry. Two of the oldest fruiting shrubs to be appreciated, even back in ancient times, are the holly and the mistletoe.

THE APPEAL OF FRUIT

Fruit, either as berries, seed pods or even fluffy heads, often enhances the appearance of a shrub, especially if the fruit is brightly-coloured. Fruit bushes, such as gooseberries and red currants, can be fan-trained or grown as standards, and many berried shrubs have been specially bred to increase the range of colours. The firethorn (*Pyracantha*) can now be found with red, orange or yellow berries, for example.

Berries and fruit are not only attractive to gardeners, but to birds and other animals, so if you want to keep the berries buy a shrub like skimmia which will not be eaten by them.

One thing to bear in mind with berrying shrubs is that the male and female flowers may be on separate plants (skimmias and hollies, for example). Although they will both flower, only the female with bear fruit. So if you want fruit or berries, make sure you buy a male and a female.

Left: *Pyracantha makes a very decorative display of berries in the autumn. There are several varieties to choose from, with the berry colour varying from yellow, through orange to red. The berries are not only attractive but good food for the birds.*

Below: *It is important when buying pernettyas* (Gaultheria mucronata) *that you buy both a male and a female plant to ensure that pollination takes place. One male will suffice for several females that carry the berries.*

BERRIED SHRUBS

Chaenomeles (japonica)
Cotoneaster
Crataegus (hawthorn)
Daphne
Euonymus europaeus
Hippophaë rhamnoides
Ilex (holly)
Ligustrum
Rosa
Symphoricarpo
Viburnum opulus

Right: Piptanthus *is not totally hardy and is normally grown against a wall for protection. After its yellow flowers in spring, it produces these attractive pods, which decorate the plant in midsummer.*

Left: *When buying holly, ensure that you buy a berry-bearing form as not all carry them. Seen here in flower is* Ilex aquifolium *'Ferox Argentea'.*

Right: *Skimmias are good plants for the winter garden as they have very large, glossy berries, with the advantage that the birds do not like them, so they remain for a long period. Ensure you get a berrying form and buy a male to pollinate them.*

Below: *The cotoneasters produce a brilliant display of berries, as well as having attractive leaves and flowers. The berries are not too popular with birds and are often left until all the other berries have been eaten.*

Above: *Rose heps or hips provide an extension to the rose's season. The colour varies from variety to variety, with some being red and others orange, and some, such as* R. pimpinellifolia, *bearing black berries.*

Shrubs for Containers

Such is the versatility of shrubs that they can be grown successfully in containers as well as in the open ground. Container shrubs can be positioned on hard surfaces such as patios, walls or on steps. They can also be grown in roof gardens, on balconies or in basement plots.

WHY CHOOSE CONTAINERS?
If the garden is small or paved, there is no reason why all the plants should not be grown in containers, particularly because they can be attractive in their own right. Any kind of shrub can be grown in a container, so long as the shrub is not too big or the container too small.

One advantage of growing shrubs in pots is that you can tailor the soil to the shrub's requirements. Probably the best thing about this is the fact that it is possible to grow acid-loving plants, such as rhododendrons and azaleas, in areas where the soil is naturally alkaline and where such plants would not normally grow. Camellias, pieris, gaultherias, vacciniums and heathers are among other such plants which need special soil.

Above: *A glazed ceramic container is used to house a combination of lavender and* Euonymous fortunei *'Emerald Gaiety'; as long as they do not outgrow their container, such combinations can create a most attractive picture.*

Right: *Most elders make a large shrub after a few years, but they can still be used as pot plants, especially if cut to the base each spring. Here* Sambucus racemosa *'Plumosa Aurea' is growing in a large substitute-stone container. It is used as part of a larger planting.*

Above: *Fuchsias make exceptionally attractive container plants. The more tender varieties need to be over-wintered inside or started again each year, but hardier varieties can be left outside in milder climates.*

Above: *It is often possible to plant shrubs that form large bushes in containers for a few years while they are still small and then replace them with the same or another plant. Here* Cornus mas *'Aureoelegantissima' which could eventually grow to 6 m (20 ft) or more is being used.*

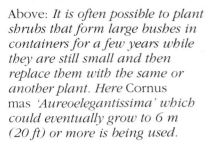

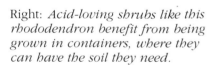

Right: *Acid-loving shrubs like this rhododendron benefit from being grown in containers, where they can have the soil they need.*

SHRUBS FOR CONTAINERS

Ballota pseudodictamnus	*Ilex* (holly)
Buxus sempervirens (box)	*Indigofera*
Callistemon citrinus (bottlebrush)	*Kalmia*
Camellia	*Laurus nobilis* (bay)
Convolvulus cneorum	*Lavandula* (lavender)
Cordyline australis	*Myrtus communis* (myrtle)
Cotoneaster	*Olearia* (daisy bush)
Erica (heather)	*Phormium* (New Zealand flax)
Fuchsia	*Rhododendron*
Hebe	*Rosa*
Helianthemum	*Rosmarinus* (rosemary)
Hydrangea	*Skimmia*
Hypericum	*Yucca*

Planting Shrubs in Containers

There is no great difficulty in growing plants in containers, so long as you remember that the pots are likely to need watering every day, except when it rains, and possibly more often than this in the summer.

CONTAINER CARE

When planting shrubs in containers, it is essential to use a good potting compost (potting soil) that contains plenty of grit or sharp sand, to help with drainage, and to add small stones to the pot so that excess water can drain away. In addition, a slow-release fertilizer and some water-retaining granules will encourage the plant to flourish.

Bear in mind that your plant will not grow indefinitely if it is kept in the same pot or compost (soil mix) for ever. Every year or so, remove the shrub and repot it using fresh compost. If the shrub is becoming pot-bound, that is,

the roots are going round the edge of the container, forming a tight knot, either put it in a larger pot or trim back some of the offending roots.

POSITIONING CONTAINERS

If you have a large enough garden, it is possible to keep the containers out of sight and only bring them into view when the shrubs are at their best, in full flower, for example. In a smaller garden, where this is more difficult, move the pots around so that the best ones are always in the most prominent position and even hiding the others if this is possible.

1 All containers should have a drainage hole in the bottom. Loosely cover this and the bottom of the pot with broken pottery, bits of tile or small stones, so that any excess water can freely drain away.

2 Partially fill the container with compost (soil mix) and then mix in some water-retaining granules. These essential granules will swell up and hold many times their own weight in water to give up to the plant's roots when they want it. While not considerably reducing the amount of water needed, water-retaining granules will make it easier for the shrub to come through really hot and dry times in midsummer. Follow the instructions on the packet as to quantities you need for the size of the pot you have.

3 Place the container in the position you finally want to have it and continue filling it with compost (the pot will be heavy to move once it is fully-planted). Plant the shrub to the same level as it was in its original container. Firm the compost down lightly and top up, if necessary, with some further compost.

4 Most composts contain fertilizers but the constant watering will soon leach (wash) it out. A slow-release fertilizer can be mixed with the compost or a tablet, as here, can be added to the pot, which will give six months' supply of nutrients. Read the packet for any special instructions.

5 Leave the top of the compost as it is, or cover it with stones of some sort, such as large pebbles, as here, or gravel. These not only give the container an attractive finish but help keep the compost cool and prevent water from evaporating.

6 Finally, water the container thoroughly and continue to do so at regular intervals. During hot weather, this is likely to be at least daily.

7 You may want to keep the newly-planted pot out of sight until the shrub has matured or comes into flower. However, if the container is large, it is often best to fill it *in situ*, because it will be very heavy once filled with compost.

Right: *This variegated pieris, which likes an acid soil, would soon languish and die in a chalky garden.*

Shrubs for Topiary

Most shrubs are grown naturally. They may be cut back if they get too big, or trimmed if they are part of a hedge, but their natural shape is not generally altered. However, there is one class of shrub-growing in which the shape is drastically altered, so much so that it takes a close look to identify the plants involved. These are topiaries.

PRODUCING A SHAPE

Topiaries can be cut to any shape the gardener desires. They can be formed into abstract or geometrical shapes, such as balls, cones or pyramids, or they can be made into something more intricate, perhaps depicting a bird, a person or even a teapot. There is little limit to what the imagination can produce in topiary.

Tight, slow-growing shrubs are the ones to choose for topiary, with yew and box being the best. Holly (*Ilex*), privet (*Ligustrum*) and box-leaf honeysuckle (*Lonicera nitida*) are also recommended. Several others can also be used, but they need a lot more attention to keep them neat.

The simplest topiaries are "carved" out of solid shrubs, particularly if they are yew or box, because these will easily regenerate and slowly fill out to their new shape. However, the most satisfactory way to produce topiary is to train the shrubs to their shape from the very beginning. A metal or wooden former or template helps with this. The shoots are tied in and trimmed as they grow, until the shrub has acquired the desired shape. Some formers are just a rough guide to the shape, intended to hold the main pieces in position, especially if they are

vulnerable, such as a peacock's tail, but others are shaped like the finished work and can be used as a trimming guide when the work is complete.

Topiaries can take several years to reach completion, so do not get too impatient. Several projects can be started in pots at the same time, so there is always something going on to keep the interest alive.

TOOLS FOR TOPIARY

Unless the topiary is on a large scale, avoid using powered tools. It is too easy to lose concentration or momentary control and disaster follows. In preference, use hand tools, which take longer but which give you more control. For cutting thicker stems, especially in the initial training, use secateurs (pruners), snipping out one stem at a time. Once the shape has been formed, trim it over with normal hedging shears or a pair of clippers of the type usually used for sheep-shearing. The latter give excellent control, but can only be used for light trimming, such as removing the tips of new growth. If the topiary is made from a shrub with large leaves, then use secateurs to trim it to avoid cutting the leaves in half, otherwise they will die back with a brown edge and the overall appearance will be spoiled.

Above: *In this topiary a four-masted ship in full sail glides across the garden. Here, the complicated design is slightly obscured by other topiaries in the background.*

Above: *This practical piece of topiary has a wooden seat worked into the bottom of the shrub, supported on a metal frame. A complete set round a table would be a novel feature for a barbecue or outdoor meal.*

Above: *These simple shapes worked in box can be used to advantage in a wide variety of positions in the garden. They will take several years of dedication to produce, but the effort is definitely worth it.*

Above: *Gardens do not have always to be serious: there is a sense of fun about this jolly witch, sitting around her cauldron with her cat and its mouse, which would cheer up anybody looking at it.*

Above: *Topiary shapes can be as precise or as free as you wish. In this free interpretation of a simple windmill, cut from yew, you can sense the pleasure of the person who created it.*

SHRUBS FOR ALL SEASONS

Shrubs in Spring

Shrubs come into their own in the spring. This is the time when everything is waking up and looking fresh and the gardener's own enthusiasm is at its greatest.

SPRING FLOWERS

Many shrubs flower in spring, which gives them ample time to produce seed and for it to ripen and be distributed to ensure the next generation.

The one big enemy of spring-flowering shrubs is the severe late frosts that occur in some areas. A false start to the spring brings warm weather and then a sudden frost kills all the new shoots and knocks off the flower buds. Rhododendrons, azaleas, pieris, magnolias and many others frequently suffer this fate. One solution is to give some protection if hard frost is forecast. Placing a sheet of fleece over them is often sufficient.

It is tempting to put all the spring shrubs together, for one glorious display, but resist this or, at least, mix in a few later-flowering ones as well or the area could become dull for the rest of the year. One solution is to plant *viticella* clematis through them. These are cut back to the ground in late winter so that they do not interfere with the shrubs' flowering, but grow up and cover them in blooms from midsummer onwards.

Try and finish planting any new shrubs by early spring and, as the various shrubs finish flowering, prune them as necessary. Remember to feed those that are in containers.

Above: *Camellias flower from the late winter through to the middle of spring. They are best planted where they do not get the early-morning sun, as this will destroy the buds if they have been frosted overnight.*

Right: *One of the earliest shrubs to flower is* Spiraea *'Arguta' which produces a frothy mountain of pure white flowers over quite a long period. Sometimes it will even produce a few blooms in midwinter, to brighten the gloom.*

Above: *The flowering currant,* Ribes sanguineum, *is a beautiful spring-flowering shrub, but its foliage has a distinctive 'foxy' smell that not everyone likes.*

Above: Exochorda x macrantha *'The Bride' is a showy, spring-flowering plant. When in full flower, it is so covered in pure white flowers that the leaves are barely visible. Here, many of the flowers are still in bud, forming attractive ribbons of white balls.*

Above: *Rhododendrons are many gardeners' favourite spring shrub. They need an acid soil and a position out of hot sunlight. They can be bought in a wide variety of colours, some soft and subtle and others bright and brash.*

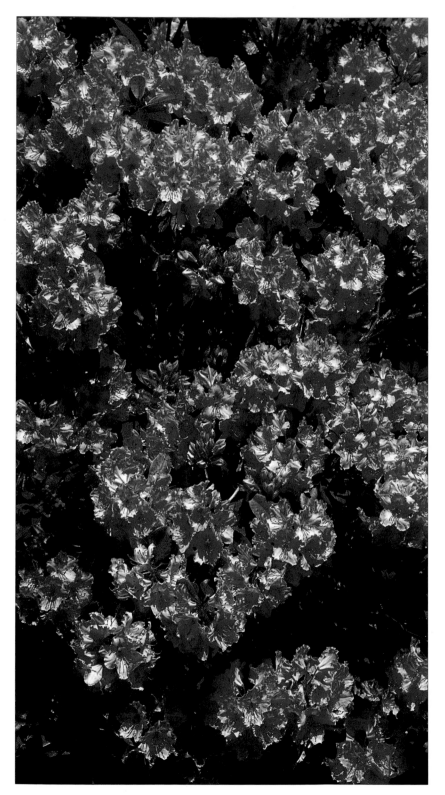

Above: *Forsythia creates one of the biggest splashes of colour in the spring. Here it is used as an informal hedge. It should be cut immediately after flowering to ensure that new flowering shoots grow in time for next season.*

Right: *One of the best-loved spring shrubs is* Magnolia stellata. *Each year it is a mass of delicate star-like flowers in glistening white or tinged with pink. The effect is enhanced because the flowers appear on naked stems, before the leaves develop.*

Left: *Azaleas are a form of rhododendron. There are ever-green and deciduous forms, both producing masses of flowers in a good year. Many of the deciduous forms have a wonderful scent. Like other rhododendrons, they need an acid soil and shelter from hot sun.*

Left: *Berberis are versatile plants, because they are attractive for much of the year: they have spectacular flower displays in spring and good foliage until summer, which then becomes beautifully tinted in the autumn. As an extra, many varieties produce red berries, which often last throughout the winter. Shown here is* Berberis linearifolia *'Orange King'.*

Left: *Lilac (*Syringa*) flowers in the late spring. It has one of the most distinctive smells of all spring-flowering shrubs and is popular for cutting to take indoors. When the flowers die they can look ugly, especially the white forms, and should be removed.*

Above: *A close up of a berberis in flower. This one is* Berberis *'Goldilocks'. Many varieties have sweetly-scented flowers, and all are much loved by bees.*

SPRING-FLOWERING SHRUBS

Berberis	*Magnolia*
Camellia	*Mahonia*
Chaenomeles	*Pieris*
(japonica)	*Prunus* (cherry)
Corylopsis	*Rhododendron*
Corylus (hazel)	*Ribes* (currant)
Cytisus (broom)	*Rosmarinus* (rosemary)
Daphne	*Salix* (willow)
Exochorda	*Spiraea*
Forsythia	*Viburnum*

Shrubs in Summer

While spring is noted for its fresh, young flowers, summer, especially early summer, is the time of mainstream flowering. This is the time for heady scents, particularly on long, warm, summer evenings. It is also a time when insects are at their busiest, with flowering shrubs full of bees and butterflies. Buddleja, in particular, is good for both.

ENJOYING THE SUMMER

Mix in a few summer-flowering shrubs with those from earlier in the year, so that the garden or borders have some form of continuity. Plant fragrant shrubs near where you sit or relax, and use those with thick foliage to create areas of privacy.

There are many types of shrub or dwarf tree that can be used for producing fruit. Currants, gooseberries, cherries, plums and apples can all be grown as small shrubs. These have decorative blossoms in the spring and then provide the delights of picking your own fruit in the summer and autumn. They need not be in a special fruit garden; grow them in ordinary borders, but beware that the soft fruits may need netting, as they ripen, to prevent birds from eating them.

In a small garden, use large shrubs, rather than trees, to create a shady sitting area. There are many that can be used and they are better suited to being cut to shape than trees.

Generally, there is not much to be done to shrubs during the summer. If the garden is in a town or near a road where there is a lot of dust and grime, wash off the leaves with a sprinkler, or spray if there is a prolonged period of drought, because the film over the surface of the foliage will impair the shrub's ability to make food. Also water, if necessary. Continue to feed those shrubs in containers until the end of the summer.

Above: *In summer the bush* Olearia x haastii *resembles a snowy mountain. Shown in full flower, this one is delicately fronted by a variegated grass,* Phalaris arundinacea *'Picta', more commonly known as "gardener's garters". Always consider the relationship between plants, rather than simply putting them in at random.*

Left: *Roses are at their best in summer. Some are once-flowering and do so in the early summer, but many go on flowering throughout the whole summer. Some gardeners prefer to have a separate garden or special beds for roses, while others like to mix them in with other plants. This lovely old rose is* R. *'Stanwell Perpetual'.*

Above: *From midsummer onwards, the hydrangeas begin to flower. There is a wide range available. The delicate lace-caps are popular because of the shape of the flowers. Here, the beautiful* H. quercifolia, *or oak-leafed hydrangea, combines good flowers and good foliage. Another very attractive hydrangea to consider is* H. aspera *'Villosa', which has soft, furry leaves and subtle, mauvish-blue and pink flowers.*

Above: *Many hydrangeas have white flowers. On the whole, they prefer a shady position and here the whites come into their own, illuminating their surroundings.*

Left: *The vexed question with these mop-headed (*H. macrophylla*) varieties of hydrangea is the colour. The same plant can have blue flowers on acid soil, red ones on a neutral soil and pink ones on an alkaline soil. It is possible to vary the colour by changing the acidity of your soil but, in the long run, it is more satisfactory to go with what you have. If you want to have different colours, plant hydrangeas in containers with the appropriate soil.*

Left: *The rock roses, or* Cistus, *make very fine summer-flowering plants. They are especially good in hot summers as they need a dry soil and can happily cope with droughts. The flowers only last a day, but are replaced by fresh ones the following morning. Some species drop their petals in the early afternoon so they are not much use to the evening gardener. This one is* C. x skanbergii, *with white-centred pink flowers set off against soft, greyish-green foliage.*

Below: *The kalmias are not seen so frequently as they should be. This may be because they need an acid soil and light shade, but even gardeners with alkaline soils should be able to grow them in containers. They flower in early summer, covering the branches with pink or red flowers. These are held in bunches, each flower being cup-shaped in a way that is unique to the plant.*

Above: *Allied to the rock rose, and liking the same kind of hot, dry conditions, are the halimiums. These are evergreen, with white or yellow flowers, some varieties having brown blotches at the base of the petals. This one is* Halimium x pauanum, *a form with pure golden flowers. Again, the flowers are produced afresh each day over a long period through the summer and sometimes well into autumn.*

Above: *The lavateras have become popular with gardeners, and justifiably so. They produce flowers over a long period, from early summer right through to the first frost. Sometimes, after a severe winter, the stems are cut to the ground and, because the new shoots take a time to grow, the flowering does not start until much later in the summer. They are not long-lived plants and it is wise to take cuttings regularly, which is not a difficult task as they root easily.*

Above: *Californian lilacs, Ceanothus, are good-value plants. Although a few of them are deciduous, the majority in cultivation have evergreen foliage that stays attractive throughout the year. In the early summer, they are covered with masses of blue flowers, the shade of blue varying from light to dark, depending on the variety. This is the dwarf form, 'Pin Cushion'.*

Above: *Being closely related, the halimiums and the cistus produce crossbreeds of which this* x Halimiocistus revolii *is an example. The first part of the name is a combination of those of its parents. This shrub makes a low-spreading carpet of green foliage, which contrasts well with its myriad snow-white flowers.*

Above: *The New Zealand tea tree,* Leptospermum *is becoming increasingly popular, especially in milder areas. They flower over a long period, with masses of small, saucer-shaped flowers in red, pink or white, often with a dark centre. There are also double-flowered varieties and several dwarf forms that are good for rock gardens. This one is* L. scoparium *'Lyndon'.*

Above: *The New Zealand hebes are amongst some of the best summer-flowering plants. They make beautifully-shaped shrubs, with good foliage and masses of flowers that are produced over a long period. The long spikes of flowers seem to whizz around in all directions, like fireworks.*

SUMMER-FLOWERING SHRUBS

Abutilon	*Hydrangea*
Brachyglottis	*Hypericum*
Buddleja	*Indigofera*
Callistemon (bottlebrush)	*Jasminum*
Carpenteria	*Kalmia*
Ceanothus (Californian lilac)	*Lavandula* (lavender)
Cistus (rock rose)	*Lavatera*
Cornus (dog wood)	*Leptospermum*
Deutzia	*Leycesteria*
Erica (heather)	*Olearia* (daisy bush)
Fremontodendron	*Philadelphus* (mock orange)
Fuchsia	*Potentilla*
Halimium	*Rosa*
Hebe	*Sambucus* (elder)
Hibiscus	*Viburnum*
Hoheria	*Weigela*

Above: *Another plant from the same region as the New Zealand hebes is the Australian bottlebrush,* Callistemon. *This shrub has curious bottle-shaped flowers, that explain its common name. Being of Australian origin, they are on the tender side, but some can be brought through to survive most winters by planting against a warm wall. If in doubt, plant in a container and keep inside during the cold months. This species is* C. sieberi.

Right: *Various forms of* Abutilon vitifolium *are appearing in more and more gardens, because it is realized that they are frost hardy. They will not survive a severe winter, but they are quick-growing and can easily be replaced. They come in a range of colours, including red, white and mauve, as here.*

Shrubs in Autumn

Autumn sees the closing of the annual growing cycle. With it come the autumn tints and hues both of the foliage and of the many berries and other fruits. Autumn is the season of reds and browns.

LONG-FLOWERING SHRUBS

There are not many shrubs that flower just in the autumn, but some summer ones continue right through to the frosts. Fuchsias are particularly useful. Buddlejas, hibiscus, hydrangeas, hypericums and indigoferas also continue to flower. One of the true autumn-flowering plants is *Osmanthus heterophyllus*, with its fragrant flowers more reminiscent of spring than of summer. Other plants that are associated with autumn flowering are the ceratostigmas and Eucryphia glutinosa.

AUTUMN LEAVES

The true glory of the autumn belongs to foliage. In a small garden, in particular, it is a wise choice to make every plant earn its keep, and those that provide a fiery end to the year's gardening certainly deserve their place. Berries and other fruit are an added bonus; they are not only attractive but also supply birds and other animals with food for the harsh months ahead.

Autumn is the time to start preparing beds for new planting and indeed to actually start planting. It is also a time to check that those plants that need staking are still securely held in place, before the winter winds begin. Once the leaves have fallen, it is a good idea to go round and examine each shrub, removing any dead or dying wood. Autumn is also the time for clearing up fallen leaves and stopping them from smothering other plants and lawns. Do not waste them by burning or throwing them away. Compost them and return them to the soil once they have rotted.

Right: *While the best-known Osmanthus flower in the spring,* O. heterophyllus *flowers in late autumn, perfuming the air.*

Below: *Hydrangeas are really summer-flowering shrubs, but their flowers last such a long time that they are still flourishing well into autumn, when their leaves lose their green colour and take on autumn tints.*

SHRUBS WITH GOOD AUTUMN FOLIAGE

Amelanchier
Berberis thunbergii
Ceratostigma willmottianum
  (leaves and flowers)
Cotinus (smoke bush)
Enkianthus
Euonymus alatus
Fothergilla
Rhus hirta
Stephandra incisa

SHRUBS WITH GOOD AUTUMN FLOWERS

Buddleja
Ceratostigma
Eucryphia glutinosa
Fuchsia
Hibiscus
Hydrangea
Hypericum
Indigofera
Osmanthus heterophyllus

Above: *The Judas tree is a curious shrub. In spring, purple flowers fill the naked branches; in autumn the leaves take on beautiful colours.*

Left: *Some of the most brilliant of autumn colours are presented by the spindle trees and bushes,* Euonymus. *The colourful* E. alatus 'Compactus' *is suitable for the smaller garden. Interest in winter is maintained by its corky wings on the stems.*

Above: *Berberises provide the gardener with a valuable group of plants. They are attractive at all seasons of the year, providing flower, berry and foliage interest. Most produce fiery-coloured foliage and waxy red berries in the autumn, including this* B. thunbergii 'Red Pillar.'

Above: *Blue is not a colour that one normally associates with the autumn; indeed there are not many shrubs that produce flowers of this colour at any time of year.* Ceratostigma willmottianum *has piercingly blue flowers that carry over from summer well into autumn.*

Right: *Most of the* eucryphias *soon become large trees, but* E. glutinosa, *although it can become large, usually remains small enough to be considered a shrub. The beauty of this plant is the late-season flowers. They are glisteningly white bowls, with a central boss of stamens.*

Left: *As well as its beautiful flowers,* Eucryphia glutinosa *is deciduous, and its leaves take on autumnal tints.*

Above: *Fothergill* (Fothergilla major*) is another good-value shrub with good flowers in late spring or early summer and wonderfully-coloured foliage in autumn. It is very slow growing and although it can eventually become quite large, it will take many years to do so.*

Below: *Many of the cotinus, or smoke bushes, have foliage that is attractive throughout the growing seasons.*

Above: Amelanchier lamarckii *frequently grows into a small tree but, if required, it can be pruned to produce several stems instead of a trunk, so that it becomes a large shrub. It is covered with delicate white flowers in spring and then in autumn its leaves colour beautifully.*

Shrubs in Winter

Winter is often considered the dead month in the garden and many may be tempted to stay indoors. But, in fact, there is a lot going on. A number of shrubs flower at this time of year, some of them with beautiful scents that are particularly noticeable on warm winter days. There are also evergreen shrubs that can look particularly good in the low winter light, especially those with shiny leaves.

WINTER TASKS

There is a lot going on during the winter months and the garden should reflect this. Because many of the shrubs that provide winter interest are dull at other times, they should be planted in less prominent positions. In this way, they will show up in winter when other plants have died back, but will be masked by more interesting plants for the rest of the year.

If the weather is fine and the soil not waterlogged, work can proceed. The more achieved during these winter months, the less there will be to do later in the year. If all the beds are forked over, the weeds removed and the soil mulched, the need for weeding throughout the spring and summer will be considerably reduced. Indeed, one hour spent weeding in winter will save several later on. Provided that the ground is neither waterlogged nor frozen, this is also the best time of year for planting and moving shrubs.

During snowy weather, make certain that shrubs, especially evergreen ones, are not weighed down and broken by excessive falls. Knock the snow off at the earliest opportunity. Light falls should be left if there is a cold wind, because these will help protect the plants.

Above left: *The winter jasmine,* Jasminum nudiflorum, *is truly a winter plant, flowering from the end of autumn through into the early spring, totally ignoring the frost and snow. Stems taken indoors make attractive winter flower decorations.*

Above right: *The winter hazels,* Corylopsis, *make excellent winter plants, with yellow catkins that defy the frosts.*

Right: *Witch hazels,* Hamamelis, *produce curious flowers like clusters of ribbons. As well as being attractive, they have a strident smell that fills the air on sunny days.*

SHRUBS WITH WINTER INTEREST

Corylus (hazel)
Cornus mas (dog wood)
Corylopsis
Hamamelis (witch hazel)
Jasminum nudiflorum
Lonicera purpusii
Lonicera standishii
Lonicera fragrantissima
Mahonia
Viburnum bodnantense
Viburnum farreri
Viburnum tinus

Above and below: *Like many winter-flowering shrubs, the mahonias are beautifully scented. This is possibly to make certain that they attract what few insect pollinators there are at this time of year. Mahonia is a prickly subject and plants can look a bit tatty at some times of year, but in winter it is supreme, with its long spikes of yellow flowers and wafting scent.*

Left: *Viburnums are a versatile group of plants, with at least one variety in flower at each time of year, including two or three in winter. Viburnum tinus is evergreen and is covered with flat heads of flowers throughout most of the winter and often through to the spring as well. On warm days the flowers have a delicate perfume.*

Shrubs with Coloured Stems

Those shrubs that have coloured bark and are grown for their winter stems such as *Rubus cockburnianus, R. thibetanus* and *Salix alba* 'Britzensis' are very worthwhile and are of great value to the winter gardener.

WINTER STEMS

When the leaves have fallen from the shrubs it is time to appreciate what is left: the bare outline of the stems and branches and, more importantly, the colour of the bark. Not all shrubs are coloured in this way but a number provide a wonderful display, especially if they are planted so they catch the low winter sunshine. The shrubs are best cut to the ground each spring, so that there is new growth for the following winter.

SHRUBS WITH COLOURED WINTER STEMS

Cornus alba
Corylus avellana contorta
Rubus cockburnianus
Rubus thibetanus
Salix alba 'Britzensis'

Above: *The red glow of the stems of* Cornus alba *is seen here on a typical winter's day.*

Above: *The ghostly stems of* Rubus cockburnianum *shine out in the winter landscape. The white is a "powdery" bloom, which is lost on older stems, and the whole plant should be cut to the ground each spring to produce new stems for the following winter.*

Above: Cornus stolonifera *'Flaviramea' is quite vibrant with its yellowish green bark. If left to mature, the stems lose their rich colour and hard pruning every spring will ensure plenty of new growth for the following winter.*

Above: Rubus 'Golden Veil' is an extremely attractive plant, with bright yellow foliage in the summer and white stems in the winter. Here the leaves have nearly all fallen, revealing the attractive winter stems beneath.

Right: *Several of the willows have beautiful winter stems as well as providing their distinctive catkins or pussies at the end of the season.* Salix alba *produces some of the best coloured stems. Here it is represented by* S.a. vitellina *and its variety* S.a.v. 'Britzensis'. *The stems should be cut back each spring to encourage new growth for the following winter.*

Left: *Here* Salix gracilistyla 'Melanostachys' *displays the catkins typical of so many willows in the winter. As well as being attractive in the garden, the stems are very popular for adding to indoor winter flower arrangements.*

CLIMBERS

Climbers do not seem to have any shape: they
just go straight up – or do they? When you stop to
think about it you realize they are actually much
more versatile. For a start, they can be trained to
spread sideways, thus covering a considerable area,
or even grown through trees and shrubs. Climbers
are slightly more difficult to grow than shrubs,
simply because they need something to climb up
and usually an element of training. However, the
choice of training method gives the gardener
plenty of scope. Climbers can be grown on walls
with a variety of supports, including wires and
trellis panels. Trellising can also be used to form
fences or screens, either around the outside of the
garden or within it. Archways, arbours and pergolas
are other ideal supports for climbers.

Left: *The golden hop* (Humulus lupulus *'Aureus') is an attractive,
self-supporting perennial climber with bristly twining stems.*

TYPES OF CLIMBERS

Annual Climbers

When considering climbers, most gardeners automatically think of woody climbing plants, such as clematis or roses, and forget about the annuals. However, annual climbers are extremely useful plants and should never be overlooked.

INSTANT COLOUR
One of the great virtues of annual climbers is that they are temporary; they allow the gardener the opportunity of changing the plants or changing their position every year. This means that it is possible to fill gaps at short notice or simply to change your mind as to the way the garden should look.

Another virtue of annuals is that they come in a wide range of colours, some of which are not so readily available in other climbers. The "hot" colours – red, orange, yellow – in partic-ular, are of great use. Annuals, on the whole, have a very long flowering season, much longer than most perennials. This also makes them very useful.

The one drawback of annuals is that they must be raised afresh each year. Many can be bought as young plants from garden centres but all can be raised from seed. This doesn't require a lot of time or space: the majority will germinate quite happily on a kitchen windowsill. With the exception of sweet peas, which are hardy and should be sown in winter, most annuals should be sown in spring, pricked out into pots, hardened off and then planted out in the open ground as soon as the threat of frosts has passed.

Annuals can be grown up any type of support, both permanent and temporary. Although they are only in place for a few months, some, such as *Cobaea scandens* (cathedral bells), can cover a very large area. Nasturtiums (*Tropaeolum*) are also annuals that can put on a lot of growth in a season.

Above: *Many climbers can be used as trailing plants as well as climbing ones. Annual nasturtiums are a good example of this. Here the nasturtium 'Jewel of Africa' is seen around a purple-leaved* Canna *'Wyoming'.*

Above: *Not all "annuals" are strictly annual.* Eccremocarpus scaber, *shown here, is really a perennial but it is often treated as an annual and planted afresh every year. It is shown with an everlasting pea,* Lathyrus latifolius.

Above: *Annuals are not restricted to just flowers. Many vegetables also make attractive climbers as well as being productive. Here, scarlet runner beans are grown up a wigwam (tepee) of canes. This is not only attractive but allows the gardener to produce quite a large crop in a small space.*

Above: *Sweet peas are amongst everyone's favourite climbers. Not only do they look good in the garden; they are also wonderful flowers for cutting for the house. Most have a delicious scent.*

Right: Cobaea scandens *is a vigorous annual climber. For success it must be planted in a warm position, preferably against a wall, and given as long a growing season as possible.*

Left: *The morning glories, Ipomoea, are just that, glorious. Soak seeds overnight before sowing and germinate in a warm place or propagator. Harden off thoroughly before planting or they are unlikely to do well. Plant them in a sheltered sunny position.*

Evergreen Climbers

Climbing plants are mainly valued for their flowers, but there are a few that hold their place in the garden because of their evergreen foliage. Probably the best known is ivy. Its glossy, three-pointed leaves make a permanent cover for whatever they climb up.

FOLIAGE SCREENS

One of the best uses of evergreens is as a cover for eyesores. They can be grown directly over an ugly wall or allowed to clamber over trellising judiciously positioned to hide a fuel tank or messy utility area. There are some places in the garden, moreover, where it is preferable that the appearance does not change with the seasons. A gateway, perhaps, may be surrounded by an evergreen climber over an arch, so that it presents the same familiar image to the visitor all year round.

From a design point of view, evergreen climbers provide a permanent point of reference within the garden. They form part of the structure, around which the rest of the garden changes season by season.

Plain green can be a little uninspiring; green works extremely well, however, as a backdrop against which to see other, more colourful, plants. Climbers such as ivy have glossy leaves, which reflect the light, giving a shimmering effect as they move. Evergreen leaves can vary in shape, and they can also be variegated, providing contrasting tones of green and sometimes colour variation.

Right: Laurus nobilis *provides attractive green foliage.*

EVERGREEN CLIMBERS
Clematis armandii
Clematis cirrhosa
Fremontodendron
  californicum
Hedera (ivy)
Lonicera japonica
Solanum crispum
Solanum jasminoides
Vinca major (periwinkle)

EVERGREEN WALL SHRUBS
Azara
Callistemon citrinus
Carpenteria californica
Ceanothus
Coronilla glauca
Cotoneaster
Desfontainea spinosa
Elaeagnus x ebbingei
Elaeagnus pungens
Escallonia
Euonymus fortunei
Euonymus japonicus
Garrya elliptica
Itea ilicifolia
Laurus nobilis
Magnolia grandiflora
Piptanthus laburnifolius
Pyracantha (firethorn)
Teucrium fruticans

Above: *Variegated ivies can make a big impact. Those with golden variegation are excellent for lighting up dark corners and they are especially good in helping to brighten the grey days of winter.*

Above: *Although the flowers of ivy are insignificant, the evergreen leaves make a valuable contribution to the garden. Here, three different varieties make a dense screen.*

Right: *This* Solanum crispum *'Glasnevin' is one of the very best climbers. Unless the weather gets very cold, it retains its shiny leaves throughout the winter and then is covered with its blue flowers from late spring right through to the autumn. The leaves may drop during severe winters, but they soon recover.*

Above: Vinca major *(periwinkle) can be considered a shrub if it is kept rigorously under control by cutting back, but it is often used as a climber, scrambling through shrubs and hedges, as here. It retains its glossy green leaves throughout the winter and produces bright blue flowers from midwinter onwards.*

Below: *There is a brightly variegated periwinkle, 'Variegata', which looks good against dark hedges.*

Climbers with Spring Interest

Spring is one of the most joyous times of the year in the garden; the winter is over and ahead lie the glories of summer. Many of the plants that flower at this time of year have a freshness about them that almost defies definition.

PROTECTING FROM FROST

Spring is a time of varying weather and plants can suffer badly from late frosts. This is made worse when frosts are preceded by a warm spell, in which a lot of new growth appears. These young shoots are susceptible to sudden cold weather and can be burnt off. Buds are also likely to be harmed and it is not uncommon to see a *Clematis montana*, for example, covered in buds and full of promise one day, only to be denuded of buds the next after a night of hard frost. This, however, should never deter you from growing spring-flowering climbers; such frosts do not occur every year and, in most springs, these climbers perform at their best. If frosts are forecast, it is possible to guard against them.

Many of the more tender early-flowering shrubs need walls for protection and are usually grown as wall shrubs. Shrubs such as camellias are particularly prone to frost damage and so are grown in this way.

Once they have finished flowering, many spring-flowering climbers are a bit dreary for the rest of the year. One way to enliven them is to grow another, later-flowering, climber through their stems. This is very useful where space is limited.

SPRING-FLOWERING CLIMBERS AND WALL SHRUBS

Abeliophyllum distichum
Akebia quinata
Akebia trifoliata
Azara serrata
Ceanothus arboreus 'Trewithen Blue'
Chaenomeles (japonica or ornamental quince)
Clematis alpina
Clematis armandii
Clematis macropetala
Clematis montana
Forsythia suspensa
Garrya elliptica
Lonicera (honeysuckles)
Piptanthus laburnifolius
Ribes laurifolia
Rosa (early roses)
Schisandra
Solanum cripsum 'Glasnevin'
Wisteria

Above: *Spring is the time when all plants are beginning to burst forth. Clematis are some of the earliest climbers, one of the earliest and most impressive being* C. montana, *which frequently has so much bloom that the leaves cannot be seen.*

Right: Clematis armandii *is one of the few evergreen clematis. It is also one of the earliest to flower, doing so in late winter or early spring.*

Above: *Another early clematis, more delicate in appearance, is* C. macropetala. *It is here seen with* C. montana, *which will flower a week or so later.*

Above: *Honeysuckles* (Lonicera) *are a great feature of the spring. This one* (L. periclymenum) *is in a natural habitat – scrambling through a bush. In this case, the supporting plant is a* berberis, *whose purply-bronze leaves make a good contrast to the yellow flowers.*

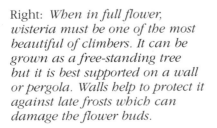

Left: Rosa *'Maigold' is one of the many roses that although strictly a shrub, have a tendency to climb. They can be used as low climbers up pillars, as here, or on tripods, trellis or low walls. It starts flowering early in the season and often repeats later in the year.*

Right: *When in full flower, wisteria must be one of the most beautiful of climbers. It can be grown as a free-standing tree but it is best supported on a wall or pergola. Walls help to protect it against late frosts which can damage the flower buds.*

Climbers with Summer Interest

Summer is when many climbers are at their best. Clematis and roses, in particular, produce plenty of blooms, covering pergolas and arches as well as climbing up walls and through trees and shrubs. They make a valuable contribution to the summer scene, giving vertical emphasis to a garden that would otherwise be flat and less interesting.

SUMMER CLIMBERS

Campsis
Clematis
Cobaea scandens (cathedral bells)
Eccremocarpus scaber (Chilean glory flower)
Fallopia baldschuanica (Russian vine)
Ipomoea (morning glories)
Jasminum (jasmines)
Lapageria rosea
Lathyrus (peas)
Lonicera (honeysuckles)
Mutisia
Passiflora (passion-flowers)

Phaseolus coccineus (runner beans)
Plumbago auriculata (Cape leadwort)
Rosa (roses)
Schisandra
Schizophragma
Solanum crispum 'Glasnevin'
Solanum jasminoides
Thunbergia alata (black-eyed Susan)
Trachelospermum
Tropaeolum (nasturtium)
Wisteria

SHADE AND FRAGRANCE

During hot, sunny summers, climbers are most welcome for providing dappled shade as they cover arbours and pergolas. There is nothing better than to sit on a summer's day in the shade of an arbour or relax there with a meal or a drink in the evening after work. Relaxation is further enhanced if the climbers are fragrant – and many are. Roses, honeysuckle and jasmine are three of the most popular scented climbers.

Many shrubs and trees are spring-flowering and climbers can be used to enliven them during the summer months, when they are, perhaps, at their dullest. *Clematis viticella* is probably the best to use for this purpose; because it is cut back almost to the ground during the winter, it doesn't smother the tree or shrub when it is in flower. Later in the season, when the tree or shrub has finished flowering, the clematis grows up through its branches and produces its own colour, usually over a long period.

Similarly, climbers can be used in herbaceous borders, where there are gaps left by perennials that flower early in the season and are then cut back. Clematis can be left to scramble through the border, either without any support or over a simple framework of twigs.

Above: Campsis radicans *is a beautiful climber for the second half of the summer. Its large tubular flowers, here just opening, contrast well with the green of the foliage. It is not a common climber but it is not difficult to find or to grow.*

Above: Clematis florida *'Sieboldii' is a very distinct clematis, with creamy white outer petals and an inner button of purple ones. It is a beautiful flower even when still in bud and while opening.*

Right: Clematis *'Perle d'Azur' must be one of the best of the blue clematis. It produces flowers of a delicate lilac blue in tremendous profusion around midsummer.*

Above: *Bougainvillea is a climber from hot climates. In more temperate areas, it has to be grown under glass, such as in a conservatory, but, in warmer districts, it can be grown outside. Its brilliant colours continue for months as it is the papery bracts rather than the flowers that provide the colour.*

Right: *Scrambling plants are a neglected area. There are very many of them and they can provide a lot of vertical interest through the summer months. Here a* Euonymus fortunei *'Emerald Gaiety' scrambles up through a large bush, with* Geranium x oxonianum *pushing its way up through both.*

Left: *Unlike the sweet pea, the perennial* Lathyrus grandiflorus *does not smell, but it is a most beautiful small climber. The round pea flowers are large and full of rich colour. They are best planted under shrubs, through which they will happily scramble.*

Above: *Another scrambler is* Tropaeolum speciosum. *This, like* Lathyrus grandiflorus, above, *has a more common annual relative, the nasturtium. However,* Tropaeolum speciosum *is a perennial and has small flowers of an intense flame red. It will scramble up through any shrub.*

Right: Tropaeolum peregrinum *(canary creeper) is tender to frosts, but if protected will flower throughout the summer.*

Left: *Not all climbers need to climb to great heights to be attractive. This herbaceous climber scrambles up through other plants with gay abandon. It is* Convolvulus althaeoides *and has delicate pink flowers, which are set off well against its silver foliage. It likes a sunny, well-drained spot.*

Above: *Passion-flowers are tender climbers, best grown against walls. Most should be grown under glass but* Passiflora caerulea *is hardy enough to be grown outside. The flowers are amongst the most extraordinary of all climbers.*

Right: *For many people, roses are the best summer climbing plants. They can be grown in a wide variety of ways, including up tripods, as seen here. This is* Rosa *'Dortmund'.*

Climbers with Autumn Interest

Most climbers have finished flowering by the time the autumn arrives but many have qualities that make them still desirable in the garden at this time of year.

FOLIAGE AND BERRIES

Perhaps the biggest attraction of autumn climbers is the change in colour of the leaves, prior to their fall. Many take on autumnal tints, some of the most fiery red. This will completely transform the appearance of the climber itself and, often, that of the surrounding area. Another benefit that some climbers have to offer is that they produce berries or fruit. Most produce seed of some kind or other but these are often visually insignificant; others produce an abundance of bright berries – honeysuckle (*Lonicera*), for example – or large luxurious fruit, such as the passion-flowers (*Passiflora*). Others carry their seeds in a different but, none the less, very attractive way. The fluffy or silky seed heads of clematis, for example, always make an interesting feature.

As well as providing an important visual element in the garden, the berries and other forms of seed are also a good source of food for birds. Birds will be attracted to the fruit for as long as they last, which may be well beyond the autumn and into the winter. Not only birds like fruit: man also likes the garden's edible bounty and many fruiting plants, ranging from currants and gooseberries to apples, plums, pears and apricots, can be grown against a wall, which provides not only support but also warmth and protection. Fruiting trees, such as apples and pears, also make good plants to train up and over arches and pergolas.

AUTUMNAL-FOLIAGED CLIMBERS

Actinidia (kiwi fruit)
Akebia quinata
Campsis
Chaenomeles (japonica or
   flowering quince)
Clematis alpina
Clematis flammula
Clematis tibetana vernayi
Cotoneaster
Fallopia baldschuanica
   (Russian vine)
Hydrangea anomala petiolaris
Hydrangea aspera
Hydrangea quercifolia
Jasminum officinale (jasmine)
Lonicera tragophylla
   (honeysuckle)
Parthenocissus (Boston ivy or
   Virginia creeper)
Passiflora (passion-flower)
Ribes speciosum
Rosa (roses)
Tropaeolum (nasturtium)
Vitis (grapevine)

Right: Pyracantha *offers the choice of yellow, red or orange berries, depending on the variety. This is* P. *'Orange Charmer'*.

BERRIED AND FRUITING CLIMBERS AND WALL SHRUBS

Actinidia (kiwi fruit)
Akebia
Clematis
Cotoneaster
Hedera (ivy)
Humulus lupulus (hop)
Ilex (holly)
Lonicera
   (honeysuckle)

Malus (crab apple)
Passiflora
   (passion-flower)
Prunus (plums,
   apricots, peaches)
Pyracantha (firethorn)
Pyrus (pears)
Rosa (roses)
Vitis (grapevine)

Above: Clematis cirrhosa *flowers in late autumn and carries its fluffy seed heads well into winter.*

Left: *The berries of* Cotoneaster horizontalis *are set off well against the foliage of* Helleborus foetidus.

Above and right: Parthenocissus
henryana *is seen here in both its
summer and autumn colours.*

Left: *Clematis display a mass of
silky heads as beautiful as any
flowers throughout the autumn.*

Below: *Fruit trees are attractive
as wall shrubs as they carry
blossom in spring and fruit in the
autumn. This pear, 'Doyenne du
Comice', has attractive foliage, too.*

Climbers with Winter Interest

While there are not many climbers that are interesting in winter, they are still a group of plants that are worth thinking about. Valuable wall space should not be taken up with plants that do not earn their keep for the greater part of the year, but it is often possible to find space for at least one that brightens up the winter scene.

WINTER-FLOWERING CLIMBERS

Surprisingly, there is one clematis that is in full flower during the bleaker winter months. *Clematis cirrhosa* is available in several forms, some with red blotches on their bell-shaped flowers. *Clematis armandii* appears towards the end of winter and heralds the beginning of a new season. There are three honeysuckles that flower in the winter and, although they are, strictly speaking, shrubs, they can be grown against a wall. As an added bonus, these are very strongly scented and they will flower throughout the whole of

the winter. Another wall shrub that flowers early is *Garrya elliptica*, with its long, silver catkins. This is the more valuable because it will grow on a north-facing wall.

One of the most commonly grown wall shrubs is the winter jasmine, *Jasminum nudiflorum*, which produces a wonderful display of bright yellow flowers. Unfortunately, unlike its summer relatives, it is not scented.

EVERGREEN CLIMBERS

While not so attractive as the flowering plants, evergreen climbers, such as ivy (*Hedera*), can be used as winter cover both for walls and for other supports. These evergreen climbers afford valuable winter protection for birds and insects, especially if grown by a warm wall. Different green tones and, especially, variegated leaves, can add a surprising amount of winter cheer, even on dark days.

Climbers and wall shrubs that still carry berries from the previous autumn can add interest in the winter. Cotoneaster and pyracantha are good examples.

WINTER CLIMBERS AND WALL SHRUBS

Chaenomeles (japonica or flowering quince)
Clematis armandii
Clematis cirrhosa
Elaeagnus x ebbingei
Elaeagnus pungens
Garrya elliptica
Hedera (ivy)
Jasminum nudiflorum (winter jasmine)
Lonicera fragrantissima (winter honeysuckle)
Lonicera x purpusii
Lonicera standishii

Above: Hedera colchica *'Dentata Variegata' is in perfect condition even in these frosty conditions. The gold variegation is good for lightening up dark winter days.*

Above: *The winter jasmine,* Jasminum nudiflorum, *flowers throughout winter, supplying cut flowers for indoors and decorating walls and fences outside.*

Right: Clematis armandii *flowers in late winter, with a wonderful display of pure-white flowers.*

Above: Garrya elliptica *is an excellent plant for winter. It has beautiful silver catkins and is one of the few plants suitable for growing on north-facing walls.*

Above: Clematis cirrhosa *is the earliest clematis to flower, starting in early winter and continuing until spring. The many varieties include this one, 'Balearica'.*

Right: Chaenomeles, *known as* japonica, *or Japanese or ornamental quince, flowers from midwinter to spring, then has hard fruit that often lasts through until the next spring.*

Fragrant Climbers

When choosing plants, the main consideration is, often, what the flowers are like, followed by the foliage. Something that is often forgotten, or just considered as a bonus, is fragrance; and yet it is something that most people enjoy and it enhances the pleasure of all uses of the garden.

USING FRAGRANCE

Climbers include some of the loveliest and most scented plants in the garden. Some of them, such as honeysuckle or jasmine, will perfume the air over a long distance. They are always worth growing on house walls near windows that are often open, so that the beautiful smells waft in and fill the rooms. Another good place to locate fragrant climbers is over an arbour or where there is a seat. Fragrance can be a tremendous aid to relaxation: just think about the idea of sitting in the evening, after a hard day, with the air filled with the smell of honeysuckle, for example.

Most scented climbers are at their best in the evening. This is a bonus if you are at work all day and, again, makes them very suitable for planting where you relax or have your evening meal. Some scented climbers, such as sweet peas, make ideal flowers for cutting to bring indoors.

Check carefully that a climber is fragrant. Honeysuckles (*Lonicera*) are amongst the most fragrant of climbers, but not all of them are scented, by any means. *Lonicera tragophylla* and *L. × tellmanniana* are both very attractive honeysuckles, but neither has any smell at all. Roses, too, vary in the intensity of their scent, and it is worth finding out which ones you like

best. Another thing to be beware of is that not all smells are nice. The privets (*Ligustrum*), which are sometimes used as wall shrubs, have a smell that many people find revolting.

FRAGRANT CLIMBERS AND WALL SHRUBS

Azara
Clematis montana
Itea ilicifolia
Jasminum (jasmine)
Lathyrus odoratus (sweet peas)
Lonicera (honeysuckle)
Magnolia grandiflora
Osmanthus
Passiflora (passion-flower)
Rosa (roses)

Above: *The fragrance of this* Rosa 'Wedding Day' *climbing through a tree will be carried far in the warm summer evenings.*

Above: *Honeysuckle has a very heady perfume, from flowers that first appear in spring and then continue through the summer; odd flowers are still being produced in autumn.*

Left: *Not all honeysuckles are fragrant but* Lonicera periclymenum *and its varieties are amongst the best. They can be vigorous growers and need strong supports.*

Above: *Growing* Rosa *'Zéphirine Drouhin' around a summer house is ideal. This rose has a delightful perfume and flowers on and off throughout the summer and well into the autumn. It has the advantage that it is thornless and so is safe to use near places where people are sitting or walking.*

Above: *Jasmine has a very distinctive fragrance and is most appreciated on a warm summer evening. This variety,* Jasminum officinale *'Aureum', has gold-splashed leaves. This gives the climber an attraction even when it is out of flower.*

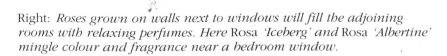

Right: *Roses grown on walls next to windows will fill the adjoining rooms with relaxing perfumes. Here* Rosa *'Iceberg' and* Rosa *'Albertine' mingle colour and fragrance near a bedroom window.*

Wall Shrubs

Not all plants that one sees climbing up walls or supported on trellis are true climbers. Many are just ordinary shrubs that are growing against a wall for a variety of reasons. In the wild, some of these might scramble through others if they are next to them, but, generally, they are free-standing shrubs. These shrubs are used as surrogate climbers in the garden, partly because they look good in positions where climbers are grown and partly because some need the protection that walls and fences provide.

WALL SHRUBS	
Abutilon	*Ficus carica* (fig)
Azara	*Fremontodendron californicum*
Carpenteria californica	(fremontia)
Ceanothus (Californian lilac)	*Garrya elliptica*
Chaenomeles (japonica,	*Itea ilicifolia*
ornamental quince)	*Jasminum* (jasmine)
Clianthus puniceus	*Magnolia*
(parrot's bill)	*Pyracantha* (firethorn)
Cotoneaster	*Teucrium fruticans*
Euonymus fortunei	(shrubby germander)

ADVANTAGES OF WALL SHRUBS

From the design point of view, wall shrubs are often more compact and controllable than climbers. They can be used in smaller spaces, which climbers would soon outgrow. If so desired, they can be clipped into topiary shapes and they will retain their shape for some time, unlike climbers, which have a constant tendency to throw out new shoots. Wall shrubs increase the range of flowering colours and periods available to the gardener, as well as offering a greater range of foliage effects.

Walls offer winter protection to many shrubs that could otherwise not be grown. The warmth that comes from a house wall might horrify the conservationally minded but, to the gardener, it offers the opportunity to grow plants, such as *Ceanothus*, which might otherwise succumb to the cold weather and die.

It is sometimes difficult to tell what is a climber and what is a wall shrub. *Pyracantha* cut tight against a wall, for example, has every appearance of being a climber, as has a large *Magnolia grandiflora*. *Euonymus fortunei*, which grows like any other shrub in the open ground, will, given the chance, shin up a wall as if that were its normal habitat. But, in fact, the difference between climbers and wall shrubs does not matter. Most gardeners are concerned about the appearance of the garden and are not worried about categories. Sad would be the case if a plant were banished from a wall or some other support simply because it was not, strictly speaking, a climber.

Above: Piptanthus nepalensis *blooms in the spring, producing bright yellow, pea-like flowers. As summer moves on, so these attractive pods are formed, adding yet another dimension to the plant. Both the flowers and pods show up well against a brick wall.*

Left: Fremontodendron californicum *is usually grown against a wall. Wear a mask when pruning or handling as the stems are covered with fine hairs that can get into the lungs.*

Right: *Although most frequently used as a free-standing shrub,* Euonymus fortunei *'Emerald 'n' Gold' will happily climb up a wall or fence.*

Above: Carpenteria californica *is one of the glories of the summer, with its large white flowers, surmounted by a boss of yellow stamens. These are set off well by the dark green foliage. This plant is usually grown as a wall shrub, because it is slightly tender and appreciates the protection of the wall.*

Left: Calistemon citrinus, *with its curious, bottle-brush-like flowers, is a tender shrub that needs the warm protection of a wall if it is to survive. It flowers during the summer months.*

Above: Ceanothus *produces some of the best blue flowers of any wall shrubs. Many can be grown free-standing, but most do best if grown against a wall or a fence as here.*

TRAINING CLIMBERS

Training Methods 1

Training is an important aspect of growing climbers. The general shape and well-being of the plant is taken care of by pruning, but how it is trained and where it is positioned are the most important things to consider when thinking about how your climber will look.

POSITIONING THE PLANT

The overall shape of the plant depends on its position. Those against a wall, for example, need to be tied in so that they do not protrude too far. Similarly, climbers over arches must be constrained on at least the inner side, so that they do not catch people walking through the arch. In some places, the plants can be left to show off the way they froth out over their supports. Vigorous climbers covering large trees, for example, are best left natural and untrained. Plants on trellis can be allowed a certain amount of ebullient freedom but they may also need some restraint.

EARLY DAYS

At the time of planting it can be a good policy to train individual stems along canes until they reach the wires, trellis or whatever the support may be. This will prevent them from all clustering together, making it difficult to train them at a later stage. Once the plant starts to put on growth, tie this in rather than tucking it behind the trellis or wires. This will enable you to release it at a later stage to re-organize it.

Above: *Tying in climbers under overhanging tiles can be a problem, because it may be difficult to find anchor points. A criss-cross arrangement of vertical wires can normally be fixed between the end of the eaves and the wall below the tiles; it makes an attractive feature in its own right. Here,* Rosa *'Zéphirine Drouhin' is supported on wires.*

SPREADING OUT THE STEMS

The climber's natural tendency is to go straight up through its support or host until it reaches the light. This frequently means that the climber forms a tight column without much deviation on either side. To make a good display the gardener should spread out the stems at as early a stage as possible so that the main stems fan out, covering the wall, fence or trellis. This not only means that the climber covers a wider area but also that its stems all receive a good amount of light, and thus flowering is encouraged at a lower level.

Right: *Horizontal training produces some of the best flowering. Here,* Rosa *'Seagull' has been trained along swags of rope suspended between wooden pillars. Do not pull the ropes too tight: a graceful curve gives a much better effect. If it is not self-clinging, tie the climber in well to the rope or it will become loose and thrash about.*

Above: *A similar effect to climbing on ropes can be had by training the climber along poles attached to pillars. These form a rustic trellis and can look very effective, even during the winter when the climber is not in leaf. Here, Rosa 'Felicia' clambers over the structure.*

Right: *Vigorous climbers, such as rambling roses, some clematis and Russian vines, can be grown through trees. This is an easy way of training because, once the plant has been pointed in the right direction (by tying it to a cane angled into the tree), it can be left to its own devices. Make certain that the tree can support the weight of the climber, especially in high winds. Here Rosa 'Paul's Himalayan Musk' begins its ascent.*

Training Methods 2

ENCOURAGING FLOWERS

Once the climber has thrown up some nice long shoots, bend these over in a curving arc and attach them to the wires or trellis. From these will come new shoots which should be treated in the same manner so that the wall, fence or trellis is covered in a increasing series of arching stems. This method has the advantage, besides creating a good coverage of the wall, of making the plant produce plenty of flowers. The chemistry of the stems is such that flower buds are laid down on the top edge of the curving branches. Roses, in particular, benefit greatly from this method of training.

Curving branches over to encourage growth can also be used for climbers growing around tripods or round a series of hooped sticks, where the stems are tied around the structure rather than in a vertical position. This will encourage a much thicker coverage and many more blooms as well as allowing you to use vigorous plants in a limited amount of space.

CHOOSING YOUR METHOD OF TRAINING

There are endless possibilities for training your climber, and really the choice will affected by the constraints of the garden and personal choice. You may have something particular in mind – for example, you may want to construct a shady arbour or romantic walkway – or you may have simply bought a climber you took a fancy to and now want to find a good place for it where it will flourish and add to the beauty of the garden.

TRAINING CLIMBERS OVER EYESORES

Climbers that grow quickly and produce lots of flowers are well-suited to covering unsightly features in the garden such as refuse areas, grey concrete walls belonging to a neighbouring property or ugly fences you are not allowed to pull down.

CLIMBERS TO TRAIN OVER EYESORES

Clematis montana
Clematis rehderiana
Fallopia baldschuanica (Russian vine)
Hedera (ivy)
Humulus (hops)
Hydrangea anomala petiolaris
Lonicera (honeysuckles)
Rosa (roses)

CLIMBERS AND WALL SHRUBS FOR NORTH- AND EAST-FACING WALLS

Akebia quinata
Camellia
Chaenomeles (Japonica or ornamental quince)
Clematis 'Marie Boisselot'
Clematis 'Nelly Moser'
Euonymous fortunei
Jasminum nudiflorum
Hedera (Ivy)
Hydrangea anomala petiolaris
Lonicera x tellemanniana
Parthenocissus (Boston ivy or virginia creeper)
Pyracantha (Firethorn)
Rosa 'New Dawn'
Schizophragma

Above: Rosa *'New Dawn' has a very long flowering period and has the added benefit that it can be grown on a north-facing wall. Here it has been tied into trellising on a wall.*

Left: *Climbers planted near doorways should be kept under control to avoid injury. Clematis, such as this C. 'Rouge Cardinal', are safer than roses as they have no thorns to catch the unwary.*

Above: *When roses are well-trained they can produce an abundance of flowers. The curiously coloured R. 'Veilchenblau', shown here growing up a wooden trellis, puts on a fine show during midsummer.*

Above: *If possible, train climbers that have scented flowers near open windows, so that their fragrance can be appreciated indoors. Here Rosa 'Albertine' is in full flower, while beyond is a wisteria that has finished flowering.*

Right: *To obtain extra height for the more vigorous roses a trellis can be erected on top of a wall. When well-trained they present a backdrop of colour against which to view the border in front and below.*

Growing Climbers on Wires

If a large area of wall is to be covered with non-clinging climbers, wires are the only realistic way of supporting them. Alternative methods, such as covering the whole wall with wooden trellis, are expensive and, if the wall is at all attractive, may detract from its appearance.

HOW TO USE WIRES

Wires can be used for most types of climbers, except for clinging ones, which should be able to cling directly to the surface of the wall. If the wires are too far apart, however, plants with tendrils may have difficulty finding the next wire up and may need to be tied in. Wires are also suitable for wall shrubs, which while not needing support, benefit from being tied in to prevent them from being blown forward by wind rebounding from the wall. Wires are unobtrusive and can be painted the same colour as the wall, to make them even less visible. Galvanized wire is best, as it will not rust. Rusty wires are not only liable to break but may also cause unsightly rust marks that may show up on the wall. Plastic-covered wire can be used but the coating is not as permanent as a galvanized one.

Do not use too thin a wire or it will stretch under the weight of the plants. If there is a chance that the wires will stretch, use bottle screws or tension bolts at one end. These can be tightened as the wire slackens.

1 Before it is fixed to wires, the young plant is loose and growing in all directions.

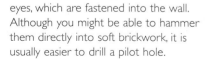

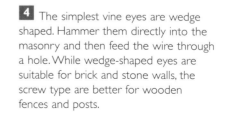

2 The wires are supported by vine eyes, which are fastened into the wall. Although you might be able to hammer them directly into soft brickwork, it is usually easier to drill a pilot hole.

3 If you are using vine eyes with a screw fixing, you need to insert a plastic or wooden plug in the wall first. The eye is then screwed into the plug. This type of vine eye varies in length, the long ones being necessary for those climbers, such as wisteria, that grow large and need wires further from the wall.

4 The simplest vine eyes are wedge shaped. Hammer them directly into the masonry and then feed the wire through a hole. While wedge-shaped eyes are suitable for brick and stone walls, the screw type are better for wooden fences and posts.

5 Thread the galvanized wire through the hole in the vine eye and wrap it round itself, forming a firm fixing. Thread the other end through the intermediate eyes (set at no more than 180 cm/6 ft intervals and preferably closer) and then fasten the wire round the end eye, keeping it as taut as possible.

6 Curve over the long stems and attach them to the wires, using either plastic ties or string. Tie at several points, if necessary, so that the stems lie flat against the wall and do not flap about.

7 When all the stems are tied in, you should have a series of arches. Tying them in like this, rather than straight up the wall, covers the wall better and encourages the plant to produce flowering buds all along the top edge of the stems.

Above: *Climbers such as roses and clematis can be trained up the whole side of a house with wires. Here* Rosa *'Madame Isaac Pereire' completely covers its wires.*

Fixing Trellis to Walls

Permanent wooden trellis, fixed to a wall, is not only a strong method of supporting climbers but also an attractive one. However, large areas of trellis can look overpowering, especially on house walls; wires are a better choice for these situations. Apart from self-clinging plants, which support themselves, any type of climber can be held up by such trellis.

HOW TO USE TRELLIS

The trellis should be well fixed to the wall, preferably with screws. It should be held a short distance from the brickwork or masonry, so that the stems of the climber can easily pass up behind it. This can be simply achieved by using spacers – wooden blocks will do – between the trellis and the wall.

If the wall is a painted one, or might need future attention for other reasons, it is possible to make the trellis detachable. The best method is to fix hinges along the bottom edge of the trellis. This allows the framework to be gently eased away from the wall, bringing the climber with it, so that maintenance can

take place. The top is held by a catch. Alternatively, the trellis can be held in position by a series of clips or catches. This is not so easy to manoeuvre as one held on hinges, however.

Any shape of trellis can be used, such as square, rectangular or fan shaped, depending on the climber and the effect of the shape on the building or wall. It is possible to be more imaginative and devise other shapes, perhaps creating a two-dimensional topiary. The mesh can be either square or diagonal, the former being better with brickwork, because the lines of the trellis then follow those of the brick courses rather than contradicting them.

CLIMBERS FOR TRELLIS
Akebia
Clematis
Cobaea scandens (cathedral bells)
Humulus (hop)
Ipomoea (morning glory)
Lathyrus odoratus (sweet peas)
Lonicera (honeysuckle)
Rosa (roses)
Solanum crispum
Solanum jasminoides
Thunbergia alata (black-eyed Susan)
Tropaeolum (nasturtiums)

1 Take the trellis to the wall and mark its position. Drill holes for fixing the spacers and insert plastic or wooden plugs.

2 Drill the equivalent holes in the wooden batten and secure it to the wall, checking with a spirit level that it is horizontal. Use a piece of wood that holds the trellis at least 2.5 cm (1 in) from the wall. Fix a similar batten at the base and one half-way up for trellis above 1.2 m (4 ft) high.

Vitis (vines)

3 Drill and screw the trellis to the battens, first fixing the top and then working downwards. Check that the trellis is not crooked.

4 The finished trellis should be tightly fixed to the wall, so that the weight of the climber, and any wind that blows on it, will not pull it away from its fixings.

Above: *The rose 'Dublin Bay' here climbs up a wooden trellis secured to the wall. This rose is fragrant and flowers over a very long period.*

Growing Climbers on Netting

A cheap but effective method of providing support for climbers on a wall is to use a rigid plastic netting. This can be used for large areas but it is more effective for smaller climbers, where a limited area is covered.

HOW TO USE NETTING

Rigid plastic netting is suitable for covering brick or stone walls as well as wooden walls and panel fences. It can also be wrapped around poles or pillars, to give plants something to grip. You can string netting between upright posts, as a temporary support for annual climbing plants such as sweet peas, but it is not really suitable for a permanent structure of this sort.

Netting is readily available from garden centres and nurseries. It can generally be bought in green, brown or white, which allows you to choose a colour that matches the wall, so that the netting does not show up too obviously. It is also possible to buy special clips, which make fixing the netting to a surface very simple.

The clips are designed to be used either with masonry nails or with screws. They have the advantage that they hold the netting away from the wall, so that there is room for the plant to climb through it or wrap its tendrils round the mesh, whereas if the netting is nailed directly to the wall there is no space between them.

A further advantage of this method of fixing is that the net can be unclipped and eased away from the wall, allowing the latter to be painted or treated with preservative before the net is clipped back into position.

Plastic netting can be used either with plants that support themselves with tendrils or by twining, or with plants that need to be tied in. It does not look as attractive as the more expensive wooden trellising but, once it has been covered with the climber, it is not noticeable, especially if the right colour has been chosen. After a few years you will not be able to see the netting at all; it will be covered in a mass of foliage and flowers.

1 Position the first clip just below the top of where the net will be and drive in a masonry nail. Alternatively, drill a hole, plug it and screw the clip into it.

2 With a spirit level, mark the position of the other upper clip, so that it is level with the first. Fix the second clip.

3 Place the top of the net in position, with one horizontal strand in the jaw of the clip. Press it home so it is securely fastened. Repeat with the other clip.

4 Smooth the net down against the wall and mark where the next set of clips will come. They should be at about 60 cm (2 ft) intervals down the wall. Move the net out of the way, fix the clips and press the net into the clips. Follow the same procedure with the bottom clips.

5 When the netting is securely in place, train the climber up into it. Even those that are self-supporting may need tying in to get them going. If the plant is a little way out from the wall, train it towards the netting along canes.

Above: *Netting is rather ugly and it is best used with vigorous climbers that will soon cover it. Here, the netting has only been used well above the ground, where the main support is needed. Unsightly supports won't show around the base of the climbers, where the main stems make an attractive feature in their own right.*

Trellis and Fences

One of the simplest and yet most decorative ways of displaying climbers is to grow them over free-standing trellises or fences. Used in the garden, to define its major routes, this is an impressive way of bringing planting right in to the garden's fundamental structure.

BOUNDARIES AND SCREENS

Fences tend to be functional, in that they create a boundary; this is usually between the garden and the outside world but a fence is sometimes used as an internal divider. Many existing fences are ugly and covering them with climbers is a good way of hiding this fact. Those erected by the gardener need not be ugly but they still provide an opportunity for climbers.

Trellises are usually much more decorative than fences. They are not so solid and allow glimpses of what lies on the other side. They are either used as internal dividers within the garden, as screens, or simply as a means of supporting climbers. Used in this way, trellis can make a tremendous contribution to a garden design, as they can provide horizontal as well as vertical emphasis. As screens, they are useful for disguising eyesores such as fuel tanks, garages or utility areas.

ERECTING TRELLIS

The key to erecting a good trellis is to make certain that it is firmly planted in the ground. Once covered with climbers, it will come under enormous pressure from the wind and will work loose unless firmly embedded in concrete. Do not try to take a short cut by simply back-filling the post-hole with earth; unless the trellis is in a very protected position, it will eventually fall over. Panel fences are erected in a similar way.

Virtually any climber can be grown over trellis. But unless it is in a sheltered position, trellis will not offer the same protection as a wall to tender climbers.

1 Dig a hole at least 60 cm (2 ft) deep, deeper in light soils.

2 Put the post in the prepared hole and partly fill the hole with a dry-mix concrete. Check that the post is upright and not sloping, using a spirit level. Adjust the position of the post, if necessary, and then continue filling the hole, tamping down firmly as you go to hold the pole still.

3 Continue filling the hole with concrete, ramming it down firmly; frequently check that the post is still upright. The post should now be firm enough in the ground to work on and, once the concrete has "cured", it will be permanently secure.

4 Lay the panel on the ground, to work out where the next hole should be. Dig the hole, again to at least 60 cm (2 ft) deep.

5 Nail the panel on to the first post, while a helper supports the free end.

6 Place the second post in its hole and nail it to the panel, checking that the tops of the posts are level and the panel is horizontal. Fill the second hole with dry-mix concrete, tamping it down as you proceed. Check that the post is upright and adjust, if necessary.

7 Repeat the steps by digging the third post hole, nailing on the second panel, positioning and nailing the third post and so on, until the length of trellising is complete. This is more accurate than putting in all the posts and then fixing the panels, when, inevitably, some gaps will be too large and some too small.

Above: *Honeysuckles will quickly cover trellis.*

Hoops

Training over hoops allows you to direct the growth of the plant, so that it covers all the available space. If the plant is allowed to shoot heavenwards, the result can be disappointing, whereas, if you spread out the initial stems at the base when you first plant, you can encourage the plant to make a much better display.

THE AIMS OF TRAINING

Bending the new young growth into curving arches encourages flowering buds to be formed along the whole length of the stem, rather than just at the tip, as happens if the branch is tied in a vertical position. Frequently, new shoots will also develop from the curving stems and these should, in turn, also be tied into an arch, gradually encouraging the climber to cover the whole hoop. This will encourage a much thicker coverage and many more blooms.

Training plants over hoops helps keep their final height in proportion to the border in which they are growing. It is a very useful method for growing reasonably vigorous plants in a limited space. Very vigorous plants are best avoided; they will soon outgrow their space, however much training you do!

1 In early spring, make a series of hoops around the rose, pushing each end of the pole into the ground. The wood used should be pliable, hazel *(Corylus avellana)* being one of the best to use. Bend each stem carefully, so that it does not crack.

2 Allow each hoop to overlap the previous one.

3 Sort out the long shoots of the rose, carefully bend them over and then tie them to a convenient point on the hoop. In some cases, it may be easier to tie the shoot to a stem that has already been tied down.

4 To start with, the "bush" will look rather untidy but, gradually, the leaves will turn to face the light and it will produce new buds all along the upper edges of the curved stems.

5 Gradually the plant will fill out, and by midsummer it should be a mass of blooms. Every year, remove a few of the older stems and tie in all new ones. After a few years, remove the old hoops and replace them with new ones.

Above: *Roses grown over hoops form a dense bush that is covered with flowers. Here R. 'Isphahan' puts on a good display of flowers as well as putting on plenty of new growth for the following year.*

Growing Climbers up Tripods

Tripods provide a useful opportunity for growing climbers in borders and other areas of limited space. A tripod helps to create vertical emphasis in gardens and may become a striking focal point if eye-catching climbers are allowed to cover it with foliage and flowers.

USING TRIPODS

Tripods can be formal, made to a classic design, or they can be made from rustic poles. The former are better where they are still partly on show after the climber is in full growth. The latter, on the other hand, in spite of their rustic and informal charm, are more suitable for carrying heavy, rampant climbers that will cover them completely. Tripods provide a more substantial support than a single pole.

More formal designs can be bought complete, ready to be installed in the garden. Tripods can, of course, also be made by the competent woodworker. A rustic-pole tripod is much more basic and can easily be constructed by most gardeners. They can be made to any height, to suit the eventual height of the plants and the visual aspects of the site.

Although any type of climber can be grown up a tripod, self-clingers would not be so good because there isn't enough flat surface for them to attach their modified roots. Tripods are ideal for carrying two or more climbers at once. If possible, choose climbers that flower at different times. Alternatively, choose two that flower at the same time but look particularly well together.

An ideal combination is a rose and a *Clematis viticella*. The latter is pruned almost to the ground each winter and so is still growing while the rose is in flower and, therefore, does not smother it. Later in the summer, the clematis comes into its own when the rose is past its best.

1 Position three posts in the ground. The distance apart will depend on the height; balance the two to get a good shape. The posts can be driven into the ground but a better job is done if you dig holes at least 60 cm (2 ft) deep. For a really solid job, backfill the holes with dry-mix concrete, but it will normally be sufficient just to ram the earth back around the poles.

2 Nail cross-pieces between the posts. These will not only help support the plants but also give the structure rigidity. Rails at 40–45 cm (15–18 in) apart should be sufficient for tying in stems. If you want more support for self-clingers, wrap a layer of wire netting around the structure. The plants will soon hide it.

3 When you nail the cross-pieces to the poles, the ends may well split if they have already been cut to the exact length. Nail the pieces on first and then cut them to the right length. Alternatively, cut to length and then drill holes in the appropriate places before nailing to the poles.

4 Plant the climbers in and around the tripod. Avoid planting them too close to the upright poles as the earth here will either be rammed down hard or have been replaced with concrete. Before planting, dig in some well-rotted organic material.

5 Water all the plants in well. If the weather continues dry, keep watering until the plants have become established. Always soak the ground well: a dribble on the surface will not help the plants send roots out into the surrounding soil.

CLIMBERS SUITABLE FOR TRIPODS
Clematis
Humulus (hop)
Lonicera (honeysuckle)
Rosa (roses)
Solanum jasminoides
Tropaeolum (nasturtiums)
Vitis (vines)

6 The finished tripod will look a bit raw at first but it will soon weather and become covered in plants.

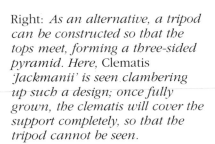

Right: *As an alternative, a tripod can be constructed so that the tops meet, forming a three-sided pyramid. Here, Clematis 'Jackmanii' is seen clambering up such a design; once fully grown, the clematis will cover the support completely, so that the tripod cannot be seen.*

Simple Pillars for Climbers

A very effective way of displaying climbers is to grow them up a single pole, which is usually called a pillar. This can look very elegant and also means it is possible to grow a large number of climbers in a relatively small space. Pillars create vertical emphasis in borders or small gardens, without creating a barrier.

CLIMBERS FOR PILLARS

Clematis
Humulus (hop)
Lonicera (honeysuckle)
Rosa (roses)
Solanum jasminoides
Tropaeolum (nasturtiums)
Vitis (vines)

USING PILLARS

A surprising number of climbers are suited to growing up pillars. Most climbing roses, for example, look particularly good growing up them, although it is probably best to avoid vigorous climbers or rambling roses.

An advantage of using pillars for your climbers is that they are inexpensive and simple to erect and take down.

The pillar shown here is permanently positioned in a border but is possible to place the posts in a collar of concrete or a metal tube, so that they can be taken down during the winter when they are bare.

Movable columns are best suited to annuals or *Clematis viticella*, which can be cut down almost to the ground before the posts are removed. Permanent climbers, such as roses, will need a permanent structure.

If space is available, a very attractive walkway can be created by using a series of pillars along a path. This can be further improved by connecting the tops with rope, along which swags of climbers can grow. This is a very good way of growing roses and creates a very romantic, fragrant route through the garden. The effect is suited to formal designs, but is so soft and flowing that it gives a very relaxing feel.

1 Dig a hole at least 60 cm (2 ft) deep. Put in the post and check that it is upright. Backfill with earth, ramming it firmly down as it is filled. In exposed gardens, a more solid pillar can be created by filling the hole with concrete.

2 Plants can be tied directly to the post but a more natural support is created if wire netting is secured to the post. Plants such as clematis will then be able to climb by themselves with little attention from you other than tying in wayward stems.

3 Plant the climber a little way out from the pole, to avoid the compacted area. Lead the stems to the wire netting and tie them in, to get them started. Self-clingers will now take over but plants such as roses will need to be tied in as they climb. Twining plants, such as hops, can be grown up the pole without the wire.

Left: Clematis *'W.E. Gladstone'* *climbing up a pillar. If the pole was covered with wire netting the plant would have more to grip on, which would prevent it suddenly collapsing down the pole under its own weight as it may do later here.*

Right: *Although single-post pillars are rather slim, they can accommodate more than one climber. Here there are two roses, 'American Pillar' and 'Kew Rambler'. Another option is to choose one rose and a later-flowering clematis.*

Above: *Single-post pillars help to break up what would, otherwise, be a dull, rather two-dimensional border. Although it is only a thin structure, when clothed with a climber it becomes a well-filled-out, irregular shape, as this 'American Pillar' rose shows.*

Growing Climbers Through Trees and Shrubs

In the wild, many climbing plants that are also used in the garden find support by scrambling up through trees and shrubs. In thick woodland or forests, they may grow to 50 m (150 ft) plus, in search of light. In the garden, supports of this height are rarely available, and, if they were, the flowers of the climbers using them would be out of sight.

CHOOSING GOOD PARTNERS

A smaller support is required for cultivated climbers in the garden, with a large apple tree, therefore, usually being the highest used. Clematis and roses will scramble through the branches, creating huge fountains of flowers. On a more modest scale, even dwarf shrubs can be used to support some low-growing climbers.

One of the advantages of growing climbers through shrubs is that it is possible to obtain two focuses of interest in one area. This is particularly true of early-flowering shrubs, which are relatively boring for the rest of the year. Through these, it is possible to train a later-flowering climber to enliven the area further on in the season. Clematis are particularly good for this, especially the later-flowering forms, such as the viticellas. These can be cut nearly to the ground during the winter, so that the shrub is relatively uncluttered with the climber when it is in flower itself earlier on in the next season.

Fruit trees that have finished their fruiting life can be given new appeal if you grow a rose through them. However, it is important to remember that old trees may be weak and that the extra burden of a large rose, especially in a high wind, may be too much for it to carry.

CLIMBERS SUITABLE FOR GROWING THROUGH TREES
Akebia
Clematis
Fallopia baldschuanica (Russian vine)
Humulus (hop)
Lonicera (honeysuckle)
Rosa (roses – vigorous varieties)
Solanum crispum
Solanum jasminoides

CLIMBERS SUITABLE FOR GROWING THROUGH SHRUBS
Clematis
Cobaea scandens (cathedral bells)
Eccremocarpus scaber (Chilean glory flower)
Ipomoea (morning glory)
Lathyrus odoratus (sweet peas)
Thunbergia alata (black-eyed Susan)
Tropaeolum (nasturtiums)
Vinca major

1 Any healthy shrub or tree can be chosen. It should preferably be one that flowers at a different time to the climber. Choose companions that will not swamp each other. Here, a relatively low *Salix helvetica* is to be planted with a small form of *Clematis alpina*. The two will make a delicate mix, especially the blue clematis flowers against the silver foliage of the *Salix helvetica*.

2 Dig the planting area at a point on the perimeter of the shrub and prepare the soil by adding well-rotted organic material. For clematis, choose a position on the shady side of the plant, so that its roots are in shade but the flowers will be up in the sun. Dig a hole bigger than the climber's rootball and plant it. Most climbers should be planted at the same depth as they were in their pots but clematis should be 5 cm (2 in) or so deeper.

3 Using a cane, train the clematis into the bush. Once the clematis has become established, you can remove the cane. Spread the shoots of the climber out so that it spreads evenly through the shrub, not just in one area.

4 If possible, put the climber outside the canopy of the shrub or tree, so that it receives rain. However, it is still important to water in the new plant and, should the weather be dry, to continue watering until the plant is established.

Above: *The beautiful white clematis 'Marie Boisselot' grows up through a small apple tree.*

Archways

Arches are very versatile features in a garden and are well suited for growing a variety of climbers. Archways can be incorporated into a dividing feature, such as a wall, hedge or fence, or can be free-standing along a path as nothing more than a means of supporting climbers.

USING ARCHES

Archways exert a magnetic effect on visitors to your garden. No matter how interesting the area you are in, an archway draws the eye to what lies beyond. It creates mystery with tantalizing glimpses of other things.

Those forming entrances are important features. They are often the first thing that a visitor is aware of on entering a garden. Arches frame the scene beyond and create atmosphere. A cottage garden, for example, looks particularly fine when seen through a rose arch, while a formal town garden may be better suited to a simple arch of foliage, such as ivy.

The possibilities of creating an arch are almost endless. They can be purchased in kit form, made to order or made by the gardener. They can be made from metal, wood, brick or stone work. Plastic ones are also available, but are neither very attractive nor long lasting. Wooden ones present the biggest range. They can be formal ones created from panels of trellis, or informal ones made from rustic poles. The choice is normally limited by cost and the appearance that is required – climbers themselves will generally climb over anything.

Always choose or make one that is big enough for people to walk through when it is fully clad with climbers – which may stick out as far as 60 cm (2 ft) or more from the supports. Make certain that the supports are well sunk into the ground, preferably concreted in. When covered with a voluminous climber, an arch may be under great pressure from the wind and a storm may push over a badly constructed one, destroying your display.

Virtually any climbers can be used with archways, although over-vigorous ones can become a nuisance – they seem to be constantly growing across the entrance itself. Other types of climbers to avoid, unless there is plenty of room, are thorned roses which may cause injury, or coarse-stemmed plants such as hops. These can be dangerous to the unwary. If you want a rose, use something like 'Zéphirine Drouhin', which is thornless.

CLIMBERS FOR ARCHWAYS
Akebia
Campsis radicans
Clematis
Phaseolus (climbing beans)
Humulus (hop)
Lonicera (honeysuckle)
Rosa (roses)
Vitis (vines)

Above: *A simple arch, constructed from rustic poles and covered with a variegated ivy. The simplicity of the foliage allows the eye to pass through to the garden beyond, without distraction.*

Above: *Wisteria makes a good covering for an arch because, once it has finished flowering, its foliage still retains a great deal of interest. It is accompanied here by* Vitis coignetiae, *whose foliage turns a magnificent purple colour in autumn. Together, these climbers provide interest from spring to autumn.*

Above: *A golden hop,* Humulus lupulus aureus, *and a honeysuckle,* Lonicera periclymenum, *combine to decorate this archway. Again, interest should be provided from spring to autumn.*

Above left: *This wonderfully romantic arch seems to come from the middle of nowhere. The roses and long grass create a soft image that provides nothing but delight.*

Left: *Roses make excellent subjects for archways. Repeat-flowering ones provide the longest interest; once-flowering roses can be combined with late-flowering clematis, to extend the season.*

Arbours

An arbour is a framework over which climbers are trained to create a shady outdoor room. It can be just big enough to take a chair or bench, but best of all is an arbour large enough to accommodate a table and several chairs, where you can sit and linger over alfresco meals.

CLIMBERS FOR ARBOURS

Clematis (some fragrant)
Fallopia baldschuanica (Russian vine – very vigorous)
Hedera (ivy – evergreen)
Humulus (hop – dies back in winter)
Lonicera (honeysuckle – many fragrant)
Rosa (roses – many fragrant)
Vitis (vines – some fruiting)

DESIGNING AN ARBOUR

The structure can be of metal or wood or the arbour can have brick or stone piers with a wooden roof. The design can be any shape that takes the fancy or fits the site. It may be triangular, semi-circular, rectangular or octagonal, to suggest but a few. The climbers can be any that you like. If you do not like bees, stick to climbers grown for their foliage. In areas designed for relaxation, fragrant climbers are most welcome. Honeysuckle provides a delicious scent, particularly in the evening. Jasmine is another good evening plant. For daytime enjoyment, fragrant roses are ideal.

An arbour may have to remain in place for many years, so make sure you build it well. Take trouble to use timbers treated with preservative (not creosote, which may kill many climbers) and make certain that it is a strong design, well supported in the ground. As with similar structures covered in heavy climbers, the wind can wreak havoc on weak construction.

Right: *Here, the overhanging fig,* Ficus carica, *and the surrounding rose, clematis and other climbers create an intimate area for sitting and relaxing, which fulfils all the functions of an arbour, even though there is no supporting structure.*

Above: *This arbour is dappled with shade from a number of roses. It is big enough for small supper parties as well as simply sitting in the evening with a drink.*

Above: *A large arbour, built for entertaining, this example is covered in a variety of climbers, including a purple grapevine. This provides a wonderfully dappled shade, as well as colourful foliage and grapes at the end of the autumn.* Clematis montana *supplies the colour in the spring and early summer.*

Above: *A dual-purpose arbour: the newly planted beans will provide shade during the hotter part of the year, as well as a constant supply of runner beans for the kitchen. As a bonus, the flowers provide an added attraction.*

Walkways and Pergolas

Extending the use of arches and trellis brings the possibility of pergolas and walkways. This is an ideal way of providing a shady path. On the whole, these are not suitable for the smaller garden, although it is surprising what can be achieved with a bit of imagination.

PLANT IDEAS

Akebia
Campsis radicans
Clematis
Phaseolus (climbing beans)
Humulus (hop)
Lonicera (honeysuckle)
Rosa (roses)

USING WALKWAYS AND PERGOLAS

Walkways are open pergolas, with no roof. They can be double-sided, that is, down both sides of a path, or you can use a single piece of trellis down one side. The simplest way is to build them out of either trellis or rustic poles. For a romantic version, use a series of pillars linked with swags of ropes.

Both can become massive structures that have to support a great deal of weight, especially when there is a strong wind blowing, so it is important to make certain that, whatever the material, the walkway or pergola is well constructed.

A wide range of climbing plants can be used to clothe the pergola or walkway; fragrant plants are especially pleasing. Roses are ideal, as long as they are either thornless or well tied in so that they do not catch passers-by with their thorns. Evergreen climbers, such as ivy, make a dark and intriguing tunnel and will keep passers-by dry in wet weather throughout the year.

Right: *An arch leads through into another part of the garden. The poles are covered with* Rosa *'American Pillar' and* R. *'Albertine'. On the side of the arch is* Clematis *'Alba Luxurians'.*

Above: *Clematis tumbling over the corner of a pergola. Here,* C. *'Etoile Violette' combines with some late flowers of* C. montana *to create an attractive picture.*

Above: *Colourful foliage makes a long-lasting covering for a pergola. Here* Vitis vinifera *'Purpurea' creates an attractive screen up a wooden pillar. As the year proceeds, the colour of the foliage will deepen, so there is a change of appearance, even without flowers.*

Above: *A romantic walkway created from a series of arches, passing along a clipped path through long grass. The arches provide a delightful tunnel effect, while the statue at the end draws the eye and adds to the romantic image.*

Temporary Supports

It is not always desirable to have fixed screens or supports for climbers. It can be fun to move them around the garden, using a different position each year. This allows a much more flexible design. While this is not really practical with perennial climbers, especially those that might take several years to establish themselves, it is entirely possible with annuals.

USING TEMPORARY SUPPORTS

In some cases, temporary supports can undertake two functions at once: to provide an attractive screen and to provide vegetables for the kitchen. Thus, peas and beans make good traditional subjects, while more novel ideas might include climbing marrows, courgettes (zucchini), gourds (squashes) and cucumbers.

Temporary screens are easy to make and a variety of materials can be used. Many are rustic in nature, such as pea-sticks simply pushed into the ground or traditional bean poles tied together in a row or wigwam (tepee). More modern materials would include plastic netting held on poles or a metal frame. However, it is best not to use materials that are unattractive, as the plants trained up temporary supports do not often get under way until the early summer, not covering them until midsummer.

Temporary structures can also be used for a few perennials that are cut to the ground each year, such as the everlasting pea *Lathyrus latifolius* or some of the clematis that are either herbaceous or a pruned to near the ground each year. Since the latter can grow quite tall, they can be supported by large branches stuck in the ground, to imitate small trees.

Left: *Climbing plants can often be used in this somewhat more horizontal way than is usual. It is an ideal way to utilize space left after spring flowers have finished blooming.*

Above: *A typical bean row, with the scarlet-flowered runner beans climbing up poles that have been tied together for support. The poles can be kept for several seasons before they need to be replaced.*

Above: *Peas growing up a wigwam (tepee) of canes. The canes are pushed into the ground in a circle, with their tops pointing towards the centre, where they are all tied together to keep them rigid. Poles of any wood or metal can be used, as well as the traditional bamboo canes shown here.*

Above right: *Sweet peas growing up a temporary screen of pea-sticks. Hazel (Corylus avellana) is one of the best types of wood, but any finely branched sticks will do. They usually only last one season and then need to be replaced.*

Right: *A framework of hazel sticks have been woven into a dome, over which a clematis is growing.*

Growing Climbers in Containers

Although most climbers are grown in the open ground, there is no reason why they should not be grown in containers. This is a particularly good idea for a balcony, roof garden or patio. While it is not really feasible to grow vigorous plants in this way, a surprising number of climbers are suitable.

SUPPORTING CLIMBERS IN POTS

The main problem when growing climbers in pots is finding a method of supporting the plant. If they are only short plants or annuals, such as black-eyed Susan (*Thunbergia*) or nasturtiums, it is perfectly feasible to include the support in the container. You can use canes or a V-shaped piece of trellising, burying the lower end in the pot.

For more vigorous plants, set the containers against a wall on which trellis has been fixed. An alternative is to have strings or tall canes rising from the pot to some suitable fixing on the wall.

One of the main secrets of success with container climbers is to keep them watered well. Feeding also becomes very important, as constant watering leaches out many of the nutrients in the soil.

1 To ensure that the compost in the container is adequately drained it is important to place a layer of small stones or broken pots in the bottom. This will allow any excess water to drain away quickly.

2 Partly fill the pot with a good-quality potting compost (soil mix). Add to this some water-retaining granules and stir these into the compost. Use the quantity recommended on the packet. The granules will expand when they become wet and hold the moisture until the plant wants it, without making the soil too wet, something that most plants hate.

3 Put the narrow end of the trellis into the container. The trellis will be held in position by the weight of the compost, so the base should be as low down in the pot as possible. This type of frame is not suitable for tall, narrow pots, which may be blown over easily.

4 Put the plant in position so that the top of the rootball comes level with the intended surface of the compost. Put in the remaining compost and lightly firm it down. Train the stems of the climber against the trellis and tie them in, if necessary.

5 Water the pot and top it up with compost (soil mix) if the level falls. Cover the top with pebbles or gravel, partly to give it a pleasant appearance but also to help suppress weeds and make watering easier. When creating such a display, put it in its final position before you fill the container as the complete container may be very heavy.

6 As an alternative, fix a piece of trellis to a wall and stand the pot next to it. This will take heavier climbers and be less inclined to blow or fall over. Being next to a wall may put the pot in a rain shadow, however, so be prepared to water it even if you have had rain.

Above: *Grouping containers together presents an attractive display. Here, Clematis 'Prince Charles' is planted in a chimney pot next to some potted chives.*

Above: *A variety of different frameworks can be used in large containers, to support annual and temporary climbers. The metal frameworks will last the longest but will be most expensive. The willow wicker support, at the back of the group, is attractive in its own right.*

ANNUALS

Annuals are tremendously popular with gardeners. In general they are easy to grow, often thriving in poor, dry soil, and will produce a brilliant show of colour over a long period of time. There are also many delicate, subtle colours, as well as the familiar bold and bright varieties. Annuals are perfect for bedding schemes, as formal or informal as you like, or they can be allowed to self-seed, in which case many varieties will more or less take care of themselves. However, if you only have space for a window box or a hanging basket, you can still create a stunning display. This chapter is the perfect introduction to the possibilities that annuals offer, from advice on design to practical information that will enable you to achieve your gardening goals.

Left: *The fluffy purple flowers of* Ageratum *'Blue Horizon' and delicate yellow-green* Euphorbia stricta *combine well with flowering shrubs in a mixed border.*

ANNUALS DEFINED

What is an Annual?

The definition of annuals is not quite as straightforward as it might seem at first sight. Fundamentally, annuals are plants that grow and die within one year, but in gardening terms, we usually think of them as plants that we use during the course of one year only and then discard, even though they might, in certain conditions, live longer. This means that the definition also encompasses biennial plants as well as a few tender and short-lived perennials.

TRUE ANNUALS

True annuals are those that grow from seed each year, flower and then die, with only the seeds surviving to the following year. Some annuals, such as those used as bedding plants or for containers, *Lobelia* for example, have a very long season and will flower from the beginning of summer right through until the middle or end of autumn. Others, however, such as the amusingly named poached egg plant (*Limnanthes douglasii*), have a brief but dramatic flowering of perhaps only a couple of weeks or even less. In addition to length of flowering, there are also other characteristics that differentiate different types of annuals.

HARDY ANNUALS

One of the most useful types of annual, especially for use in mixed plantings, are the hardy annuals. These can be sown directly into the soil or in trays or pots to be planted out in autumn where they will survive the winter unprotected, ready to produce flowers in the late spring or early summer, well before the more tender bedding comes into flower. Forget-me-nots (*Myosotis*) are a good example of this.

HALF-HARDY ANNUALS

Half-hardy annuals will not tolerate frost and should be either grown from seed in a greenhouse or conservatory and planted out once the danger of frosts has passed or sown directly into the soil once temperatures are guaranteed to be above freezing. Those sown directly into the soil will flower much later than those that have been raised under glass in the spring and planted out as almost mature plants, and in some cases as fully mature plants in full flower. Anything grown under protection needs to be fully hardened off before it is planted outside. Examples of half-hardy annuals include French marigolds (*Tagetes patula*) and cosmos. Sometimes a distinction is made between half-hardy annuals and tender ones (see below).

TENDER ANNUALS

Tender annuals originate in tropical and sub-tropical climates and must be raised under heat in a greenhouse in order for them to flower within a year. If they were sown in the open soil after the danger of frosts had passed, they would not have a long enough season to mature and flower before the autumn frosts. The castor-oil plant (*Ricinus*) is a good example.

SOME POPULAR ANNUALS

Ageratum (floss flower)
Amaranthus caudatus (love-lies-bleeding)
Antirrhinum (snapdragon)
Calceolaria
Centaurea cyanus (cornflower)
Cosmos
Godetia
Ipomoea

Limnanthes douglasii (poached egg plant)
Myosotis (forget-me-not)
Nigella damascena (love-in-a-mist)
Papaver somniferum (opium poppy)
Petunia
Tagetes (marigold)
Tropaeolum (nasturtium)

Top: *This drift of the annual* Cleome *'Pink Queen' combines well with perennials in a mixed border. The effect of the foliage of these plants is nearly as striking as that of the flowers.*

Left: *Tender perennials are particularly good subjects for containers because they can be moved inside at the end of the season. Here a scented pelargonium, variegated fuchsia and* Persicaria captita *are displayed behind a creeping thyme.*

Right: *Brightly-coloured pelargoniums and mesembryanthemum create a spectacular display when used in this colourful bedding scheme. The scheme is unusual in that it has been created in a rock garden.*

What is a Biennial?

True annuals have a life-span of less than 12 months, and always flower within this time span. On the other hand, there are also biennials which take longer to flower. Biennials germinate in the first year, overwinter as a rosette of leaves and then flower during the following spring or summer. Occasionally biennials may be slow growing in their first year. If this is the case, the flowers may take an extra year to appear, blooming only in their third year.

TYPICAL BIENNIAL

The well-known foxglove, *Digitalis purpurea*, is a typical biennial. It is sown in the spring of the first year, either in trays or directly into the ground, and then it quickly germinates. Foxgloves grow on throughout the year with their basal leaves reaching almost full size before the start of the winter. They are fully hardy and need no winter protection. As spring of the second year approaches foxgloves grow rapidly, forming the familiar tall flower spike, which by early summer forms a statuesque spire of flowers.

SELF-SOWING

If left after flowering, foxgloves will produce copious amounts of seed which self-sow to produce another crop of plants. There are quite a number of biennials that behave in this way, which can save the gardener a lot of time. All that is required is to remove any excess or unwanted plants as well as any that have sown themselves in the wrong place.

Some plants often skip a year, the seed lying dormant then germinating the following year. *Delphinium staphisagria* and the Scotch thistle (*Onopordum acanthium*) often behave like this, but after a few years there is enough residual seed in the soil for at least some to germinate every year giving a succession of flowers every year.

DIRECT SOWING

Many biennials and some short-lived perennials that are treated as biennials, such as wallflowers (*Erysimum*) and sweet William (*Dianthus barbatus*), are sown directly into the soil. They can also be sown in trays but do better in the ground. They should be sown in shallow drills in the late spring and thinned out when they have germinated. They are left in the rows until the autumn, when they will be big enough for transferring to their final flowering positions, which will often be an area of border that has just been cleared of the current year's annuals after the flowers have faded.

SOME POPULAR BIENNIALS

Anchusa capensis (Cape forget-me-not)
Brassica oleracea (ornamental cabbage)
Campanula medium (Canterbury bells)
Delphinium staphisagria
Dianthus barbatus (sweet William)
Digitalis purpurea (foxglove)
Echium vulgare (viper's bugloss)
Eryngium giganteum (Miss Willmott's Ghost)
Erysimum, syn. *Cheiranthus* (wallflower)
Exacum affine
Glaucium flavum (horned poppy)
Hesperis matronalis (sweet rocket)
Lunaria annua (honesty)
Matthiola incana (Brompton stock)
Oenothera biennis (evening primrose)
Onopordum acanthium (Scotch thistle)
Papaver nudicaule (Iceland poppy)
Silybum marianum
Verbascum (mullein)

Left: *Biennials, such as this foxglove,* Digitalis purpurea, *usually form a rosette during their first year. After overwintering, they grow during the next spring to flower in the summer.*

Above: Eryngium giganteum, *which is also commonly known as Miss Willmott's Ghost, produces steely blue flowers and has silver, prickly foliage. It is a good flower for drying.*

Right: Lunaria annua *is, in spite of its name, a biennial. Also known as honesty, its delicate silvery seed cases are very valuable in dried flower arrangements and decorations.*

Above: Hesperis matronalis *or sweet rocket is an old-fashioned cottage garden plant that has a most delightful scent, which is especially apparent around dusk.*

What is a Tender Perennial?

Gardeners are often unaware that many of the 'annuals' they grow every year are, in fact, perennials, which in their wild state will go on flowering year after year. There are two reasons why these plants are treated as annuals in temperate regions. Some are short-lived while others are tender and would not survive a frosty winter. With care, both types could be treated as perennials, but their natures are such that it is advisable to discard the plants at the end of the year and then start afresh the following year.

SHORT-LIVED PERENNIALS
These can be typified by wallflowers (*Erysimum*), snapdragons (*Antirrhinum*) and sweet Williams (*Dianthus*

barbatus). Traditionally, these are sown afresh each year for flowering the next. However, if they are grown in soil that does not become too water-logged,

and are trimmed back after flowering, they will flower again the following year, and even the next. However, with each year the flowering becomes a little less successful and to get the best show it is best to treat them as an annual or biennial and sow each year.

Being perennial they can also be propagated vegetatively. If the sown seed produces a wallflower that has an interesting colouring, it is possible to ensure that you have it again the next year by taking cuttings from non-flowering stems. Treat these as ordinary cuttings, potting them up when they have rooted and planting out in the autumn for flowering the following year.

TENDER PERENNIALS
Different types of tender perennials are treated in various ways by gardeners. Some, including petunias, are grown exactly like annuals, which means that they are sown every year and discarded after flowering. Another group, which includes pelargoniums and fuchsias, can be propagated by cuttings in the autumn, overwintered in a greenhouse or on a windowsill, and then planted out the following spring after the danger of frosts has passed. A third group includes dahlias and tuberous begonias, and these have tubers which are simply lifted, stored in a frost-free place over the winter, and then planted out again.

SOME POPULAR TENDER PERENNIALS

Abutilon
Alonsoa warscewiczii (mask flower)
Alternanthera
Antirrhinum majus (snapdragon)
Argyranthemum
Begonia semperflorens
Bellis perennis (daisy)
Browallia speciosa
Capsicum annuum (ornamental pepper)
Celosia cristata
Chrysanthemum
Cobaea scandens (cup and saucer vine)
Coleus blumei (syn. *Solenostemon scutellarioides*)
Commelina coelestris
Coreopsis (tickseed)
Crepis rubra
Cuphea miniata
Dahlia
Eccremocarpus scandens (Chilean glory flower)
Erysimum (syn. *Cheiranthus*) *cheiri* (wallflower)
Erysimum hieraciifolium
Felicia amelloides (blue marguerite)
Gaillardia aristata (blanket flower)
Gazania
Gomphrena globosa

Helichrysum
Heliotropium arborescens (syn. *H. peruvianum*)
Hesperis matronalis (sweet rocket)
Humea elegans
Impatiens (busy Lizzie)
Limonium sinuatum
Melianthus major (honeybush)
Mimulus
Mirabilis jalapa (marvel of Peru)
Nicotiana langsdorfii
Nierembergia rivularis
Osteospermum
Pelargonium (geranium)
Polygonum capitatum (syn. *Persicaria capitata*)
Primula
Ricinus communis (castor-oil plant)
Rudbeckia hirta (coneflower)
Salvia farinacea
Senecio cineraria (syn. *S. maritima*)
Solanum pseudocapsicum (Jerusalem cherry)
Tanacetum ptarmicaeflorum
Thunbergia alata (black-eyed Susan)
Verbena × *hybrida*
Viola × *wittrockiana* (pansy)

Above: *Several salvias, including this* Salvia farinacea, *are popular 'annuals', but they are, in fact, perennials and can be overwintered in warmer areas.*

Left: *Dahlias are an ideal choice for bringing the summer to a colourful end. However, dahlias are frost tender and must be lifted and stored in a frost-free place, such as a greenhouse or conservatory, before the weather turns cold. This striking, rich orange variety is 'David Howard'.*

Right: Begonia semperflorens *will flower non-stop from early summer through to the end of autumn when it will be killed by the first frosts if it is not moved inside.*

USING ANNUALS

Choosing a Scheme

Although large bedding schemes are not as popular as they once were, there is a revival of interest in the various ways that annual plants can be used and they are being appreciated anew. One of the main advantages of using annuals is their great versatility: they can be mixed with other plants or they can be used on their own.

ANNUAL VARIETY

The great thing about annuals is that they only last for one year. This may seem rather a waste, but the advantage is that once they have been planted you are not tied to a particular scheme for more than a year. If you so wish you can repeat it again the following year, but, on the other hand, you can do something completely different every year. You can simply vary the way you use the plants, that is by choosing another pattern or colour scheme, or you can use quite different plants.

THINKING AHEAD

While annuals provide summer and early autumn enjoyment in the garden, they can also be a source of much pleasure during the winter months as you plan your planting schemes for the following year. While this may simply appear to be a pleasant way of spending a winter's evening, such advance planning is very important, especially if you wish to use annuals on any scale. You need to have worked out well in advance exactly what you want to do and what you will need to achieve it. There is nothing more annoying than

devising a scheme only to discover that when you come to lay it out several plant varieties or colours are missing or you cannot get hold of them.

You can always obtain a few plants from the local garden centre or nursery, but buying in any quantity can become expensive, and you may be restricted in your choice. A much better plan, if you have time and space, is to grow your own plants. This way you can grow as many as you need (plus a few spares), and to your own satisfaction, rather than being limited to what may be second-rate plants from some other source.

INSPIRATION

Some people can invent their own schemes but many others need to look for inspiration elsewhere. Look at gardening books and magazines and visit as many gardens as you can.

Above: *This arrangement is simplicity itself. Scarlet pelargoniums with decorative leaves can be used to provide a very sophisticated display simply by growing them in terracotta pots and lining them up on top of a wall. You can, of course, use as many pots as you want.*

Right: *Busy Lizzies* (Impatiens) *create a colourful bed that contrasts well with the surrounding green hedge. Planting in blocks of the same colour rather than mixing colours is more restful to the eye.*

Above: *Annuals can be planted to create striking points of interest, as this casual display of evening primroses (*Oenothera biennis*) shows.*

Right: *Annuals are excellent plants for edging borders. Here, French marigolds (*Tagetes patula*) line a small patio bed.*

Above: *Annuals have been used here to create a large bedding scheme of subtle colouring. These bedding schemes are very effective but need a lot of careful planning.*

Informal Schemes

One of the most common ways of using bedding plants is to plant them in an informal way. Whether roughly grouped or arranged in some form of pattern, they are basically planted in a glorious mixture that is rather reminiscent of old cottage gardens. While the longer-lasting bedding plants can produce a lovely display, and are invaluable for those with limited time, you can create much more interesting effects by using some of the more unusual annuals with relatively short flowering periods, thus changing the picture as the season progresses.

DESIGN WITH CARE

Mixing plants without any real thought to their placement may well produce a riot of colour, but it can equally produce a chaotic mess. Most gardeners have probably come across examples of front gardens covered in a garish mixture of red, white, blue and orange all stirred up leaving an uncomfortable spectacle on which there is no place for the eye to rest. Take care when mixing the colours in beds and borders and try not to make the effect look too random and unplanned. Make the colours blend, the soft colours creating a restful scene, the brighter ones livening up the overall picture.

SEASONAL ANNUALS

In an informal setting, rather than the more typical bedding plants, less garish plants can often be used to create a bed that has more lasting interest. In spring, the soft colours of forget-me-nots (*Myosotis*), with foxgloves (*Digitalis*) pushing up through them and starting to flower before the forget-me-nots are over, are delightful. These can be followed by nigellas growing around the foxgloves which in turn can be replaced by stately mulleins (*Verbascum*). Later in the season both the yellow Mexican poppy (*Argemone mexicana*) and the white (*A. grandiflora*) might add their own charm. *Crepis rubra*, a short-lived perennial, and *Silene pendula* can be used to add a soft pink note to the planting. Pale cream could also perhaps be introduced by planting *Collomia grandiflora*.

All these mixed colours will vary from week to week, creating a constantly changing, soft misty background against which splashes of eye-catching colour, perhaps the bright red of field poppies (*Papaver rhoeas*), can be added to liven it up.

Top right: *Cottage-garden simplicity and informality has been created by weaving* Collomia grandiflora *through perennials and other annuals.*

Right: *A closer shot of the above showing the way informal plantings can be random without looking too 'bitty'.*

236

Right: *A mixture of annuals and perennials draws the eye along a path to the front door. Here, the informality creates a wonderfully welcoming atmosphere. This contrasts well with the more formal outlines of the house. Remember that this type of gardening is not restricted to quaint cottages.*

Below: *A mass of different annuals creates the effect of a colourful meadow. Such plantings are not easy to achieve but are well worth the effort.*

Below right: *This is a semi-formal scheme in which the annuals have been beautifully planted in blocks but not to any overall pattern.*

Formal Patterns

Patterns have always played an important part in garden design, especially in the larger gardens where there was space to lay things out on a grand scale. The grand designs are now seen only in municipal plantings, especially on the coast and in parks and other public spaces. For many years they have languished, but now a new generation of gardeners has produced a revival with some very imaginative plantings. There is no reason why the gardener with only a small plot should not produce scaled-down versions of these.

STRAIGHT LINES AND SQUIGGLES

All types of patterns can be used as long as they are not so intricate that the detail is lost as the plants grow. The plot to be planted can be divided up into geometrical shapes, such as straight lines, squares, rectangles, triangles, circles and so on. An alternative is to use free-form lines and shapes that interlock or at least react with one another to produce a pleasing pattern. Scrolls and teardrops might be two examples. Each of the lines or shapes can be delineated or filled in with a different colour of flower or leaf. It is worth remembering that foliage adds a great deal to these schemes.

PICTURES

For those who want to do something special, creating a picture with flowers and foliage can be quite a challenge, and can be stunning when carried out well. At a municipal park level, one often sees the town's coat of arms (emblem) picked out in plants. Another popular theme is to make a working clock from flowers and foliage, with only the hands being made of metal or plastic. These types of designs are not only complicated and challenging but need a great deal of attention, especially with clipping, to keep them from going ragged and losing their image.

FROM PAPER TO THE BED

Patterns, especially intricate ones, need a great deal of planning and thought. They should be worked out on graph paper in the same way that you might work out an embroidery or tapestry. You should then stretch a grid, using string and canes, across the plot to be planted, corresponding to the grid on the drawing. Using the string grid as a guide to position, you can then transfer the design to the ground by outlining the shapes with sand poured from a bottle.

Right: *Although the planting in this urn is informal, the overall effect, especially with the begonias around the base, is formal, without being too rigid.*

Left: *Annuals arranged in simple geometric shapes create a satisfying rhythm along this long border. Blocks of single colours are easier on the eye than random mixes.*

Right: *With plenty of space to play with, creating a scheme like this is very gratifying. However, with a little ingenuity and good planning, there is no reason why such a scheme cannot be incorporated into a much smaller garden.*

Above: *A simple scheme using bold colours.*

Above: *A rainbow of colours can look wonderfully cheerful.*

Carpet Schemes

A long-standing tradition in public parks and gardens, carpet schemes can be used in a variety of ways. You can create intricate, formal designs, as demonstrated here, or you can use blocks of colour in bold, simple shapes, or a more informal, irregular scheme. The blocks can be created by planting out bedding plants, or you can sow directly into the soil, broadcasting different seed over each area. Striking colour contrasts can be achieved with flowers, or an interesting effect can be produced using only foliage plants. Many gardeners are under the impression that they do not have enough space for a carpet scheme, but if only small, low-growing plants are used, a very impressive design can be created in a relatively small area.

PURE BLOCKS

Carpet bedding can be arranged in some form of pattern, possibly using an edging plant in a contrasting or sympathetic colour. The blocks can be regular in shape for a formal effect or they can be more random in appearance, perhaps with their edges in a series of curves if you want to achieve a more informal look.

The edges of a block are usually clear-cut, one type of plant ends and another starts, but there is no reason why they should not merge, especially if the colours blend well. The blocks can consist purely of one colour, bright red salvias for example, or they can be a subtle or contrasting mixture. Soft blue forget-me-nots (*Myosotis*) and pink tulips may be an unoriginal combination but it is nonetheless a very effective one. If you need inspiration for devising carpet bedding schemes, look at your local park or public gardens where they are common.

WORKING IN THREE DIMENSIONS

It is worth remembering at the planning stage that different plants grow to different heights and spread, so make allowances for this. Otherwise the design may look ragged. On the other hand, it may be possible to use the different heights to advantage to create a three-dimensional bed with some areas, or even certain plants, higher than others.

PLANNING

It can be fun to work out different designs for carpet bedding schemes. For a formal scheme, you will need to draw the design on graph paper and mark out the grid on the ground using canes and string. Then draw the outline of the design on the ground by pouring sand from a bottle. If you want a less formal scheme, the sizes and shapes of the blocks of colour will be less critical and you can draw the design freehand on the ground with sand.

1 Plan the scheme and draw it on graph paper. To transfer the design to the ground, first mark out a grid using canes and string, then draw out the design using distinctively coloured sand or compost (soil mix), poured from a container. If you are using plants to mark out the design, plant these first, along the lines of sand or compost (soil mix). Complete the planting by filling in between the lines with plants, following your plan. To avoid treading on the plants as you work, use a platform. Here, ladders supported on bricks, with timber planks placed along the rungs, have been used.

2 The finished scheme illustrates the benefit of patient work. Maintenance can be carried out using the same bridging technique as was used for its construction. Maintenance consists of removing any weeds and cutting back any growth that gets too long.

Left: *A wonderfully ornate bed using many of the same plants as the detailed scheme (see below). This type of scheme can be carried out on a grand scale if space allows or devised to fit a small front garden. Much fun can be had during the winter, devising the scheme and drawing up the plans.*

Left: *The plants used in this scheme are (from the left): rows 1-3 forms of* Alternanthera*; 4* Sempervivum arachnoideum*; 5* Tanacetum parthenium *'Golden Moss'; 6* Senecio serpens*; 7* Alternanthera*; 8* Sedum spathulifolium *'Cape Blanco'; 9* Echeveria glauca*; 10* Sedum spathulifolium *'Purpureum'; 11* Echeveria secunda.

Parterres

Gardeners with space to spare can create a superior bedding scheme by planting a parterre and filling it with annuals. Parterres are patterns, either geometric or free-flowing, where each element is outlined by a low hedge. Where there is enough space, patterns can become very intricate and are often best viewed from above, perhaps from the top floor of the house. However, it is possible to create a small parterre in a relatively small garden. Indeed the simplicity of such a garden and the relatively low maintenance it requires lends itself to this type of situation.

HEDGES

The only real disadvantage of this type of scheme is that you have to wait several years for the hedges to grow to the required dimensions. The best plant to use is undoubtedly box (*Buxus sempervirens*), which is, unfortunately, very slow growing. This is an advantage in that it only needs cutting once or perhaps twice a year, but it does take some years to mature. A more rapid design can be achieved by using *Teucrium chamaedrys* or the grey-leaved *Santolina pinnata neapolitana*, but both need trimming a little more frequently than box. Lavender (*Lavandula*) is more untidy but makes a very colourful and fragrant parterre.

The hedges should be about 25cm (10in) high. Prepare the ground well and be certain to remove any perennial weeds or these will cause a problem later on. Dig in plenty of organic material as the hedge is likely to be there for many years and the better the condition of the soil, the better the condition of the hedge, especially if drought conditions prevail.

THE INFILL

Make the most of the parterre and fill it with winter bedding plants as well as using it to create a colourful summer effect. Pansies are ideal for winter use. For spring, use forget-me-nots, primulas and wallflowers (*Erysimum*) as well as bulbs like tulips and narcissus.

For summer the choice is enormous. Each section of the parterre can show a different colour, or colours can be mixed. Traditional bedding plants that have a regularity in height and spread, a long flowering period and require little attention also make ideal candidates. Remember that foliage plants are excellent fillers – colourful *Coleus* (syn. *Solenostemon*), for example, or the subtle *Helichrysum petiolare*.

PERMANENCE

Since the hedges take a while to grow, the basic shapes in the parterre cannot be changed each year. This makes annuals an ideal choice for filling the beds – they will not only vary from season to season but can be completely changed from year to year.

Above: *The edges of the parterre in this walled garden are made up of box (*Buxus sempervirens*) and filled with striking* Salvia farinacea 'Victoria'.

ANNUALS FOR FILLING A PARTERRE

Begonia semperflorens
Bellis (daisy)
Coleus blumei (syn.
  Solenostemon
  scutellarioides)
Erysimum, syn. *Cheiranthus*,
  cheiri (wallflower)
Helichrysum petiolare

Heliotropium
Impatiens (busy Lizzie)
Lobelia erinus
Myosotis (forget-me-not)
Pelargonium (geranium)
Primula
Salvia patens
Tagetes (marigold)

Above: *Wallflowers (*Erysimum*) are superb plants for creating mass planting within a parterre. The variation in their colour establishes an overall effect, rather than the uneven one that mixing colours can often create.*

Left: *Complicated patterns, like this one with its sinuous curves, call for a simple planting, here fulfilled by using yellow pansies (*Viola × wittrockiana*).*

Mixed Borders

Annual plants do not have to be used exclusively on their own in borders or beds devoted to various types of bedding scheme. They can be mixed with other plants, perennials and shrubs. This has the advantage of vastly increasing the variety of plants that can be used in the border (enlarging the gardener's palette, in other words), as well as allowing the introduction of a variable element into what is otherwise a fixed planting. A perennial border will vary slightly from year to year as the influence of the seasons and weather alters timing and the amount of flowering, but generally this type of border will remain much the same in appearance. By using different annuals, perhaps introducing reds instead of blues, or yellows instead of white, the overall effect can be subtly altered.

CHOOSING PLANTS

Many of the popular bedding plants, such as red pelargoniums, are too rigid for the mixed border. It is better if possible to use annuals that look at home among herbaceous plants in a perennial or mixed border. Foxgloves (*Digitalis*) are ideal for early summer, and the opium poppy (*Papaver somniferum*) for later in the season. Both work well in a cottage-garden border. A more modern border with subtle colourings might include purple-leaved red orach (*Atriplex hortensis* 'Rubra') or soft blue love- in-a-mist (*Nigella damascena*). Foliage plants like *Helichrysum petiolare* add colour or act as linking themes between colours.

PERENNIAL ANNUALS

Some annuals self-sow regularly, reappearing every year without the gardener having to bother about sowing or planting them.

These work well in a mixed border where the seed can germinate and seedlings develop undisturbed, unlike in bedding areas where the soil is dug over every year, and self-sowing plants can be a nuisance. Many self-seeding plants, such as borage (*Borago officinalis*), also associate well with a herbaceous border.

PLANTING

If the annual plants are to be dotted about the border, as foxgloves might be, they can be planted directly in their positions. For a drift, however, or even a block of plants, it is preferable to dig over the area first and rejuvenate the soil with well rotted organic material. When planting, avoid setting out the plants in straight rows. An uneven number of plants makes this easier, three or five making a more satisfactory arrangement than, say, two or four. Remove the plants after flowering.

1 Remove any old plants and weeds from the area. Dig over the soil, avoiding disturbing the roots of nearby plants, and add well-rotted organic material if the soil has not been rejuvenated recently. If necessary, only dig the centre of the patch, where the plants will actually be positioned; their foliage will spread to fill the gap.

2 Feed the soil by scattering a slow-release general fertilizer, following the manufacturer's instructions.

3 Work the fertilizer into the soil using a rake. If you are going to sow seed, break the soil down to a fine tilth at the same time. For bedding plants, the soil need not be as fine – an attractive, even tilth is sufficient.

5 If you wish to use bedding plants to fill the gap, simply plant them out at the appropriate intervals to the same depths they were in their pots. Gently firm in each plant, then rake the soil to even it and to remove any footprints. Water thoroughly.

4 If you want to sow a drift of annuals, scatter the seed evenly over the ground. Rake in and water using a watering can fitted with a fine rose. If the ground is very dry, water and allow the water to drain away before sowing, then sow and water again. When the seedlings appear, thin them to the desired distance apart.

Above: *In this beautifully informal border, the annuals that have been chosen blend in perfectly with the perennials. Formal bedding plants would look completely out of place in such a planting scheme.*

Annuals as Edging Plants

Many annuals make perfect plants for edging features such as paths, borders or special beds. Paths in particular benefit from an edging. A straight path with edging on either side quickly draws the eye down along its length, and will often appear longer than it really is. Edging plants also act as a visual barrier between path and border, making the scene much neater as the bustle of the border stops at the line of edging plants. They can also be a physical barrier: if larger edging plants are used they actually stop the inner plants flopping over the path.

PLANTS TO USE

Any annuals can be used as edging plants but some look better than others in this defining role. Some, such as white alyssum, make compact plants that, when lined up along the edge of a bed or border, can be used almost like a narrow ribbon. These are best used where the other border plants gradually build up in height behind them. If tall plants are used immediately behind alyssum, then the latter is often swamped and the line is lost under a tangle of stems and foliage.

Other plants, such as bright red salvias, can be used to create a positive coloured line; it is impossible not to notice such a bright streak of colour.

Both alyssum and salvia make a very formal edge, but a plant with a looser nature, such as forget-me-not (*Myosotis*), will make a softer, much more diffuse edge to the border. It will merge gently with the plants ranged behind it so that it does not form an obvious line but rather a pretty ruffle along the edge of the border.

BLENDING

Edging is usually thought of as only one plant deep, but there is no reason why the line should not be thicker – two or even three plants deep. Avoid setting plants too far apart or the edge will look uneven. It is better to plant them fairly closely so that they blend together. This might be difficult to achieve with compact or upright plants, so choose your plants with care.

MAKING THE LINE

Planting edging is not difficult, but it is important to get the line straight or running parallel with the edge of the border or path as any deviation will show up clearly. Use a garden line or some other guide to ensure your row follows the correct line and use a measure of some sort to make certain that the plants are evenly spaced.

Right: *In this planting along the edge of a lawn, no attempt has been made to create a distinct line. Instead, poached egg plants* (Limnanthes douglasii) *create a mass of colour along the edge of the border.*

1 Prepare the soil thoroughly, removing any weeds and adding some well-rotted compost or soil conditioner if the soil is tired. Break the soil down to a fairly fine tilth. Set up a garden line at an even distance from the actual edge of the border. Using a standard measure, such as a length of stick, between the edge and each plant will ensure the line is even.

2 Plant the edging plants along the line at regular intervals, regulating the distance between each one with a measuring stick. Firm in each plant, rake over the soil and water. For an informal planting, you can insert a few plants behind the main row so that the edging merges into the other plants in the border.

Above: *An informal edging of* Chrysanthemum tenuiloba *'Golden Fleck' sprawls out over a path.*

Right: *Different shades of busy Lizzie (*Impatiens*) are beautifully set off by silver-leaved plants in an elaborate, formal edging.*

Above: *China pinks (*Dianthus chinensis*) make a pretty contribution to the edge of a bed or border as this vibrantly coloured variety shows.*

ANNUALS SUITABLE FOR EDGING

Ageratum (floss flower)
Begonia semperflorens
Clarkia
Crepis rubra
Dianthus chinensis (China
   pink)
Iberis amara
Lobelia

Lobularia maritima, syn.
   Alyssum maritimum
   (sweet alyssum)
Myosotis (forget-me-not)
Primula
Silene pendula
Tagetes (marigold)
Viola × wittrockiana (pansy)

Annual Climbers

We tend to think of annuals largely as temporary additions to the structure of the garden, since they only last for one year. However, there are many climbing varieties, which, although they will not continue from year to year, can put on a surprising amount of growth in one year and contribute significantly to the overall design of the garden. For example, you can add extra height and interest to a low-level border by growing annual climbers up a series of tripods (teepees).

ANNUAL CLIMBERS	
Asarina erubescens	*Lathyrus sativus*
Caiophora	*Mikania scandens*
Cobaea scandens (cup and saucer vine)	*Rhodochiton atrosanguineum*
Convolvulus tricolor	*Thunbergia alata* (black-eyed Susan)
Eccremocarpus scaber (Chilean glory flower)	*Tropaeolum majus* (Indian cress)
Ipomoea	*Tropaeolum peregrinum*, syn. *T. canariense* (canary creeper)
Lablab purpureus, syn. *Dolichos lablab*	
Lathyrus odoratus (sweet pea)	

SUPPORTS

Annual climbers can be grown up a permanent support, such as wooden trellising on a wall or in a container, or wires fixed to a wall. Alternatively, the support can be temporary, removed annually with the remains of the plant at the end of the season. Pea-sticks make excellent temporary supports, but canes or wicker pyramids are also useful.

A charming idea is to grow the annual up through a shrub. This works particularly well with shrubs that flower in the spring and perhaps look dull for the rest of the year. Once the annual starts to bloom, it will brighten up the foliage until it stops flowering. For example, grow the yellow-flowered canary creeper (*Tropaeolum peregrinum*) up through a *Spiraea* 'Arguta'.

Climbing plants can also trail, so there is no reason why many of them cannot be planted in hanging baskets and allowed to tumble down.

CULTIVATION

Climbing plants are best when they can be grown without interruption. If their growth is checked, especially by being left in the original container for too long, they will rarely grow away well. They will become weak, with yellowing leaves. Keep potting the plants on and plant them out as soon as the weather allows. Water and feed them and they will respond with vigorous growth and plenty of flowers.

Deadheading will also help the plant to produce a continuous stream of flowers. Many plants, sweet peas (*Lathyrus odoratus*) being a good example, produce shorter flowering stems as the season progresses. This is quite normal so do not think something has gone wrong.

TEMPORARY BOUNDARIES

If you are experimenting with the layout of your garden, or perhaps wish to screen off an area such as the vegetable patch, climbing annuals can make an excellent temporary boundary. A row of sweet peas, for example, can be grown up canes to create a fragrant screen, which can easily be removed at the end of the season.

Right: Ipomoea lobata *(syn.* Mina lobata*), which is also known as the cardinal climber, climbs up a metal tripod. Such plants add height to an annual border.*

Left: *Peas and beans that usually grow in the vegetable garden can be grown as decorative as well as productive plants. There are also a number of unusual varieties with different-coloured flowers and pods that are even more attractive.*

Below: Ipomoea lobata, *also known as* Mina lobata *and* Quamoclit lobata, *has masses of scarlet flowers that gradually change to orange, then fade to yellow and eventually white. When happy it will climb to 5m (16ft).*

Above: *In spite of being related to* Ipomoea lobata *(right)*, I. indica *has flowers that look quite different. This is one of the morning glories, known as the blue dawn flower. It is a tender perennial and can climb up to 6m (20ft).*

Self-sowing Annuals

One of the criticisms of annuals is that they are labour intensive, because they have to be raised from seed or cuttings each year, often cosseted in heat, hardened off and then planted out. However, all this is unnecessary for self-sowing annuals, which can also be called naturalizing annuals although the term often implies that they are growing in a wild situation rather than in a border.

WORKING WITH SELF-SOWERS

Self-sowing annuals involve little work and can simply be admired. Of course, unless you inherited the annuals when you first took over the garden, you also have to sow or plant them out first. But once they have flowered for the first time, they will produce seed that drops to the ground and germinates without any interference to produce another crop of flowers next year.

You may need to thin out the seedlings if they are too thick, which is often the case as many self-sowing annuals produce copious amounts of seed. Fortunately, most annual self-sowers have heavy seed which drops around the original plants and does not colonize the whole garden. Some, however, such as busy Lizzies (*Impatiens*) and poppies (*Papaver*), use an explosive mechanism, flinging the seed far and wide. To control the level of self-sowing, pull up some plants before they seed.

Once they have finished seeding, the plants have to be removed to the compost heap. Be warned, though, any seed remaining with the plants may survive the composting process, if it does not become hot enough, and go on to colonize areas over which it is spread. Forget-me-nots (*Myosotis*) are notorious for this.

TIDYING UP

Do not be in too much of a hurry to clear up the plants once the flowers have gone over; remember to leave them long enough for the seed to set and drop. In most cases this happens even before the last flowers have appeared, but in some, *Hesperis matronalis* for example, it can take a long time after the end of flowering. In this case, if you want to tidy up, remove most of the old plants but leave a few to produce enough seed. If you want to dig over an area or renovate it and feel that you might disturb the cycle of self-sowing and germination, collect a few seeds and sow them yourself, setting the whole process in motion once more.

USING SELF-SOWERS

Surprisingly, perhaps, most of the self-sowers are very good garden plants and are well worth growing. Every garden should include at least a few of these wonderful plants. As self-perpetuating annuals they are really only suitable for the border, but as plants they can of course be used in containers, window boxes and hanging baskets. Either dig up a few plants from the border (there are usually more than enough) or sow them from seed in the usual way.

COLLECTING SEED

1 Most self-sowing annuals will drop their seed without need for assistance. But to ensure that seed does fall on to the soil, tap ripe seed heads to dislodge and scatter the seed before discarding the dead flowers.

2 As well as scattering the seed directly on to the ground, some can be collected by tapping the seed-head over a sheet of paper. Remove any bits of seed case or other detritus and pour the seed into a paper bag, labelled with the plant's name, until it is required. Store in a cool dry place.

THINNING SELF-SOWN ANNUALS

1 Some annuals produce copious amounts of seed that result in far too many seedlings. Overcrowding leads to drawn and starved plants, so thin out the seedlings to ensure a healthy display of full-sized flowers.

3 Once you have removed all the excess plants, water the remaining ones to wash the soil down around any loosened or disturbed roots. A mulch of composted or chipped bark will help to keep the area weed-free.

2 To remove the excess seedlings, pull them out without disturbing the roots of those plants you want to keep. If you want to transplant the seedlings elsewhere, remove them carefully using a trowel or hand fork.

SELF-SOWING ANNUALS

Adlumia fungosa (Allegheny vine)
Agrostemma (corn cockle)
Alcea rosea (hollyhock)
Angelica archangelica
Antirrhinum majus (snapdragon)
Argemone mexicana (Mexican poppy)
Atriplex hortensis 'Rubra' (red orach)
Borago officinalis (borage)
Calendula officinalis (pot marigold)
Centaurea cyanus (cornflower)
Chrysanthemum segetum
Clarkia amoena
Cosmos
Digitalis purpurea (foxglove)
Eryngium giganteum (Miss Willmott's Ghost)
Eschscholzia californica

Euphorbia lathyris
Galactites tomentosa
Hesperis matronalis (sweet rocket)
Isatis tinctoria (woad)
Limnanthes douglasii (poached egg plant)
Linaria maroccana (toadflax)
Lobularia maritima, syn. *Alyssum maritimum* (sweet alyssum)
Lunaria annua (honesty)
Myosotis (forget-me-not)
Nigella
Oenothera biennis (evening primrose)
Omphalodes linifolia
Onopordum acanthium (Scotch thistle)
Papaver somniferum (opium poppy)
Silene armeria (catchfly)
Tanacetum parthenium

Annuals for Fragrance

When choosing plants for a particular design or position there are several criteria to consider. The primary ones are flower colour, good foliage and how long the plant lasts, but fragrance, which is often overlooked, is also important. Scented flowers or foliage are an added bonus in a plant and should put it at the top of your lists.

USING FRAGRANT ANNUALS

Fragrant annuals should be grown where their scent will be appreciated most. Grow some as part of a normal border so that their perfume is enjoyed when you walk past. Grow some on the patio or next to an arbour where you sit, perhaps even eat, where the relaxing atmosphere will be enhanced by the smell of fragrant flowers. These annuals can be grown in the soil or in a container. Containers are also useful for growing annuals near to windows or doors so that the perfume will waft indoors when they are open.

Heavily scented sweet peas (*Lathyrus odoratus*) are grown by many gardeners purely for cutting for the house or for giving away as fragrant posies.

TIMING

Not all fragrant annuals are perfumed all the time. The evening primrose (*Oenothera biennis*), as its name suggests, is only fragrant during the evening. The tobacco plants, *Nicotiana alata* and *N. sylvestris* in particular, are also perfumed at this time of the day. Many annuals, as with many other types of plant, will only release their odour when the weather is warm as this is when the pollinating insects that they are trying to attract will be flying. It is not worth their while to waste energy when it is too cold.

Above: *Sweet William (*Dianthus barbatus*) are related to pinks and carnations and have their own very distinctive fragrance.*

Above: *It is the foliage of many pelargoniums that are scented rather than the flowers. These pelargonium cuttings will provide a beautifully scented display. When lightly crushed they emit an aromatic scent.*

SCENTED ANNUALS

Abronia umbellatum
Brachycome iberidifolia (Swan River daisy)
Centaurea (syn. *Amberboa*) *moschata* (sweet sultan)
Datura (syn. *Brugmansia*)
Dianthus barbatus (sweet William)
Dianthus chinensis (China pink)
Erysimum, syn. *Cheiranthus* (wallflower)
Exacum affine
Heliotropium arborescens (syn. *H. peruvianum*)
Hesperis matronalis (sweet rocket)
Lathyrus odoratus (sweet pea)
Lobularia maritima, syn. *Alyssum maritimum* (sweet alyssum)
Matthiola (stock)
Mirabilis jalapa (marvel of Peru)
Nicotiana (tobacco plant)
Oenothera (evening primrose)
Pelargonium (foliage of scented-leaved only)
Phacelia
Reseda odorata (mignonette)

Above: *Sweet peas* (Lathyrus odoratus)*, one of the best-loved of all fragrant annuals, can be used as trailing plants, as here, instead of their more usual climbing habit.*

Left: *Placing scented annuals near open windows can fill the room with their fragrance. Here, the delicate scent of tobacco plants* (Nicotiana) *and heliotrope* (Heliotropium) *will waft into the house.*

Above: *The tobacco plants* (Nicotiana) *release their rich scent into the evening air and are excellent plants to use near where you sit and relax at that time of day. This one is* Nicotiana langsdorfii.

Annuals for Cutting

There is no gift more welcome when visiting than a bunch of flowers from your own garden and annuals can be ideal for making up into bouquets as well as for cutting for the house. Although not all annuals are suitable for formal arrangements, nearly all of them can be made up into bunches of one sort or another. Many of the shorter ones are useful for making little posies, and even if the flower quickly wilts, the leaves may well add something to the arrangement. Some flowers, such as sweet peas, dahlias and chrysanthemums, are grown almost exclusively to use as cut flowers, while others are used both as decoration in the borders and as the occasional cutting for the house.

Above: *Because of its pendulous habit, love-lies-bleeding (*Amaranthus caudatus*) does not strike one straight away as a plant for cutting but that very quality can make it a useful choice for flower arrangements.*

WHERE TO GROW CUT FLOWERS

It is better to allocate a special piece of ground for those flowers that are grown almost exclusively for cutting, rather than try to incorporate them into a border. The problem with growing them in a border is that every time the flowers are cut, which may be regularly, it can leave a gap. Also, the constant need for access to the plants can lead to the soil becoming compacted. Growing them in a separate plot, perhaps as part of the vegetable garden, allows much easier access for cutting as well as for tending the plants.

IN THE BORDER

While it may not be a good idea to include plants that are grown exclusively for cutting in the border, there is no reason why plants that occasionally provide a few blooms for the house cannot be incorporated. Place them in different parts of the border so that no one area is denuded after you have raided it for a bunch of flowers, and plant them where they are not too difficult to reach. Try to arrange the planting so that there are always a few flowers to cut.

GROWING CUT FLOWERS

Those plants that will be cut only occasionally can be grown in the normal manner, but those grown especially for cutting may well need special attention. They will need staking to ensure they stay upright and retain their straight stems. They will need protection against pests that may spoil the blooms: earwigs, slugs and aphids are three common pests to many plants. With many cut flowers, sweet peas (*Lathyrus odoratus*) for example, it is important to cut regularly and to remove any dead flowers as this will encourage the plant to continue producing new and reasonably sized blooms. To grow especially large blooms, it may be necessary to remove some of the buds to allow the remaining ones to develop to their full potential.

PLANTS FOR CUTTING

Agrostemma githago (corn cockle)
Amaranthus caudatus (love-lies-bleeding)
Antirrhinum majus (snapdragon)
Brachycome iberidifolia (Swan River daisy)
Calendula officinalis (pot marigold)
Callistephus chinensis (China aster)
Campanula medium (Canterbury bells)
Centaurea (syn. *Amberboa*) *moschata* (sweet sultan)
Chrysanthemum coronarium
Consolida ambigua, syn. *C. ajacis* (larkspur)
Coreopsis (tickseed)
Dianthus barbatus (sweet William)
Dianthus chinensis (China pink)
Digitalis purpurea (foxglove)
Gaillardia pulchella (blanket flower)
Gilia capitata

Godetia
Gypsophila elegans
Helianthus annuus (sunflower)
Iberis amara
Lathyrus odoratus (sweet pea)
Lavatera trimestris (tree mallow)
Limonium sinuatum
Matthiola (stock)
Moluccella laevis (bells of Ireland)
Nicotiana (tobacco plant)
Nigella damascena (love-in-a-mist)
Reseda odorata (mignonette)
Rudbeckia hirta (coneflower)
Salvia farinacea
Salpiglossis
Scabiosa atropurpurea (sweet scabious)
Tagetes erecta (African marigold)
Tagetes patula (French marigold)
Tithonia rotundifolia (Mexican sunflower)
Zinnia elegans

CUTTING ANNUALS

2 The best time to cut flowers is just as they are opening or about to open. Cut the longest available stalk, which can be trimmed back later if necessary. Plunge the cut flowers up to their necks in lukewarm water and store them in a cool shady place for a few hours before you arrange them in a vase or jug.

3 The length of time that a cut flower stays fresh and attractive varies from variety to variety. This period can be extended by adding a proprietary cut-flower food to the water at the dosage recommended on the packet.

1 Regular cutting helps to ensure a continuing supply of new flowers. If any of the flowers are allowed to run to seed, vital energy that would otherwise be channelled into producing new blooms is used up. Removing dead flowers and any developing seed helps to conserve this energy.

4 Before placing in a vase cut the stems to the required length and remove all leaves that would be below water when arranged. The style of the arrangement is up to you – experiment with different combinations, and use your imagination!

5 The finished vase will make the effort of raising and growing the plants worth while. The best place for cut flowers is in a cool, airy position away from direct sunlight.

Above: *Dahlias make excellent cut flowers and can be grown in a general border, as here, or in a separate plot, especially for cutting. This variety is 'Aylett's Gaiety'.*

Annuals for Drying

Drying annuals prolongs their useful life, allowing them to be used as decoration for a second year or even longer. (Do not keep them too long, though; there is nothing sadder than faded, dusty dried flowers.) A number of annuals are grown specifically for drying, but it is surprising how many ordinary annuals can also be effectively dried. As well as display, many can be used as components of a pot-pourri, either for their colour or their fragrance.

GROWING FOR DRYING

Annuals that are grown specifically for drying are probably best grown in separate rows, especially if they are needed in quantity. Those that are used to just add a bit of variety to an arrangement and therefore are needed in small quantities only can be grown in ordinary borders.

DRYING

There are several different ways in which to dry annuals, but air-drying is the simplest, the cheapest and in many ways the most effective.

The best time for harvesting flowers for drying is on a dry day after any early morning dew or overnight rain has evaporated. The exact time that a flower needs to be picked varies from variety to variety, but generally the best time is soon after it has opened, or in some cases while it is still in bud. You might like to include some buds in your final dried-flower arrangement.

Cut the stems cleanly with a pair of secateurs (pruners), leaving as long a stem as possible. Strip off the lower foliage, leaving bare stems. Place the stems in small bunches and bind them with rubber bands, raffia or string. The advantage of rubber bands is that they contract to take up the shrinkage that takes place as the stems dry. If carelessly tied with string the bunch may come loose, scattering the flowers and possibly damaging them.

Hang the bunches upside down in a warm, airy place. Avoid hanging them where they are in direct sunlight or anywhere where the air is liable to be damp. The ideal place is in a warm kitchen, away from any steaming kettles or pans. As well as being practical, drying flowers in the kitchen can also be very decorative. An airing cupboard is another perfect place.

The flowers are ready to use when they are completely dried. Check the thickest part of the flower or stem, breaking one if necessary to test it.

Individual flowers for use on home-made greetings cards or bookmarks for giving as gifts can be dried by pressing with a heavy weight between sheets of blotting paper or by burying them in silica gel crystals.

Right: *Cornflowers* (Centaurea cyanus) *are valuable as they add the colour blue to the dried-flower arranger's palette.*

FLOWERS FOR DRYING

Ageratum (floss flower)
Amaranthus caudatus (love-lies-bleeding)
Ammobium alatum
Atriplex hortensis
Briza maxima (greater quaking grass)
Briza minor (lesser quaking grass)
Calendula officinalis (pot marigold)
Celosia argentea
Celosia cristata
Centaurea cyanus (cornflower)
Centaurea (syn. *Amberboa*) *moschata* (sweet sultan)
Clarkia
Consolida ambigua, syn. *C. ajacis* (larkspur)
Gilia capitata
Gomphrena globosa
Gypsophila elegans
Helichrysum bracteatum, syn. *Bracteantha bracteata* (everlasting flower)
Helipterum roseum (syn. *Acroclinium roseum*)
Hordeum jubatum (squirrel tail grass)
Lagurus ovatus (hare's-tail grass)
Limonium sinuatum
Lunaria annua (honesty)
Moluccella laevis (bells of Ireland)
Nicandra physalodes (apple of Peru, shoo-fly)
Nigella damascena (love-in-a-mist)
Onopordum acanthium (Scotch thistle)
Salvia horminum (syn. *S. viridis*)
Scabiosa atropurpurea (sweet scabious)
Setaria italica (foxtail millet, Italian millet)
Stipa pennata
Tagetes erecta (African marigold)

Above: *Pot marigolds* (Calendula officinalis) *tend to shrivel slightly when dried but are good because of their strong orange colour.*

Right: *The bells of Ireland* (Moluccella laevis) *dry to a pale green that soon changes to soft cream.*

Above: Limonium sinuatum *is one of the classic plants for drying. It can be grown, as here, as part of a border, but is often grown separately, especially for cutting and drying.*

Finding the Right Annual

There is a tremendous range of colours in annual plants, so wide that with a little thought and imagination you can paint any picture you like.

USING COLOURS

Each colour has many tones and shades, and annuals reflect all the possible nuances. On the whole, though, most annuals are of a bright nature and this must be taken into account when using them.

Since so many annuals come from hot, Mediterranean-type climates, they often have bright colours, which are necessary in harsh, bright light for attracting passing pollinators. Many gardeners take advantage of this, using annuals to provide strong impact in the garden. A sudden splash of bright red pelargoniums or salvias, for example, will always catch the eye. However, bright colours are not always easy to combine as they may clash with one another or create a confused picture in which there is nowhere for the eye to rest. Hot, vibrant colours can get lost in the hurly-burly of a mixed border and tend to look better when used as part of a design for bedding plants. They can look even better when used to enliven the façade of a building, possibly in window boxes or hanging baskets. This is where bright pelargoniums and trailing petunias come into their own.

Many annuals, nonetheless, are subtly coloured and can be combined to create a more romantic image. The misty blues of love-in-a-mist (*Nigella damascena*), the soft, silky pinks of lavateras, the smoky lavenders of some of the opium poppies (*Papaver somniferum*), or the apricots of *Collomia grandiflora* can be used singly in drifts or combined to form a restful image.

COMBINING COLOURS

Some colours mix better than others. Near neighbours on the artist's colour wheel combine together much more sympathetically than the contrasting colours that are opposite each other. Thus, red flowers merge seamlessly with purple ones, but orange will stand out quite starkly against blue. Combining colours can be used to great effect, but try to avoid creating a restless image as a result of combining too many colours at once. Drifts of colour are much easier on the eye.

When you grow plants from seed you can use particular colour strains which are almost guaranteed to come true. However, if you buy mixed seed, the plants could turn out to be any colour and this must be borne in mind when planting them out. Similarly, when you buy seedlings from a garden centre or nursery it may be a good idea to see at least some in flower before you buy to ensure you get what you want. Your carefully planned scheme could be ruined by a wishy-washy pink appearing where you expected a strong yellow.

Left: A lot of careful thought needs to be given to colourful bedding schemes like this. Drawing them out on a piece of graph paper with coloured pencils helps with planning – it can be an enjoyable way to pass a winter evening.

Above: *Foliage plays an important part in any colour scheme. Here the delicate pink of this opium poppy* (Papaver somniferum*) is beautifully set off against the grey leaves.*

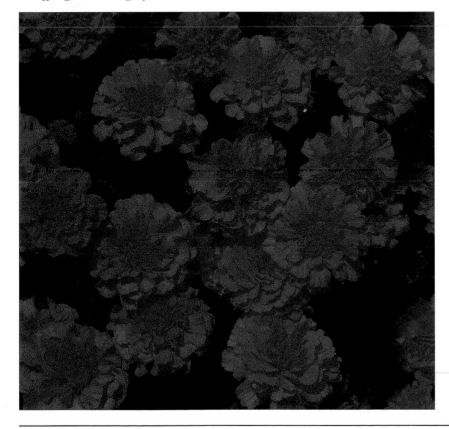

Above: *Sweet peas* (Lathyrus odoratus*) come in a wide range of colours and can be mixed, as here, or grown separately.*

Left: *One of the benefits of modern breeding methods is the consistency in colour that can be produced. Here the French marigold,* Tagetes patula *'Aurora Primrose', produces a batch of identical flowers.*

Purple and Violet

Purple and violet are borderline between blue and red: purple is red with a dash of blue while violet is blue with a dash of red. Purple has a richness about it, which is why it has always been a sign of luxury and class. It is a strong colour – paler shades would be described as mauve. Similarly, violet is a deep colour, with lighter forms becoming mauves or lilacs.

USING PURPLE

Purple is a solid colour, because of its depth, and a patch of it always appears as a strong block of colour, never as a misty haze. However, the over-use of purple can have a deadening effect, creating a rather leaden appearance. A hanging basket of purple petunias can look stunning, but ten such baskets hung in close proximity lose all their impact and can be positively dull. As purple tends to sink back into green foliage, making it even more difficult to see, contrast it with silver or grey foliage for a better effect.

While purple is a sombre colour, violet is a more lively one, and has still more vibrancy when on the dark side. While it is less leaden than purple, it should still be used with care and discretion.

Both purple and violet can be used more extensively if they are mixed with other colours. Lighter colours, such as yellows and whites, contrast with and stand out against purple. Purple also harmonizes well with purple reds and purple blues, but if these are too dark, the colours tend to blend too much, creating a leaden effect. Lime-green flowers such as lime zinnias and the foliage of *Helichrysum petiolare* 'Limelight' make

excellent companions. These are colours that need to be experimented with to some degree. Try a range of different combinations until you find something that you are pleased with, but do not always expect everybody to agree with your choice of colours.

POPULAR PURPLE AND VIOLET ANNUALS

Antirrhinum 'Purple King'
Callistephus chinensis (China aster – purple and violet varieties)
Centaurea cyanus 'Black Ball'
Cleome spinosa (syn. *C. hassleriana*) 'Violet Queen'
Collinsia grandiflora
Eschscholzia californica 'Purple-Violet'
Eustoma grandiflorum
Exacum affine
Heliotropium
Hesperis matronalis (sweet rocket)
Impatiens (busy Lizzie – purple varieties)

Limonium sinuatum 'Midnight'
Limonium sinuatum 'Purple Monarch'
Lunaria annua (honesty)
Malva sylvestris mauritiana
Orychiophragmus violaceus
Papaver somniferum (opium poppy – purple varieties)
Petunia (purple varieties)
Salvia horminum, syn. *S. viridis* (purple varieties)
Salvia splendens (violet varieties)
Senecio ciliocarpa
Trachelium caeruleum (throatwort)

Left: *The deep purple flowers of honesty (*Lunaria annua*) have a luminous quality that looks attractive both in the evening light and also in the gloom of a woodland or other shady setting.*

Right: *Silene armeria 'Electra' is a good bedding plant, forming a sheet of magenta-purple flowers for a short season in the summer.*

Above: *The delightful* Galactites tomentosa *is a non-troublesome thistle that produces light purple flowers. These look wonderfully striking against the variegated foliage. This is a particularly good plant for including in the mixed border.*

Above right: *Ageratums make perfect bedding plants with their small powder-puff flower heads that last throughout the summer and well into the autumn. This rich reddish-purple variety is 'North Star'.*

Right: Brachycome iberidifolia, *the Swan River daisy, comes in a variety of shades that range from blue to violet and even include rich purple.*

White and Cream

White flowers are very fashionable. Long associated with purity, peace and tranquillity, they are much in demand for wedding bouquets and as cut flowers. The purity and clarity of white gives it a touch of class and sophistication that other colours can rarely match. Cream is white with a little yellow added. It is a more sensuous, luxurious colour, and lacks the more clinical qualities of pure white.

USING WHITE

White is a good colour for brightening up a planting scheme or container display and can be used to illuminate dark corners of the garden. White busy Lizzies, for example, in a hanging basket against a dark background or in shade will shine out. White also has a magical quality as the light fades in the evening, standing out long after other colours have disappeared in the gloom. This makes it an excellent choice for use in containers and other displays, especially in areas where you sit in the evening.

White will mix well with other colours, although it can sometimes be a little too stark in contrast with some. Cream will often blend in more sympathetically, especially with colours on the orange-red side of the colour spectrum.

One big drawback with white flowers is that they so often refuse to die gracefully. Once they have finished flowering you are left with shrivelled brown petals that stand out far too well against the remaining white flowers. To keep such displays at their best, it is essential to deadhead at least once a day.

POPULAR WHITE AND CREAM ANNUALS

Alcea rosea (hollyhock – white varieties)
Antirrhinum 'White Wonder'
Argyranthemum (syn. *Chrysanthemum*) *frutescens* (white varieties)
Centaurea (syn. *Amberboa*) *moschata* 'The Bride' (sweet sultan)
Clarkia pulchella 'Snowflake'
Cleome spinosa (syn. *C. hassleriana*) 'Helen Campbell'
Consolida ambigua (syn. *C. ajacis*) 'Imperial White King'
Cosmos bipinnatus 'Purity'
Dianthus (carnation, pink – various varieties)
Digitalis purpurea alba (white foxglove)
Eschscholzia californica 'Milky White'
Eustoma grandiflorum (white varieties)
Gypsophila elegans 'Giant White'
Helianthus annuus 'Italian White'
Helichrysum bracteatum (syn. *Bracteantha bracteata*) 'White'
Hibiscus trionum (flower-of-the-hour)
Iberis amara
Impatiens (busy Lizzie) Super Elfin White
Lathyrus odoratus (sweet pea – various varieties)
Lavatera trimestris 'Mont Blanc'
Limonium sinuatum 'Iceberg'
Lobelia erinus 'Snowball'
Lobularia maritima, syn. *Alyssum maritimum* (sweet sultan)
Malope trifida 'Alba'
Matthiola (stock – white varieties)
Nemesia 'Mello White'
Nemophila maculata
Nicotiana alata, syn. *N. affinis* (tobacco plant)
Nicotiana sylvestris
Nolana paradoxa 'Snowbird'
Omphalodes linifolia
Osteospermum 'Glistening White'
Papaver somniferum (opium poppy – white varieties)
Pelargonium (various white forms)
Petunia (various white forms)
Tripleurospermum inodora 'Bridal Robe'
Viola × wittrockiana (pansy – white varieties)

Left: *The tender perennial* Osteospermum *'Prostratum' is a lovely pure white, but it needs plenty of sun, as the flowers only open in sunlight.*

Right: *Cream is a good colour to combine with a wide range of other colours, especially schemes planted with hot yellows and orange reds. The marigold* Tagetes *'French Vanilla' demonstrates clearly the true beauty of this colour.*

Above: Iberis crenata *is rather more lax than other species of candytuft, and produces an abundance of stunning white flowers. These emerge from the mauve buds that are still held in the centre of the flower head.*

Above: *Many flowers also have white forms including this foxglove,* Digitalis purpurea alba.

Above: *For ethereal, billowing clouds of white flowers it is hard to beat* Gypsophila, *which brings an elegant tracery to a planting scheme. This annual form is* G. elegans *'White Elephant'.*

Above: *The old-fashioned annual* Collomia grandiflora *produces beautiful flowers at the height of summer that are the most wonderful peach-cream colour.*

Orange

Orange is a warm, friendly colour. It is predominantly a colour of late summer and autumn, but it is welcome at any time of the year. It has quite a wide range of shades, from deep gold (the lighter golds are closer to yellow) through to almost flame red. At the deeper end of the spectrum, it is a hot colour, exciting and vibrant. At the golden end it is warm rather than hot and can be used a bit more freely.

USING ORANGE

Orange mixes well with most colours although the redder shades are not so complementary with the bluer reds, including purple and pink, unless you like to combine colours that clash. The more yellow colours mix better with blues.

Orange shows up well against green foliage and can be picked out at a distance. It can be used wherever annuals are appropriate and is frequently found in the form of African marigolds (*Tagetes erecta*) and French marigolds (*T. patula*), in large bedding schemes.

Although orange is most widely seen in autumn gardens, not only in flowers such as chrysanthemums but in trees and shrubs with coloured foliage and berries, there are also many annuals that can add a vibrant orange note throughout the year. The winter-flowering pansies (*Viola × wittrockiana* Universal Series) include orange varieties which continue flowering into the spring, and wallflowers (*Erysimum*), snapdragons

(*Antirrhinum*) and pot marigolds (*Calendula*) then come into their own, the latter often flowering quite early if it has been left to self-sow. During the summer, nasturtiums (*Tropaeolum*) in various shades will follow.

Right: *Although osteospermums have the annoying habit of closing up on dull days, they can still make a splash with their bright colours. This pure orange variety is* O. hyoseroides *'Gaiety'.*

POPULAR ORANGE ANNUALS

Alonsoa warscewiczii (mask flower)
Antirrhinum majus (snapdragon – various varieties)
Calceolaria (various varieties)
Calendula officinalis (pot marigold – various varieties)
Emilia coccinea, syn. *E. flammea* (tassel flower)
Erysimum (syn. *Cheiranthus*) *cheiri* 'Fire King'
Erysimum (syn. *Cheiranthus*) *cheiri* 'Orange Bedder'
Eschscholzia californica
Helichrysum bracteatum, syn. *Bracteantha bracteata* (various varieties)
Impatiens (busy Lizzie) Impact Orange
Impatiens 'Mega Orange Star'
Mimulus (creeping zinnia – various varieties)
Nemesia 'Orange Prince'
Rudbeckia hirta (coneflower – various varieties)
Tagetes erecta (African marigold – various varieties)
Tagetes patula (French marigold – various varieties)
Tithonia rotundifolia 'Torch'
Tropaeolum majus (Indian cress – various varieties)
Viola × wittrockiana (pansy – various varieties)
Zinnia (various varieties)

Above: *Cannas can be used to make strong extrovert statements in a bedding scheme. Many have bright orange flowers and this one, 'Roi Humbert', has contrasting purple foliage as an added bonus.*

Above: *Calceolarias have curious slipper-shaped flowers. The bedding varieties come in shades of yellow, orange or red. This bright orange variety is 'Kentish Hero'.*

Mixed Annuals

The flowers of many annuals are not, of course, restricted to a single colour. Each flower may consist of several colours although there may be one basic colour. For example, salpiglossis have dark or differently coloured throats and very prominent veining, which help to disguise or alter the overall appearance of the base colour. This means that flowers that are basically coloured orange will have quite a different effect in a display than totally orange flowers, such as calendula.

USING MIXED COLOURS

Some plants have several colours in their flowers, without any one being dominant, and planning precise colour schemes with this type of flower is very difficult if you are not to avoid a chaotic mixture. This is not to say that they are not worth growing, simply that they have to be handled differently and rather carefully. You must decide what their overall effect is likely to be when used in a specific planting scheme. You should also be careful when mixing them with other plants that have mixed colours as the general effect may become rather uneven and restless. Sometimes it can be effective to echo one of the colours in an adjacent planting.

There is an increasing tendency on the part of seed merchants to market packets of mixed colours rather than just a single one. For instance, some merchants may only have mixed colours of snapdragon (*Antirrhinum*) available. You can sometimes achieve a lovely cottage-garden effect with these mixtures, for example of sweet peas, but if you do want a more planned scheme, check in different catalogues and with

luck you should find the specific colours you want. Surprisingly, it is often the smaller companies that offer a better service in this respect.

A similar problem arises when buying plants from a garden centre or nursery. Sometimes it can be impossible to find the colour you want and you have to make do with a mixture. At other times the packs of plants may not be labelled. Although it is not always a good idea to wait for annuals to flower before buying, it may sometimes be necessary to ensure that you get the right colours.

If you save your own seed, of snapdragons for example, there is no guarantee that the resulting seedlings will be the same colour as the parent from which the seed was collected. This is further complicated by the fact that some plants are more likely to come true than others.

Right: *These marigolds* (Tagetes) *are two-toned but the colours are relatively close to each other on the colour wheel and so they blend well together giving a harmonious effect.*

POPULAR MIXED ANNUALS

Mixed Colour Annuals
Dianthus barbatus (sweet William
Dianthus chinensis (China pink)
Nemesia
Primula
Salpiglossis
Schizanthus (butterfly flower, poor man's orchid)
Tagetes (marigold)
Viola × wittrockiana (pansy)

Mixed Colour Seeds Available in Packets
Alcea rosea (hollyhock)
Antirrhinum majus (snapdragon)
Callistephus chinensis (Chinese aster)
Cosmos
Erysimum (wallflower)
Eschscholzia californica
Lathyrus odoratus (sweet pea)

Above: *Many flowers change colour as the flowers mature and finally fade. This* Verbena *'Peaches and Cream' goes through several stages.*

Below: *A common coloration is where one colour shades into another. In this pelargonium the dark pink merges into a much softer one.*

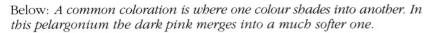

Above: *Where two colours are strongly contrasted, as in this nemesia, the overall effect is much more startling and eye-catching.*

Annuals for Foliage

There is a tendency to think of annuals only in terms of their flower-power, but they have a lot more to offer. Indeed, many are useful solely for their foliage, which can be wonderfully coloured, but there are a few that are notable for both their foliage and their flowers. Even plain green foliage often comes in attractive and interesting shapes, setting off the flowers very effectively.

FOLIAGE COLOUR

In annuals, foliage colours are far from being restricted to green. Red orach (*Atriplex hortensis* 'Rubra') has rich purple leaves which go well with pinks and silvers, and it is a marvellous plant for dotting about a mixed border of soft colours. Several silver-foliaged annuals, which are particularly good for setting off blues and pinks, can be used as part of a formal bedding scheme or in a more mixed planting. The statuesque Scotch thistles (*Onopordum acanthium*) are too big for most bedding schemes but they fit well into large borders or stand as individual plants.

As well as these striking single colours, there are some annuals with variegated foliage: *Euphorbia marginata* has a cool white and green combination, while the tender shrub *Abutilon megapotamicum* 'Variegatum' has dark green leaves liberally splashed with gold. *Coleus* (syn. *Solenostemon*), in particular, comes in a wide range of colours and markings, and will often outshine a display of flowers.

OTHER QUALITIES

The shapes of leaves are also of value. The castor-oil plant (*Ricinus communis*), with its large-fingered leaves, for example, is very eye-catching.

The grey or silver leaves of melianthus are also very architecturally shaped.

Scent can add another dimension to interesting foliage. The scented-leaved pelargoniums, for example, come in many varieties with different fragrances, and are delightful in containers positioned where you can crush a leaf as you pass.

Cannas, tender perennials that are usually treated as annuals, have wonderful green or bronze leaves twirled around the stems as well as large brightly coloured flowers. The leaves are large and shiny, which, along with the hot flower colours, adds a touch of the exotic and tropical to any planting scheme.

WINTER

For winter schemes, ornamental cabbages (*Brassica oleracea*) are extremely valuable. The variegated leaves, in shades of pink or white, add a welcome touch of colour at a time when it may be in short supply.

Right: *The beautiful silver of the leaves and the wings on the stems of this* Onopordum acanthium, *or Scotch thistle, gives the plant a stunning appearance. This dramatic shape makes it one of the best architectural plants for beds and borders.*

POPULAR FOLIAGE ANNUALS

Abutilon megapotamicum 'Variegatum'
Ammobium alatum
Atriplex hortensis 'Rubra' (red orach)
Bassia (syn. *Kochia*) *scoparia trichophylla*
Beta vulgaris
Brassica oleracea (ornamental cabbage)
Canna
Coleus blumei (syn. *Solenostemon scutellarioides*)
Euphorbia marginata
Galactites tomentosa
Helichrysum petiolare
Impatiens (busy Lizzie – bronze-leaf forms)
Melianthus major (honeybush)
Ocimum basilicum 'Purple Ruffles'
Onopordum acanthium (Scotch thistle)
Pelargonium (geranium – scented-leaved forms)
Perilla frutescens
Ricinus communis (castor-oil plant)
Senecio cineraria (syn. *S. maritima*)
Silybum marianum
Tropaeolum majus 'Alaska'

Above: Helichrysum petiolare *is a tender perennial that is frequently used in both containers and bedding schemes, mainly for its furry, silvery-grey foliage.*

Above: *A favourite plant for self-sowing is the purple-leaved red orach (*Atriplex hortensis *'Rubra'). It looks best in a position in which the sun can shine through and light up the leaves.*

Right: *The red markings on this unusual and very striking annual,* Medicago echinus, *combine beautifully with the perennial* Geranium phaeum *'Samabor'.*

Annual Grasses

Annual grasses are not as popular as they deserve to be, possibly because in many people's minds annuals are synonymous with flowers, and grasses, perhaps, are associated with lawns. Ornamental grasses do have flowers but they are hardly brightly coloured things when compared with busy Lizzies (*Impatiens*) or pelargoniums. However, grasses have their own subtle charm, and are extremely useful for adding a quietening note to a scheme and for the swaying elegance they bring to mixed borders.

NATURAL GRACE

What grasses lack in colour they more than make up for in grace and beauty. They have elegant shapes; whether they are tall and wispy or stout clumps, grasses always exhibit the same kind of linear form. The leaves are long and straight. The flower stems are also long and narrow, and even in short grasses are usually taller than the leaves. Even the flowerheads tend to be long and narrow, but if they are spreading then the individual components are narrow, creating a wonderfully diffuse effect.

The numerous flower stems erupt like fountains, taking the eye with them and giving the display an upward thrust. At the same time their simplicity means that there is something cool about grasses. They move gracefully in the slightest breeze. They are gentle, even soothing to the eye, especially after the hurly-burly of conventional, colourful annuals.

USING GRASSES

Grasses can be used by themselves to create a distinct feature or they can be mixed in with other annuals. You are most likely to use them as a whole bedding scheme or as part of one, although they can also be grown in containers, particularly the taller ones. Generally, they are not much use in hanging baskets, but some of the arching types can be effective if used with care.

Most grasses are extremely good at catching the sunlight and can look superb when lit from behind. Place them so that they are between the viewer and the evening sun for some of the most stunning effects. Squirrel-tail grass (*Hordeum jubatum*), for example, creates a wonderful arching, feathery effect, and looks fantastic when it catches the sunlight.

Unfortunately, most of the annual grasses are quite short, although ornamental maize (*Zea mays*) will grow up to 2.4m (8ft) in a season, which is tall enough for most purposes. Most annual grasses have green leaves, but some have a distinct bronze tinge, while others, including ornamental maize, are variegated.

Many annual grasses can be dried and used as indoor decoration. Hare's-tail grass (*Lagurus ovatus*), which has chunky but very soft heads, is a popular drying grass. The feather top (*Pennisetum villosum*), strictly a perennial but a tender one, has more open heads, but again is wonderfully silky.

Below: *Soft grasses look very effective when they are backlit by sunlight, as this squirreltail grass* (Hordeum jubatum) *shows. Stirred by the breeze the effect is even more enchanting.*

<table>
<tr><td colspan="2">POPULAR ANNUAL GRASSES</td></tr>
<tr><td>

Agrostis nebulosa
Briza maxima
  (greater quaking grass)
Briza minor (lesser
  quaking grass)
Hordeum jubatum
  (squirreltail grass)
Lagurus ovatus (hare's-tail
  grass)

</td><td>

Lamarckia aurea (golden top)
Panicum capillare (old-witch
  grass)
Pennisetum setaceum
  (African fountain grass)
Pennisetum villosum (feather
  top)
Sorghum nigrum
Zea mays (ornamental maize)

</td></tr>
</table>

Above: *Not all grasses associate well with flowering plants, but in this planting scheme squirreltail grass* (Hordeum jubatum) *makes a very effective partner for* Dahlia *'Yelno Harmony'*.

Above: *Arching grasses have a pleasing, often restful, effect. Here the tender perennial* Pennisetum setaceum *'Cupreum Compactum' adds a tranquil note, in contrast to more colourful plants.*

Above: *Many grasses are useful for drying as well as creating a decorative effect in the garden. The hare's-tail grass* (Lagurus ovatus) *is one such plant.*

Annuals in Pots and Planters

In the past annuals were mainly used as bedding plants in borders, but with the increased interest in container planting, including hanging baskets and window boxes, annuals have taken on a new lease of life, and they make the most perfect container plants.

USING ANNUALS

Containers are an immediate way of gardening, almost like flower arranging except that the flowers have roots. One minute the pot is empty, the next it is full of flowers. Annuals lend themselves to this style of gardening. They have such a short life cycle that they flower very early in their lives, soon after planting out, or they may already be in flower when planted.

Many have a long flowering period, often covering the whole of the summer and most of the autumn as well. They are also colourful, a factor that most people want in their containers. An added bonus is that they are relatively easy to look after: they just need watering and a bit of dead-heading.

Almost any annuals can be used in containers, though the very tall ones will usually be less successful. Scotch thistles (*Onopordum acanthium*), for example, would look out of proportion in a small pot, but could be effective in the centre of a large arrangement.

CONTAINERS

Containers can be used singly or in groups. An advantage of containers is that they can be moved around. Groups can be reformed or split up, constantly changing the scene. If one pot begins to look a bit straggly or the flowers fade, then it can be moved out of sight and perhaps another used to replace it. Collect as many different types and sizes of container as you can and use them imaginatively.

PLANTING TECHNIQUES

When planting a container, you will have to add crocks to the bottom in order to aid drainage. Plants in containers need plenty of water, but they do not like sitting in stagnant water, so it is important to ensure that any excess water can drain away easily. The compost (soil mix) can be either a general one or one that has been especially formulated for use in pots and other containers.

As care and attention are usually lavished on containers by way of daily watering and regular feeding, you can pack plants more tightly than you normally would in a bed or border. Keep the plants neat by removing dead heads and any straggly growths. The perfectionist always has a few spare plants tucked away out of sight to use as replacements if one of the plants in the container dies or begins to flag.

Left: *An evergreen cordyline has been livened up for the summer by the addition of colourful annuals. As the flowers die, different ones can replace them according to the seasons. For example, winter pansies are good plants to add interest to an evergreen shrub as they bloom non-stop right through the gloomier months and are not particularly affected by the weather.*

Below: *As this lovely container planting shows, there is nothing to beat the striking combination of pink and purple flowers with silver foliage.*

PLANTING CONTAINERS WITH ANNUALS

1 Before you start to plant, assemble all the materials you need: a container, crocks, perhaps a stone, compost (soil mix), water-retaining crystals, slow-release fertilizer, and your chosen plants and a trowel if you are using one. Pots can be heavy when they are filled with wet compost, so it is best to fill them where they are to be sited.

2 Ensure the container has drainage holes. Partially cover any large holes with an irregularly shaped stone, to prevent the compost (soil mix) falling out, then place other crocks in the bottom of the container to aid drainage.

3 Nearly fill the container with compost (soil mix) and add water-retaining crystals, following the manufacturer's instructions. Compost in containers dries out very quickly and these help reduce the amount of watering required. They swell up into a jelly-like substance, enabling the compost to retain much more water than it normally would.

4 Constant watering washes away many of the nutrients in the compost (soil mix) before the plants can take them up, so it is important to feed them regularly. Adding a slow-release fertilizer to the compost before planting provides food for several months, so you do not have to apply liquid feed regularly.

5 Fill the container with compost (soil mix) almost to the top and gently firm down. Make planting holes using a trowel or your hand and insert the plants to the same depth as they were in their pots or trays. Once all the plants are in position, firm and tidy up the compost, then water well.

6 Tidy up the container by cutting off any damaged stems. Tease out the stems to make the plants look natural and as if they have been planted for some time.

7 The finished container will look even more effective if grouped together with others. Remember to water containers regularly: even in winter, sun and wind can be quite drying, and in a hot summer they may need watering more than once a day.

Annuals in Window Boxes

By making use of wall space, window boxes allow for vertical gardening. This is particularly important where ground space is restricted, but it also helps to create a three-dimensional garden. Also, they are useful for transforming what otherwise may be a rather dull building or wall.

SAFETY
Window boxes are heavy when filled with moist soil, so if the site is windy and exposed, it is important that they are fixed securely. A falling window box is not only a broken and wasted window box, but it is extremely dangerous to anyone underneath. If you do not feel competent to fix it, ask a professional to do the job; it will be cheaper than any possible litigation resulting from a window box falling on someone's head.

MATERIALS
Window boxes are made of various different materials. Terracotta and replica stone look good but are heavy. Plastic ones usually look what they are, but they are lightweight and if covered with trailing plants cannot be seen. Wood is a compromise; it looks good and is reasonably lightweight, but it will eventually rot. Wood's big advantage is that the box can be tailor-made to fit the space.

PLANTS FOR WINDOW BOXES
The range of plants for window boxes is more limited than for pots. Choose a few upright, bushy plants for the rear and trailing ones for the front. For winter and spring use, it is often a good idea to use a few dwarf conifers or evergreen shrubs to give the box structure. You can also do this for summer, but with so many varieties of plants at your disposal it is not so necessary.

PLANTING TECHNIQUES
Place crocks in the bottom of the box to allow easy drainage. There are specially formulated composts (soil or planting mixes) for window boxes, but a general compost is usually more than adequate. Set the plants close together so that when they are in full growth no soil shows; a thinly planted window box can look rather sad and messy.

Keep the box well watered; every day is likely to be necessary. A special pump-action water dispenser with a long nozzle can be used to water them from the ground, but higher ones have to be watered from the window (site the box well below the window so that it will open) or from a ladder. Exercise caution if you use a ladder.

POSITIONING WINDOW BOXES
The obvious place for a window box is outside a window, but their shape and size means that they are suited to other positions. They are good for placing on the top of walls, for example, or on the ground, perhaps together with round pots.

POPULAR ANNUALS FOR WINDOW BOXES

Ageratum (floss flower)
Antirrhinum (snapdragon)
Begonia
Bidens
Brachycome
Cerinthe
Chrysanthemum
Dianthus (carnation, pink)
Echium
Felicia
Fuchsia
Helichrysum
Impatiens (busy Lizzie)
Laurentia (syn. Isotoma)
Lobelia
Myosotis (forget-me-not)
Nicotiana (tobacco plant)
Pelargonium (geranium)
Petunia
Sanvitalia
Schizanthus (butterfly flower, poor man's orchid)
Senecio
Tagetes (marigold)
Tropaeolum (nasturtium)
Viola × wittrockiana (pansy)

Above: *Cheerful-looking pansies and lobelias are excellent plants for window boxes because they last for a long time and are very little trouble. Some varieties of pansy can also be used for winter displays. As this trough shows, long, box-like containers can be used successfully on the ground as well as on windowsills.*

PLANTING A WINDOW BOX WITH ANNUALS

1 Assemble all the ingredients: these include a window box, irregularly shaped stones, good quality compost (soil mix), water-retaining crystals, slow-release fertilizer, plants and a trowel if you are using one. If the box is light, assemble it on the ground. If it is heavy, make it up in position, especially if it is to be fixed high up.

2 Stagnant water can be a problem in inadequately drained boxes, so always buy, or make, boxes with holes in the bottom. Place irregularly shaped stones over the bottom of the box to help water drain down towards the holes. Partially cover the holes with these to stop compost (soil mix) falling through.

3 Partially fill the box with compost (soil mix), then mix in water-retaining crystals following the manufacturer's instructions. Continue to fill the box with compost, then gently firm down.

4 Make planting holes with a trowel or your hand and insert the plants to the same depths as they were in their pots or trays. Since you will be constantly watering and feeding the plants, it is possible to plant much more closely together than you would in open ground.

5 Since the window box will be watered frequently, the nutrients in the compost (soil mix) will quickly get washed away, so regular feeding is very important. This is traditionally done by adding a liquid feed to the water every week or so. Alternatively, slow-release fertilizer can be added, either in tablet form, as shown here, or as granules mixed into the compost (soil mix) before planting. Both of these should supply sufficient food for the season.

6 Water the window box thoroughly. The box still looks under-filled, but the plants will soon grow and spread out to fill the whole box. If it is possible to plant a box away from its final position, it can be filled with plants and left for a while until they are all in full flower before being displayed.

7 Boxes that are heavier than this one should be filled in position so that they do not have to be carried and lifted. As well as avoiding physical damage to the gardener, it also prevents the plants being damaged in transit.

Annuals in Hanging Baskets

Hanging baskets are ever increasing in popularity and seed merchants and plant suppliers are constantly searching out new annuals to feed demand. There are now so many bushy and trailing plants to choose from, you can really let your imagination run riot. There is even a trailing variety of tomato, 'Tumbler', which not only looks attractive but provides the added bonus of a crop of delicious fruit.

THE BASKETS

Baskets consist of three parts: the basket, a liner and a support, frequently a chain. The baskets are usually made from plastic-coated wire. Increasingly they are also available in just plastic but these do not look as good (if you can see them under the plants) and can become brittle.

Liners can be made of compressed paper, coir (coconut fibre) matting or moss. Moss is the most natural-looking but stocks in the wild are being threatened by over-collecting. Paper is recycled and coir is cultivated, so both of these are environmentally acceptable.

You can use either a good general-purpose compost (soil mix) or a specially formulated hanging-basket compost which includes water-retaining gel or crystals. In this case, do not add further gel or crystals, as excessive quantities would cause problems when they expand.

PLANTING HANGING BASKETS

Most hanging baskets include tender annuals so they cannot be placed outside until after the last frosts, but they can be made up in advance and left indoors until the danger of frosts has passed, by which time the basket will have filled out and with luck be in full flower.

Plant the hanging basket tightly so that there are few spaces between the plants. This is acceptable as there should be no shortage of moisture and nutrients if the basket is regularly watered and fed. As well as planting the surface of the compost (soil mix), it is also possible to make holes through the liner so that plants can be inserted around the sides. The most successful baskets are those in which the framework cannot be seen, as it is entirely masked by plants. In many cases, the hanging basket will look like a ball of plants.

A wide range of plants are available for baskets and an increasing number of trailing ones are being introduced. Many plants, such as pelargoniums and petunias, have trailing varieties as well as the more common bushy ones. Even snapdragons have been bred with a trailing habit. Any combination of plants can be used to create different schemes. A wonderful pot-pourri of colours can be achieved with a mixed planting, although a much more sophisticated effect can be created if you use plants in the same colour or even plants of just one variety. Baskets can be used individually or grouped together to produce a grander effect.

Above: *Hanging baskets like this can be very heavy so make sure that the fixing point is strong enough. Check each year that it is still secure before replanting the hanging basket.*

POPULAR ANNUALS FOR HANGING BASKETS

Anagallis	*Laurentia* (syn. *Isotoma*)
Antirrhinum (snapdragon)	*Lobelia*
Asarina	*Myosotis* (forget-me-not)
Begonia	*Nicotiana* (tobacco plant)
Bidens	*Pelargonium* (geranium)
Brachycome	*Petunia*
Camissonia	*Sanvitalia*
Cerinthe	*Schizanthus* (butterfly flower,
Chrysanthemum	poor man's orchid)
Diascia	*Senecio*
Echium	*Tagetes* (marigold)
Felicia	*Tropaeolum*
Fuchsia	(nasturtium)
Helichrysum	*Viola* × *wittrockiana* (pansy)

PLANTING A HANGING BASKET WITH ANNUALS

1 Assemble all the ingredients for making up the hanging basket, including compost (soil mix), water-retaining crystals and slow-release fertilizer.

2 Stand the basket on a large pot or bucket to make it easier to work with. Carefully place the liner in position so that it fills the basket.

3 Half fill the liner with compost (soil mix), then mix in some water-retaining crystals following the manufacturer's instructions to help prevent the basket drying out. Also add some slow-release fertilizer; this will remove the necessity to feed throughout the summer.

4 Cut holes about 4cm (1½in) across in the side of the liner. Shake some of the earth off the rootball of one of the side plants and wrap it in a strip of plastic. Poke it through the hole, remove the plastic and spread the roots out. When all the side plants are in place, fill up the basket with compost (soil mix), adding more water-retaining crystals and slow-release fertilizer.

5 Plant up the rest of the basket, packing the plants much more tightly together than you would in the open ground. Smooth out the surface of the compost (soil mix), removing any excess or adding a little more as necessary. Water, then hang the basket indoors until all danger of frost has passed.

Above: *The various types of pelargoniums are well suited to planting in a hanging basket. They make very cheerful planting partners. Here they are contrasted with verbena and trailing lobelia.*

DESIGNING WITH PERENNIALS

Choosing a Scheme

One of the great advantages of using perennial plants in the garden is their versatility. The same basic selection of plants can be arranged in several ways to produce quite different results. In each situation, a plant will combine with its neighbours and take on the character of the scheme. Lady's mantle (*Alchemilla mollis*), for example, has a wonderfully old-fashioned look when combined with other such plants in a cottage garden. In a more formal arrangement, it can be used to provide an even block of yellowish-green, and, when it is grown near water, it takes on an entirely new character.

PERENNIAL USES

The versatility of perennials provides gardeners with the means to create whatever kind of garden appeals to them. Perennials can be planted in precise patterns, whereby symmetrical blocks of colour and shape are used to create a formal garden, while, at the other end of the spectrum, they can be allowed to run riot in the controlled chaos of a cottage garden. Between the two extremes is the herbaceous border, where the essential freedom of the cottage garden is married with the conscious arrangement of plants in the formal garden to create a bed that is very pleasing to the eye.

THE RIGHT PERENNIAL

Although perennial plants are versatile and, on the whole, forgiving, it is essential that when you plan your garden, whatever the proposed style, you

bear in mind the origins of the plants you wish to include. Plants always grow best in conditions that are similar to their natural habitat. An extreme example is pond plants, which are unlikely to grow in dry sand. In this case, the need to match the plant's location in the garden to its natural habitat will be obvious to most gardeners. However, many gardeners fail to consider the more subtle aspects of a plant's origins. For example, plants that naturally grow in full sun rarely do well in shady conditions, and nearly all the silver-leaved plants, which love the sun, will languish and die if planted in shade.

The design of your garden must, therefore, take into consideration the type of conditions that prevail in your local area. Most of the brightly coloured flowers appear on plants that grow in direct sun, for instance, whereas woodland

or shade planting relies on less colourful subjects and is more dependent on shapes, texture and the subtle colour variations of foliage.

While it is true that plants are best grown in conditions that are similar to those to which they are used in the wild, there is no reason why the conditions in your garden cannot be changed – to some extent, at least – to suit the plants you want to grow. For example, many plants like deep, rich soil, so it is hopeless trying to grow them on a light,

Above: *The fresh, bright colours of these stream-side plants make for a very attractive planting association. The jumbled colours create an informal effect.*

sandy soil. However, with effort, the conditions can be altered by adding plenty of well-rotted organic material, so that these plants can be grown.

The key to using perennials is to work with, rather than against, nature, because this is much more likely to produce satisfactory results.

Above: *Contrasting flowers and foliage produce an interesting picture. Here, the foaming flowers of lady's mantle* (Alchemilla mollis) *with the green, infertile fronds and the brown, fertile fronds of the royal fern* (Osmunda regalis) *create a perfect contrast, which is ideal for a formal or informal setting.*

Above right: *Try to blend the colours of foliage and flowers. Here, the silky, silver leaves of* Stachys byzantina *and the soft, bluish-purple flowers of* Nepeta × faassenii *combine to create a soft romantic image.*

Right: *This is a perfect example of the jumble of shapes, sizes and colours that produces the informality of the cottage garden.*

Cottage Gardens

Many people regard the traditional cottage garden as the epitome of beauty, a wonderful mixture of plants that seems to spill out in all directions. Indeed, such gardens often look as if the planting is out of control and the plants have been dotted here and there, seemingly at random. Cottage gardens may have looked like this a century ago, but today many gardeners are much more design-conscious in their approach and prefer to impose some form of discipline.

COTTAGE GARDEN STYLE

In the true cottage garden, plants were positioned where there was room, and there seemed to be no organization or overall design, with the resulting effect being a riot of plants and colour. The plants were situated close together, and any gaps were soon filled by self-seeded plants, again appearing at random. The tightness of the planting had the advantage of preventing weeds from surviving or even germinating, thus reducing the amount of work involved.

Modern cottage gardens, however, are rather more organized than the traditional ones. For example, species and varieties are kept together in clumps, rather than dotted about in a haphazard way. There is a tendency to ensure that the adjacent colours of the perennials blend with each other, rather than clash – we seem to be much more colour-conscious than our ancestors used to be. There is also more control in terms of the positioning of the plants, so that the smaller ones are at the front of the border and the taller ones are at the back.

That said, however, there is no reason why you should not let things run riot, if you so wish, and create a truly old-fashioned cottage garden.

OLD-FASHIONED PERENNIALS

One of the elements that gives the cottage garden its particular atmosphere is the use of "old-fashioned" plants, which may be described as plants that were grown by our ancestors and that are still grown today, largely unchanged. Apart from aesthetic reasons, there are other grounds for growing old-fashioned plants. The most important is that these plants have survived because they are tough. They are sufficiently resistant to the weather, pests and diseases to have lasted for several centuries. This means that many of them are relatively free of problems, making gardeners' lives easier.

Another reason for the enduring popularity of old-fashioned perennials is their appearance: they are, quite simply, attractive. They may not have the big, blowsy flowers in bold, bright colours that many modern plant breeders would have us like, but they are, nonetheless, usually covered in glorious flowers, often in subtle pastel shades, with occasional splashes of bright colour to liven up the border.

Modern plant breeding has concentrated so much on size and colour that scent has almost been bred out of many flowers. One advantage of the species and old varieties found in traditional cottage gardens is that they are often highly perfumed, an important quality in the make-up of a romantic cottage garden.

Left: *Spring in the cottage garden heralds the appearance of primulas, forget-me-nots, columbines and bluebells; all of these perennials are firm favourites with those who adopt this ever-popular style of gardening.*

Above: *A typical cottage garden path with plants spilling over it. A colour scheme of pinks and purples has been loosely followed, with the plants mixed together and allowed to self-seed.*

Above: *The tight planting of a cottage garden allows little room for weeds to grow. Here, a mixture of self-sown annuals and planted perennials creates a wonderfully relaxed picture.*

Above: *Columbines (*Aquilegia*) contrast with the filmy foliage of fennel (*Foeniculum vulgare*).*

Above: *Greater masterwort (*Astrantia major*) has a lovely, old-fashioned quality that makes it a perfect subject for including in a cottage garden.*

COTTAGE GARDEN PERENNIALS

Alcea rosea (hollyhock)
Anemone × hybrida (Japanese anemone)
Aquilegia vulgaris (granny's bonnet)
Aster novae-angliae; A. novi-belgii
Astrantia major (masterwort)
Bellis perennis (double daisy)
Campanula persicifolia; C. portenschlagiana; C. poscharskyana
Centaurea cyanus (cornflower); *C. montana* (perennial cornflower)
Chrysanthemum
Delphinium
Dianthus (carnations, pinks)
Dicentra spectabilis (bleeding heart, Dutchman's trousers)
Doronicum (leopard's bane)
Galium odoratum, syn. *Asperula odorata* (woodruff)
Geranium ibericum
Geum rivale (water avens)
Lathyrus (vetchling)
Lupinus (lupin)
Lychnis chalcedonica (Jerusalem cross, Maltese cross)
Lysimachia nummularia (creeping Jenny)
Meconopsis cambrica (Welsh poppy)
Monarda didyma (bee balm, bergamot)
Myrrhis odorata (sweet cicely)
Paeonia officinalis (peony)
Polemonium caeruleum
Primula
Pulmonaria (lungwort)
Ranunculus aconitifolius (bachelor's buttons)
Saponaria officinalis (bouncing Bet)
Sedum spectabile (ice-plant)

Formal Gardens

As the name implies, formal gardens tend to be highly organized, with each plant in its place and no chance of self-sown seedlings appearing to disrupt the design. The overall plan is based on the use of symmetry, straight lines and smooth curves. It is this combination of regular lines and carefully positioned plants that makes the formal garden so different to the cottage garden, in which it can be said that anything goes.

FORMAL EFFECTS

A strictly formal garden is designed with precise regularity. The garden itself may be square or rectangular, but there should be a set piece in the centre, as well as borders around the edges. The planting on each side of the square or rectangular garden should be mirrored on the opposite side. Certain plants may also be repeated at intervals along the borders to create a sense of rhythm.

A formal garden may take the form of a parterre, in which the borders are contained by low hedging. This may be provided by a shrubby plant, such as box (*Buxus*), or by plants like santolina or germander (*Teucrium*), which are technically shrubs or sub-shrubs, but usually regarded as perennials in the garden. Within the hedges, perennials of a uniform colour and size are set out in blocks, or a variety of plants are laid out in a pattern that is then echoed elsewhere in the design.

Not all formal gardens are symmetrical. Some schemes that may be considered formal have no real formality at all, depending more on simplicity for the effect they produce. In this type of garden the number of plants is severely restricted. There might be, for example, one or two well-chosen plants, sited in telling positions. Alternatively, there may be a formal pond, with plants in one corner – a tall reed, perhaps, or three plants, a taller one with two others in front, forming a close triangle. Other arrangements might include a single clump of tall grass or bamboo in a gravelled area.

Plants in a formal garden often play a lesser role than features such as hedges, paths, statuary, large ponds and fountains. When plants are introduced, they are often selected for their architectural qualities – a single clump of flax lily (*Phormium*), for example. A cabbage tree (*Cordyline*), with its even spread of pointed leaves, is another perfect plant for such a garden, whether planted directly in the ground or grown in a container.

Stark formality is not really the business of this book. We are more concerned with the use of perennials, and formal gardens, attractive though they often are, do not use as many different perennials as most gardeners would like. However, if you feel that a formal garden is the right choice for you, remember that there are many occasions when perennials can be organized in a formal way, while many of the plants that are suggested for less formal gardens can also be used to create an eye-catching, symmetrical scheme.

Above: *Grasses have simple, elegant shapes that rarely look fussy. This makes them suitable for formal settings, either used as single specimens or planted in groups, as is the case here.*

Above: *Foliage is often more important than flowers in a formal setting, as is demonstrated by this group that is dominated by* Euphorbia mellifera. *The coolness of the greens looks very striking in combination with the white stone planter.*

Above right: *Rhythm and repetition in a garden create a feeling of formality, as does the use of straight lines and simple shapes. The clipped box balls in this formal garden contribute to the overall effect by creating a satisfying rhythm down the length of the garden.*

Right: *This large sunken garden shows how a formal layout can be softened with well-placed plants such as lady's mantle (*Alchemilla mollis*), whose foaming, lime-green flowers are spilling out over the edges of the paths.*

Herbaceous Borders

A herbaceous border is simply a border devoted to herbaceous plants. At the end of the year all the plants die back, but then sprout anew the following spring. A large herbaceous border in full flower is a wonderful sight and more than compensates for the empty winter months when there are fewer perennials to see.

THE SIZE OF THE BORDER

In the past, herbaceous borders tended to be extensive and required the attention of a large number of gardeners. However, a successful herbaceous border need be neither large nor labour-intensive. It is perfectly true that a huge herbaceous border several hundred metres (yards) long is an incredible sight, but then so is one that extends for only about ten metres or less. Unlike the Victorians, we do not necessarily believe that the size of a border is a measure of its effectiveness. We are probably more concerned with the plants that are growing there.

When it comes to the amount of labour needed to maintain herbaceous borders, it is a mistake to think that you need a staff of full-time gardeners to ensure that they look their best. You will definitely need help if your borders are several hundred metres long, but the borders that can be accommodated in most of today's private gardens can be looked after by the owner. As long as the ground is well prepared in the first place and work is carried out early in the year, before the weeds can get a hold, herbaceous borders are easy and, in fact, pleasurable to maintain.

SEASONAL CHANGES

The winter months can be a problem for those who feel that the garden must offer something all year round. In the old days herbaceous borders were often part of a larger garden, in which there were plenty of other areas to see during the winter months, including, in the very largest gardens, tropical glasshouses!

Today, however, many gardeners are as interested in the dried remains of the perennials as they are in their appearance when in full growth. Many plants die very gracefully, and their bare, dead stems can be unexpectedly attractive. Grasses, in particular, are useful in this respect, but there are many other plants, either in clumps or as individual stems, that are eye-catching in dull, winter light. These remains also, of course, provide invaluable food and shelter for birds and insects.

CHOOSING THE COLOURS

The design of a herbaceous border is a matter of personal preference, and individual tastes can all be accommodated using the incredible range of plants now available. The perennials are usually grouped so that the colours blend harmoniously. They are often arranged so that the hotter colours are in the centre and the cooler tones at the ends of the border. It is also possible to create borders that are restricted to only one colour or to a group of colours – pastel shades or hot colours, for example. Some gardeners prefer a white border or one that is limited to plants that have yellow and blue flowers and foliage. The number of variations on these themes is almost limitless, and each offers the possibility of a border that is unique.

Below: *This is a typical layout, with twin herbaceous borders separated by a wide path. Such a planting scheme is unbeatable in midsummer.*

Above: *An informal herbaceous border that relies on both foliage and flowers for its effect, contrasting grasses and hostas with Welsh poppies* (Meconopsis cambrica) *and columbines* (Aquilegia).

Above: *A vivid contrast between the purple of this* Phlox *and the silver foliage of the* Anaphalis *brings alive this section of the border. Too much contrast, however, would create an uncomfortable effect.*

Above: *A daylily (*Hemerocallis*) peeping through the delicate, silver foliage of an* Artemisia *makes for a wonderful contrast of flower and foliage.*

Right: *Dedicated colour schemes can produce particularly striking results. Here, a gravel-edged border has been filled with perennials in a range of hot colours, creating a bright, cheerful atmosphere.*

Mixed Borders

An increase in interest in the mixed border came with the decline in popularity of the herbaceous border earlier this century. The mixed border is so-called because, of course, it contains a mixture of plants. It is not restricted solely to herbaceous plants, but can also include shrubs and even trees.

THE ADVANTAGES

Devotees prefer the mixed border to the traditional herbaceous border for several reasons. The main reason is that including trees and shrubs gives the border a clear structure and a permanent framework. Even in winter there is something to see, especially if the shrubs are evergreen. Although many herbaceous plants have a relatively long season of interest, many have only a brief one. This can be regarded as an advantage in many ways – borders that are dynamic and ever-changing make for a much more interesting garden. The sudden blooming of a clump of red flowers, for example, not only provides a point of interest, but also changes the whole appearance of the border. The advantages of a mixed border are easier to understand if you contrast this type of border with, say, an annual bedding scheme, which remains largely the same throughout the summer and autumn.

COMBINING THE PLANTS

Some gardeners do not like too much change in the garden but prefer to have one or two anchor points that provide a permanent structure within which the perennials can be allowed to weave their constantly changing thread. In some respects, reducing the amount of change in a border emphasizes what remains.

Including trees and shrubs widens the scope of plants that can be used in a border and introduces a wider variety of shapes and textures into the overall design. In general, trees and shrubs also have a more "solid" appearance, which is important, whether they are dotted around the border, grouped together or even used as a backdrop. This structure is particularly important if there is no proper background to the border, such as a hedge or wall.

Many perennials often look their best when grown with shrubs. A clump of day lilies (*Hemerocallis*), for example, peeping out from between two shrubs, can look superb.

Another advantage of incorporating trees and shrubs into a border is that they provide shade. Although many gardeners try to avoid shade, it does provide a habitat for a wider range of perennials than could otherwise be grown in a border.

Left: *Most cottage gardens are a delightful mixture of annuals, perennials, shrubs and climbers. A cottage garden made up of borders with a well-chosen mixture of annuals and perennials will give you a long-lasting display of flowers, with ever-changing points of interest.*

Above: *Annuals, perennials and shrubs all play a part in this tightly packed planting scheme. The colours, textures and shapes of the plants are used to good effect to create an eye-catching border.*

Above: *Combining perennials with shrubs – here* Sisyrinchium striatum *is growing with* Rosa *'Félicité Perpétue' – allows for a greater variety of planting and hence a more interesting scheme than could be achieved using perennials alone.*

Right: *Some shrubs are regarded as "honorary" perennials. Herbs, such as the sage shown here, as well as lavender and rosemary, are frequently seen in association with perennials.*

Island Beds

Although they have long been a part of the bedding plant tradition, it is only relatively recently that island beds have become an acknowledged element of the perennial scene. Island beds are simply borders that you can walk around completely, and so view from all angles. They may be positioned in the centre of a lawn or within a paved area, or they can be circumnavigated by a path.

SHAPES AND SIZES

The shapes of island beds can vary enormously. In more formal gardens, the shapes should be regular, including circles, ovals and squares. However, triangles should be avoided, unless they are large, because it is difficult to plant the corners of a triangle satisfactorily, especially if they come to a sharp point.

Formal shapes do not, however, lend themselves particularly well to the informality of most perennial plants, for which larger, free-form beds are usually much more satisfactory. By this is meant a self-contained bed that has a sinuous edge. The line of the edge should not be determined at random, however, since it always looks better if it reflects the shape of a nearby border or path, or swings out around a tree or some other garden feature.

Allied to the shape is the size of the bed: a simple rule to remember is that perennial island beds should never be too small. In fact, if the shape of the bed can be taken in at a glance, the bed is probably too small. The best island beds are large enough to accommodate some tall plants, or even some trees and shrubs in the centre of the bed in order to introduce some height. The worst beds are those in which there is not enough space for the plants to develop any height. In such beds, your eyes are likely to sweep straight across the planting to whatever lies beyond.

CHOOSING THE PERENNIALS

The idea of looking beyond the bed is an important one. When you are planning both the size and contents of the bed, always make sure that it is filled with plants of an appropriate height and density. No plant looks its best if you can see straight though it. A thin scattering of low plants usually looks unappealing and does little for the overall appearance of the garden.

One of the advantages of an island bed is that it can be sited in the open, away from the shade, with plenty of air circulating among the plants. This type of position is greatly appreciated by many sun-loving plants. In larger island beds, however, where there is a central planting of small trees and shrubs, shade will be created on one side. The shade will vary in intensity across the bed and provide an opportunity to grow a range of plants that have different growing requirements.

CREATING A CIRCULAR BED

1 Insert a post in the centre of the proposed bed. Attach one end of a piece of string to the post and the other end to a bottle filled with sand or peat.

2 Walk slowly around the post, keeping the string taut and the bottle tilted, so that the sand trickles out and marks the outline of the circle.

CREATING AN IRREGULAR BED

Use a flexible hosepipe to work out the size and shape of an irregular bed. Once you are happy with the shape of the bed, remove a line of turf around the edge of the pipe to mark it out.

CREATING AN OVAL BED

3 Once the circle is complete, the turf can be cut from within the marked area in order to produce a perfectly circular bed.

Place two posts in the ground and loosely tie a piece of string around them. Experiment with the distance between the posts and the length of the piece of string to get the size and shape of bed you require. Place a bottle filled with peat or sand inside the loop of string and walk around the posts, keeping the string taut. The sand trickles out of the bottle, creating the outline of a perfect oval.

PREPARING THE GROUND

1 With many lawn grasses, it will not be necessary to use a herbicide; simply skim off the surface grass and dig out any roots that remain.

2 Dig the soil, removing any weeds and stones. Mix in plenty of organic material as you dig to encourage the roots to grow deeply.

3 Leave the bed to weather for a few months after digging, and remove any residual weeds. Fork in well-rotted compost and rake level before planting.

Above: *This island bed is filled with an array of colourful perennials and surrounded by mown grass paths.*

Shady Plantings

Many gardeners regard areas of shade as a problem, but they can be an advantage in many ways, because they provide a greater variety of habitats, thus increasing the range of plants that can be grown. Shade is not something to worry about, as so many gardeners seem to do.

SUITABLE PERENNIALS

The golden rule when planting shady areas is to use perennials that grow naturally in the shade. If this rule is followed, you should have no difficulty in establishing a fine range of perennials. It may seem an obvious point to make, but the main reason so many gardeners dread gardening in shady areas is because they want to grow the brightly coloured plants that thrive in full sun. They plant them in shady borders, and they quickly become drawn and etiolated, as they struggle to the light; then they turn sickly because they are undernourished and short of light. This, in turn, means that they are more susceptible to disease, and, before long, the plants die. If you choose plants that like the shade, the results will be completely different.

DEGREES OF SHADE

It is important to distinguish between the different types of shade and to give your perennials the right conditions. The first kind of shade is known as light or partial shade. This includes areas that are in sun for part of the day or are lightly shaded by objects through which the sun can penetrate from time to time. The mottled light under some trees comes into this category, which also includes areas such as the north side of a building where the sun does not reach, but where there is always light from above.

Dense shade is defined as an area in which sunlight never penetrates and the low levels of light make the site gloomy. This type of shade is much more problematic. Fortunately, few gardens are entirely in dense shade, although there may be one or two small areas that are.

You can alter the level of shade in parts of the garden. If you have a large tree, for example, removing the lower branches allows more light to reach the ground beneath. The branches in the main canopy can also be thinned to create a dappled light. In a dark, north-facing area, a fence or wall opposite the site can be painted white to reflect the available light towards the shady bed.

Above: *Many hellebores, including this* Helleborus odorus, *grow well in light shade.*

Left: Geranium macrorrhizum *is one of the best perennial plants for growing in shade. Here, it is flowering well in fairly dark conditions.*

Some shade-loving perennials, such as pulmonarias and hellebores, can be planted under deciduous trees, which have lost their leaves during the perennials' main flowering season, thus providing plenty of light at the crucial time when these plants produce their flowers.

Remember, too, that the type of soil is important. Many shade-loving perennials are naturally woodland plants, and so need a woodland-like soil. This should be high in organic materials, such as leafmould, which hold plenty of moisture. Some perennials will grow in dry woodland soils – *Euphorbia amygdaloides robbiae*, for example – but for a greater range of plants it is better to modify the soil in order to create better conditions.

Above: *Both primulas and ferns relish growing in light shade. Plants always do well if given the conditions they prefer.*

Above: *Columbines are usually grown in the open border, but are frequently found in open woodland in the wild. Why not follow nature and use them in shady borders?*

SHADE-LOVING PERENNIALS

Achlys triphylla
Actaea alba (white baneberry); *A. rubra* (red baneberry)
Alchemilla mollis (lady's mantle)
Anemone nemorosa (wood anemone)
Aruncus dioicus (goat's beard)
Asarum caudatum; *A. hartwegii*
Begonia grandis evansiana (hardy begonia)
Bergenia (elephant's ears)
Brunnera macrophylla, syn. *Anchusa myosotidiflora*
Caltha palustris (kingcup, marsh marigold)
Campanula latifolia
Cardamine bulbifera; *C. enneaphyllos*; *C. kitaibelii*; *C. pentaphyllos*
Carex pendula (pendulous sedge)
Convallaria majalis (lily-of-the-valley)
Corydalis flexuosa
Dicentra
Disporum (fairy bells)
Dryopteris filix-mas (male fern)
Epimedium
Eranthis hyemalis (winter aconite)
Euphorbia amygdaloides (wood spurge); *E. amygdaloides robbiae*
Geranium (cranesbill; some)
Glaucidium palmatum
Hacquetia epipactis
Helleborus (hellebore)
Hosta
Houttuynia cordata
Iris foetidissima (stinking iris)
Jeffersonia diphylla; *J. dubia*
Kirengeshoma palmata
Lamium galeobdolon (yellow archangel)

Lathyrus vernus (spring vetchling)
Lilium martagon (Turk's cap lily)
Liriope muscari (lilyturf)
Meconopsis (blue poppy)
Milium effusum 'Aureum' (Bowles' golden grass)
Myosotis sylvatica (garden forget-me-not)
Omphalodes cappadocica; *O. verna* (blue-eyed Mary)
Oxalis acetosella (wood sorrel)
Paris (herb Paris)
Pentaglottis sempervirens
Persicaria affinis (syn. *Polygonum affine*)
Phlox divaricata (blue phlox, wild sweet William); *P. stolonifera* (creeping phlox)
Podophyllum hexandrum (syn. *P. emodi*); *P. peltatum* (May apple)
Polygonatum (Solomon's seal)
Polystichum setiferum (soft shield fern)
Primula
Pulmonaria (lungwort)
Sanguinaria canadensis (bloodroot)
Smilacina racemosa (false spikenard); *S. stellata* (star flower)
Smyrnium perfoliatum
Stylophorum
Symphytum ibericum (syn. *S. grandiflorum*)
Tellima grandiflora
Tiarella (foamflower)
Trillium (wood lily)
Uvularia (merrybells)
Vancouveria
Viola odorata (sweet violet); *V. riviniana* Purpurea Group (Labrador violet)
Waldsteinia ternata

Wild Flower Plantings

In some respects all flower gardens may be described as wild flower plantings. Every plant we grow in our gardens, including the species, which are undoubtedly wild flowers, as well as the other highly bred forms that we can buy today, originated somewhere in the wild. However, the term "wild flowers" is usually taken to mean those flowers that grow wild in the local area.

WILD FLOWER HABITATS

Increasing pressure on the countryside means that the number of wild flowers is diminishing, and, unfortunately, this is a worldwide problem. One way of combating this demise is by creating wild flower habitats within our own gardens. Such areas, in turn, have the benefit of reintroducing wildlife, especially in the form of insects, such as butterflies, which thrive on the native plants, but are less happy on many of the introduced or hybridized ones that we grow in our gardens. On the whole, most wild flowers are not as attractive individually as cultivated ones, but when they are gathered together in, say, a meadow garden, their beauty becomes much more apparent.

WILD FLOWER GARDENS

One might expect growing wild plants to be fairly easy, but establishing and maintaining a wild flower garden is one of the most difficult types of gardening. There is the natural tendency, especially in cultivated ground, for the ranker weeds to take over and smother the plants you want to encourage. Success depends largely on the way you approach the task as well as on the initial preparation.

The first method is to allow wild flowers to colonize some existing grass. If this is a lawn, you should not have many problems, but if you are lucky enough to have a field, the grasses are likely to be too rank for the flowers to survive. The first task is to spend a year mowing the grass at regular intervals to keep it short. This will kill off most of the ranker grasses and leave the finer ones.

The next step, whether you have a field or a lawn, is to put in wild flower plants at random throughout the meadow. You can scatter the seed directly over the area, if you wish, but the competition is intense, and so it is better to sow the seed in trays, prick out and grow on the plants in pots first. Plant out in spring when the perennials are strong enough to compete. Once established, they will self-sow, which is always more successful than simply scattering the seed.

The second method is to clear the ground completely, removing all traces of perennial weeds. Then, sow a wild flower and grass seed mixture that has been especially formulated for your area. There are several suppliers for this type of seed. It is worth finding the right seed mixture, as it is important to use only those

perennials that already grow, or are likely to grow, in your area. These will have the best chance of surviving. For example, there is little point in trying to naturalize plants from chalk (alkaline) downland on acid heathland soil.

Once the meadow is established, it should be cut regularly, about once or twice a year, to prevent the rank weeds from taking over. The best time is usually in summer once the main flush of plants have seeded.

Above: *Here, wild flowers are growing to great effect in a herbaceous border. Evening primrose (Oenothera biennis) and feverfew (Tanacetum parthenium) make a sympathetic planting combination.*

On a much smaller scale it is also possible to create a wild flower garden simply by sowing or planting perennials along a hedgerow, which is another natural habitat in itself.

PERENNIALS FOR WILD FLOWER PLANTINGS

Achillea millefolium
(milfoil)
Ajuga reptans
(common bugle)
Asclepias tuberosa
(butterfly weed)
*Campanula
rotundifolia* (harebell)
Cardamine pratensis
(cuckoo flower,
lady's smock)
Centaurea scabiosa
Fritillaria meleagris
(snake's head fritillary;
this is a bulb)
Geranium pratense
(meadow cranesbill)
Hypericum perforatum
(St. John's wort)

Leontodon hispidus
(rough hawkbit)
Malva moschata
(musk mallow)
Monarda fistulosa
(wild bergamot)
Narcissus pseudonarcissus
(Lent Lily; this is a bulb)
Primula veris (cowslip)
Prunella vulgaris
Ranunculus acris
(meadow buttercup);
R. bulbosus (bulbous
buttercup); *R. repens*
(creeping buttercup)
Stellaria graminea
(lesser stitchwort)
Succisa pratensis
(devil's bit scabious)

Above: *A beautiful wild flower meadow edged with red valerian* (Centranthus ruber) *that is growing in an old wall.*

Above: *Many garden flowers are forms of wild flowers.* Ajuga reptans *'Catlin's Giant' is a large form of the species.*

Above: *Wild flowers can also be planted in shade.* Anemone nemorosa *and* Ranunculus auricomis *are both woodlanders.*

Container Plantings

There is a tendency to think of perennials in terms of the herbaceous border or bed, and, while it is true that they are border plants par excellence, many can also be used as container plants. As with most of the ways in which you can use perennials, the possibilities are endless, with new ideas for container plantings appearing all the time.

PERENNIALS FOR CONTAINERS

Many of the so-called "annuals" that are used in windowboxes and hanging baskets are, in fact, perennials, but most, such as pelargoniums and petunias, are tender, and are therefore treated as annuals. Others are on the borderline of hardiness and may survive mild winters, but it is the true hardy perennials that we are considering here.

On the whole, it is much more effective to plant perennials in a container as individual species or varieties, rather than using them in mixed plantings. This is partly because they look best like this, but it also has a lot to do with the size of the plants – if you have a large flax lily (*Phormium*) in a pot, there is not much room for anything else.

When plants are grown in isolation in this way, it is also much easier to appreciate them than when they are part of a busy border. For example, the fountain-like foliage of a hosta in a pot will stand out against stone or brick paving in a way that would be impossible if the same plant were surrounded by other foliage. Similarly, the spiky appearance of a cabbage tree (*Cordyline*) can also be fully appreciated in a container on a plinth, silhouetted against a plain background or the sky.

Perennials in containers can be used in a variety of ways. Placing the container in a border may seem rather odd, but this can be a good way of filling any gaps – a pot of African lilies (*Agapanthus*), for example, can be stood in the gap left when a spring-flowering plant dies back.

When they are raised on plinths, containers also work well as focal points. For example, a large container on a plinth might be placed in a border, positioned at the end of a path, or at the edge or centre of the lawn. The eye is drawn immediately to the container, and this is the perfect way to focus a visitor's attention towards – or even away from – another garden feature. Containers can also be used to great advantage in more obvious places, notably on patios, either arranged in groups or used singly to show off individual specimens.

The other great advantage of container-grown perennials is that they can be moved around to create fresh displays, and, as the flowers of one plant go over, another coming into bloom can be moved in to replace it, producing an ever-changing scene in the border.

Containers are also the ideal way of decorating or drawing attention to a flight of stairs. They can be positioned on the highest or lowest steps to guide the eye up or down. They can also be set to stand guard on each side of a doorway or arch, thus creating a well-defined entrance to the house or garden.

SUITABLE PERENNIALS FOR CONTAINERS

Acanthus (bear's breeches)
Agapanthus (African lily)
Bergenia (elephant's ears)
Cordyline (cabbage tree)
Dianthus (carnations, pinks)
Diascia
Euphorbia (spurge)
Geranium (cranesbill)
Geum
Hemerocallis (daylily)
Heuchera (coral bells)
Hosta
Iris
Nepeta
Oenothera fruticosa glauca
  (sundrops)
Phormium tenax
  (New Zealand flax)
Primula
Sedum
Stachys byzantina,
  syn. *S. lanata* (lamb's ears)
Verbena

Left: *The beautiful mauve flowers of* Convolvulus sabatius *complement the warm, terracotta colour of the pot. Being a slightly tender plant, the convolvulus can be moved inside in its pot for the winter.*

PLANTING A CONTAINER

1 These are the materials you will need to plant a container. They include a terracotta pot, your choice of plant (in this case, a cordyline), some stones for drainage, potting compost (soil mix), slow-release fertilizer (either loose or in pellets) and water-retaining granules.

2 Cover the bottom of the container with small stones or some pieces of tile or pottery, so that water can drain freely from the pot.

3 Partly fill the pot with a good quality potting compost. Some loose slow-release fertilizer and water-retaining granules can be mixed with the compost before filling the pot.

4 Scoop a hole in the compost and insert the plant, positioning it so that the top of the rootball will be level with the surface of the compost.

5 Place any extra plants you wish to include around the edge of the main plant. Add more compost to fill any gaps, and firm down.

6 Insert a fertilizer pellet if you have decided to use one, rather than the loose fertilizer granules. Water thoroughly.

7 The plants will soon grow away and fill out the container.

Fragrant Perennials

As you would expect from a range of plants as diverse as the perennials, there are a number that are fragrant, which adds to the enjoyment of growing them.

THE SCENTED GARDEN

It is possible to create borders especially devoted to scent, but, in many ways, it is more exciting to come across a fragrance at random. If too many fragrant plants are placed together, the various fragrances may conflict with each other, so they can be appreciated neither singly nor together. Placing scented plants judiciously around the garden, on the other hand, means that individual scents can suddenly assail you as you walk around, often before you are conscious of the plants themselves.

Although it is pleasant to come across scents as you walk along a border, it is often far more enjoyable to relax on a seat or in an arbour that has perfumed plants set near to it. This is a particularly good idea if you have a patio where you can eat on a summer's evening. Many plants are evening-scented, and sitting in the garden after a hard day's work, as the light begins to fade and the scents start to float on the warm air, is one of the most pleasant and effective ways to relax and forget the problems of the day.

A similar idea is to position scented plants near doors and windows that are likely to be open, so that the scents waft in and fill the room. Planting your favourite scented plant near to the drive so that it welcomes you as you arrive home is also a sure way to emphasize the break between work and home.

CAPTURING THE SCENT

Scent can be elusive. Sometimes it travels a long way on the air and at other times you have to place your nose in the flower before it becomes apparent. Some scents have to react with the air before they can be smelt – when you are close to the flower you cannot smell anything, but move a few feet away, and there it is.

Other scents are not given off until the plant is bruised. *Artemisia*, for example, does not smell until you gently crush its leaves. Plants of this type should be planted close to paths, so that their scent is released as you brush past them. Catmint or catnip (*Nepeta cataria*) is good for this.

You should remember that not all plants are pleasantly fragrant. Your family will not be appreciative if you plant a dragon arum (*Dracunculus vulgaris*) under a window. It is a striking plant, but put it at the bottom of the garden because it has a strong foetid smell, rather like rotten flesh, which it uses to attract flies.

Remember, too, that not everyone likes the same scents – *Phuopsis stylosa*, for example, has a foxy, rather pungent smell that some people dislike. Some scents change in character during the day – for instance, *Cestrum parqui* has a strong savoury smell during the day, but a sweet fragrance at night.

Above all, remember that while much pleasure can be obtained from scented plants, they must always be used with discretion.

Left: *Lupins have a very distinctive, peppery scent, which, like many plant perfumes, is most apparent in warm weather.*

SCENTED FLOWERS

Acorus calamus (sweet flag)
Adenophora liliifolia
Aponogeton distachyos
 (water hawthorn)
Asphodeline lutea
 (syn. *Asphodelus luteus*)
Calanthe discolor
Cestrum parqui
Chrysanthemum
Clematis heracleifolia;
 C. recta
Convallaria majalis
 (lily-of-the-valley)
Cosmos atrosanguineus
 (chocolate cosmos)
Crambe cordifolia;
 C. maritima (seakale)
Delphinium wellbyi
 (syn. *D. leroyi*)
Dianthus (carnations, pinks)
Filipendula ulmaria
Helleborus lividus
Hemerocallis citrina;
 H. dumortieri;
 H. lilioasphodelus (syn.
 H. flava); *H. middendorffii*;
 H. multiflora
Hosta 'Honeybells';
 H. plantaginea
Iris 'Florentina';
 I. germanica (common
 German flag); *I. hoogiana*;
 I. pallida dalmatica;

I. unguicularis (Algerian iris)
Lobularia maritima,
 syn. *Alyssum maritimum*
 (sweet alyssum)
Lunaria rediviva
 (perennial honesty)
Lupinus polyphyllus
Mirabilis jalapa
 (four o'clock flower)
Paeonia (peony; some)
Petasites fragrans (winter
 heliotrope); *P. japonicus
 giganteus*
Phlox maculata (meadow
 phlox; wild sweet William);
 P. paniculata (perennial
 phlox)
Polygonatum × *hybridum*
 (syn. *P. multiflorum*)
Primula alpicola; *P. florindae*
 (giant cowslip); *P. secundiflora*;
 P. sikkimensis (Himalayan
 cowslip)
Romneya coulteri
 (Californian poppy);
 R. coulteri trichocalyx
Smilacina racemosa (false
 spikenard)
Tellima grandiflora
Verbena bonariensis
 (purple top); *V. corymbosa*
Yucca filamentosa (Adam's
 needle)

Above: *Not all flowers can be smelt from a distance. You need to be quite close to irises to catch their fragrance.*

Above: *The lily-of-the-valley* (Convallaria majalis) *is one of the best loved of all scented cottage garden plants.*

SCENTED FOLIAGE

Agastache foeniculum (syn.
 A. anethiodora, *A anisata*);
 A. mexicana (Mexican
 giant hyssop)
*Anthemis punctata
 cupaniana*
Artemisia (wormwood)
Melittis melissophyllum
Meum athamanticum
 (spignel)
Nepeta (catmint)
Salvia (sage)

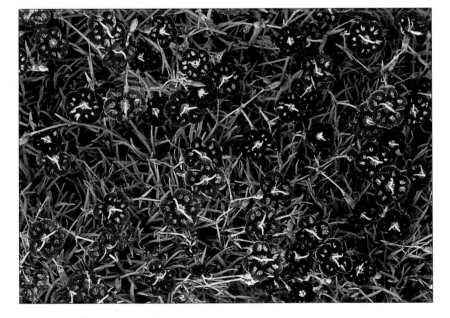

Left: *Old-fashioned cottage garden plants, such as this lupin, are more likely to have perfumed flowers than many of the modern hybrids.*

Above: *Old-fashioned pinks* (Dianthus) *have a wonderful scent, but a short flowering season. A few of the modern hybrids are also scented, but flower for longer.*

Climbing Perennials

When we think of climbing plants, it is usually the shrubby types that come to mind: roses, clematis, honeysuckles and many other cottage garden favourites. However, there are also a number of perennial climbers, some of which can be a wonderfully colourful addition to the garden.

CLIMBERS FOR SHRUBS

One of the most important points to remember about climbers is that they need something to climb up. In the wild, they usually climb up other plants such as trees or shrubs. In the garden, this is not only a possibility, but also a good idea. This is because many shrubs are at their best when they are in flower and, if this happens to be in the spring, then they are dependent on their foliage to provide interest for the rest of the year. So, one way to brighten up a shrub is to grow another plant through it that produces flowers later in the season. Flame creeper (*Tropaeolum speciosum*) is ideal for this, and will happily grow over low shrubs, producing masses of flame-red flowers.

A similar idea is to grow a climbing perennial through another more vigorous climber – the Chilean glory flower (*Eccremocarpus scaber*), for example, will grow through an early-flowering clematis and produce its flowers in late summer and early autumn. Hedges can also be used as supports, as long as the plant is robust enough to stand the competition. Greater periwinkle (*Vinca major*) is ideal for using in this way, and looks superb in spring when its blue flowers peep out from what might otherwise be a dull hedge.

Providing an artificial framework is another way to grow perennial climbers. This is best done in the perennial border by erecting wooden structures such as pyramids, tripods or even simple poles. These provide robust supports which the plants can climb up, or, if they are not self-clinging,

against which they can be tied. Most perennial climbers do not grow very high, so the supporting structures do not have to be very tall, and wicker is the perfect material in this instance. Similarly, *Clematis recta,* like many other perennial plants, only needs the help of some peasticks or metal plant supports in order to form a pleasingly rounded shape.

Some perennial climbers are quite vigorous and are suitable for growing over arches or trellises. The golden hop (*Humulus lupulus* 'Aureus') is a perfect example of such a plant. It can also be trained over a framework to make a secluded arbour. However, the stems are

rough and can cause serious weals if they rub against the skin, so it is important to make sure that you tie in all the straggling stems.

As a last resort, one way of using perennial climbers, especially if they are not too vigorous, is to leave them alone and allow them to scramble over the ground, forming a loose, straggling pile. Some clematis, such as *Clematis heracleifolia*, are particularly good for this.

Below: *Many perennials, such as these violas and armerias, will scramble quite happily through low shrubs, using them as supports in order to get closer to the light.*

PERENNIAL CLIMBERS AND SCRAMBLERS

Clematis × *eriostemon*;
C. × *durandii*;
C. heracleifolia;
C. × *jouiniana*; *C. recta*
Codonopsis (bonnet
bellflower)
Eccremocarpus scaber
(Chilean glory flower)
Humulus lupulus 'Aureus'
(golden hop)

Lathyrus sylvestris (perennial
pea)
Rhodochiton atrosanguineus
(purple bells)
Solanum dulcamara
'Variegatum' (poisonous)
Tropaeolum speciosum
(flame creeper); *T. tuberosum*
Vinca major (greater
periwinkle)

Above: Clematis recta *is an*
excellent herbaceous clematis. It
can either grow through a low
shrub or brushwood supports, or
simply be left to form a mound.

Right: *The golden hop,* Humulus
lupulus *'Aureus', puts on a*
tremendous amount of growth
each year, although it takes a few
years to reach its full potential.

Perennials for Ground Cover

Plants that act as ground cover do just that – they cover the ground. For the gardener, there are both horticultural and visual advantages to this. From the horticultural point of view, a plant that covers the ground thoroughly should be welcomed because it will, in theory, help to reduce the number of weeds in the beds and borders. This works on the principle that the plant is so dense that little light can reach the ground and any weed seedlings that do manage to germinate are starved of light, become drawn and sickly, and soon die.

HORTICULTURAL ADVANTAGES
Ground cover is not quite the answer to every gardener's dreams as is sometimes implied. Simply excluding light does not necessarily guarantee that there will be no more weeds. Before planting, it is absolutely essential to make certain that there are no perennial weeds left in the ground. In many cases, even a fragment of root can regrow into a full-sized plant, and no amount of ground cover will prevent this. If perennial weeds do reappear in ground cover there is no alternative but to dig out all of the plants and start again. Therefore, it is important to get the ground completely free of weeds right from the start.

Similarly, if the ground cover is not complete, weeds will simply grow through the gaps. Plants are often recommended as ground cover that are just not dense enough to create total shade at ground level, and such plants are, therefore, useless for ground cover in the horticultural sense. Pinks (*Dianthus*), for example, produce a mat of foliage, but weeds always manage to grow among them. Bear in mind that plants which spread quickly do not necessarily make good ground cover.

VISUAL ADVANTAGES
The other purpose of planting ground cover is to produce a solid mass of one colour as part of a design or colour scheme. For example, a drift of wood anemones (*Anemone nemorosa*) through a wood could be considered ground cover in this context, although the anemones would be useless as weed suppressants.

Allied to this is the use of ground cover plants in order to fill a patch of difficult or unwanted ground. Thus, a drift of *Euphorbia amygdaloides robbiae* could be planted in a dry, shady area to provide some sort of planting because little else would grow there, including the weeds.

When ground cover plants are used, it is often assumed that all the plants should be the same type. This is not completely true. Old-fashioned cottage gardens were often a delightful jumble of plants, planted or self-sown in close proximity. This dense planting still acted as a ground cover, however, even though there was a mixture of different plants. The same principle applies to the modern herbaceous border. Once the clumps of perennials merge in late spring and the ground is covered, the number of weeds that can germinate is greatly reduced. It is only if you leave areas of bare soil showing that you will run into trouble and find that you are constantly having to weed the border.

Left: *The foliage of these hostas provides a very dense ground cover that will help keep weeds at bay, while at the same time looking very attractive.*

DENSE PLANTS FOR MASS GROUND COVER

Acaena

Alchemilla mollis
 (lady's mantle)

Anemone × hybrida
 (Japanese anemone)

Bergenia
 (elephant's ears)

Brunnera macrophylla,
 syn. *Anchusa myosotidiflora*

Convallaria majalis
 (lily-of-the-valley)

Crambe cordifolia

Epimedium

Euphorbia
 amygdaloides robbiae
 (wood spurge)

Geranium × cantabrigiense;
 G. endressii;
 G. macrorrhizum;
 G. nodosum;
 G. × oxonianum

Gunnera

Hosta

Houttuynia cordata

Lysimachia nummularia
 (creeping Jenny)

Maianthemum (may lily)

Persicaria affinis
 (syn. *Polygonum affine*)

Petasites (butterbur,
 sweet coltsfoot)

Pulmonaria (lungwort)

Rheum (ornamental rhubarb)

Rodgersia

Symphytum (comfrey)

Tiarella cordifolia
 (foamflower)

Tolmiea menziesii
 (pickaback plant)

Vancouveria

Vinca minor (lesser
 periwinkle)

Above: Persicaria affinis *provides good ground cover, the flowers (whether in bloom or after they have gone over) as well as the foliage being very attractive for most of the year.*

Above: *The spotted foliage of lungwort (*Pulmonaria*) perfectly sets off the flowers when they appear in late winter and early spring. If sheared over, lungwort will provide excellent ground cover for the rest of the year.*

Above: *The ground-hugging creeping Jenny,* Lysimachia nummularia *'Aurea', works well as a ground cover, as long as all perennial weeds have been removed first.*

Above: *The close planting of any vigorous perennials, such as* Dictamnus, *prevents weed seedlings germinating and surviving.*

Architectural Perennials

Every plant in a border performs a different function or range of functions, contributing to the overall look of the scheme. Some owe their inclusion, at least in part, to their size, shape and sheer physical presence.

USING ARCHITECTURAL PLANTS
Architectural perennials have two roles: one is as individual plants, when they are used to create a focal point, and the other is as a part of the border, when they are used to add to the diversity of shapes and sizes. Focal points in a garden are plants or objects, such as statues or urns, for example, that draw the eye. They can be placed either in isolation – at the end of a path or at the edge of a lawn, for instance – or within a larger arrangement, such as in a border. The eye needs something on which to rest from time to time and one large plant, among many smaller ones, will certainly draw the eye and will probably be the first object the viewer notices.

A cabbage tree (*Cordyline*), for example, with its spray of tapering leaves, placed in an urn at the end of a path will pull your eye towards it so that you appreciate the length and direction of the path. Only afterwards do you draw back and begin to examine the borders on either side of the path. Similarly, a bold architectural perennial, in the middle of a host of other plants in a border, will catch the eye, which rests briefly there, enjoying what it sees, before breaking off and examining the border bit by bit.

On a more general level, a border planted with at least a few architectural perennials is much more interesting than one containing a more uniform planting. Their larger size, as well as the bold shapes of their leaves, adds structure, variety and something striking to look at. However, like most aspects of planting, overdo any one element and the impact is lost.

Strongly shaped perennials often look good in pots or other containers. They can be used in isolation or in groups, and are particularly effective when used as sentinels to a path, steps, a gateway or a door. They also make good plants for patios.

Above: *The biennial or short-lived perennial giant hogweed* (Heracleum mantegazzianum*) is a spectacular plant. However, it should be used with extreme caution as touching it can result in serious skin complaints.*

Left: Gunnera manicata *produces some of the largest leaves seen in gardens. It is bound to catch the eye, wherever it is planted.*

LARGE ARCHITECTURAL PERENNIALS

Acanthus spinosus
 (bear's breeches)
Alcea rosea
 (hollyhock)
Angelica archangelica
 (angelica)
Cordyline australis
 (New Zealand cabbage palm)
Cortaderia selloana
 (pampas grass)
Crambe cordifolia
Cynara cardunculus
 (cardoon)
Delphinium

Gunnera manicata
 (giant rhubarb)
Inula magnifica
Ligularia (leopard plant)
Macleaya cordata
 (plume poppy)
Miscanthus sinensis
Phormium tenax
 (New Zealand flax)
Rheum (ornamental rhubarb)
Stipa gigantea (golden oats)
Telekia speciosa (syn.
 Buphthalmum speciosum)
Verbascum (mullein)

Above: *The red, jagged foliage of the ornamental rhubarb,* Rheum *'Ace of Hearts', can be spectacular, particularly when, as here, it is contrasted with more simple foliage.*

Above: *Angelica (*Angelica archangelica*) can be very imposing, but it is a good plant, not only for the herb garden, but also for the wilder parts of the garden.*

Perennials for Foliage

Perennials are often valued purely for the beauty of their flowers. In a well-designed garden, however, their foliage is likely to play an equally important role. Indeed, foliage usually provides the structure and backbone of the whole border, giving greater solidity to the planting scheme.

THE VALUE OF FOLIAGE

If you were to remove all of the foliage from your garden, you would be left with just a few spots of colour. If these spots of colour were seen against one another, or against bare earth, they would not look particularly attractive. However, if you were to place these colours against a sympathetic background of foliage, the picture would be suddenly complete. Foliage helps to bring out the colours in flowers as well as to meld them together.

FOLIAGE SHAPES

Foliage is important because it brings shape, texture and colour to the garden. Of these attributes, shape is the most significant. The strap-shaped leaves of plants such as grasses and irises, for example, have a quite different quality from the large leaves of, say, an ornamental rhubarb (*Rheum*). The shape of a whole plant, which is often dictated by the foliage, also plays a part. Most grasses are tall and often grow in clumps, with the leaves forming the shape of a fountain. Irises, on the other hand, are more upright and have quite a different appearance. Some plants form hummocks; others make flat mats. The interplay of these different shapes is important to the design of a border.

FOLIAGE TEXTURES

Texture is often overlooked in a garden, but it can play a very important role. Plants with shiny leaves, for example, are valuable in shady areas, where they reflect the light, brightening up what would otherwise be a dark corner. On the other hand, velvety leaves absorb the light and give an impression of richness and luxury. There is a world of difference, both in appearance and feel, between the silky leaves of an artemisia and the rough bristles of a gunnera.

FOLIAGE COLOURS

One tends to think of foliage as simply green, but, of course, the range of greens is enormous. In addition, some plants have purple, yellow and even black foliage. These colours can also be variegated in a number of ways. Some are splashed with gold, others with cream; in some the markings are around the edges of the leaves, and in others they are in the centre.

Above: *Light and shadow play beautifully on the foliage of this crocosmia.*

Left: *A group of contrasting foliage shapes, including* Smilacina racemosa *(top left),* Ferula communis *(right) and* Morina afghanica *(bottom left).*

PERENNIALS WITH COLOURED FOLIAGE

PURPLE FOLIAGE

Ajuga reptans
  'Atropurpurea';
  A. r. 'Burgundy Glow'
Anthriscus sylvestris
  'Ravenswing'
Canna 'Roi Humbert'
Clematis recta
  'Purpurea'
Cordyline australis
  'Atropurpurea'
Dahlia 'Bishop of Llandaff'
Foeniculum vulgare
  'Purpureum'
Heuchera micrantha
  diversifolia 'Palace Purple'
Ligularia dentata
  'Desdemona'; *L. d.* 'Othello'
Lobelia cardinalis
  (cardinal flower)
Phormium tenax
  Purpureum Group
  (New Zealand flax)
Rodgersia aesculifolia;
  R. podophylla
Sedum telephium
  maximum 'Atropurpureum';
  S. 'Morchen';
  S. 'Vera Jameson'
Viola riviniana
  Purpurea Group
  (Labrador violet)

BLUE FOLIAGE

Acaena saccaticupula
  'Blue Haze'
  (syn. *A.* 'Pewter')
Elymus magellanicus
Festuca glauca
  (blue fescue)
Helictotrichon
  sempervirens
  (syn. *Avena candida*)
Hosta

GOLDEN FOLIAGE

Filipendula ulmaria 'Aurea'
Hosta
Humulus lupulus 'Aureus'
  (golden hop)
Lysimachia nummularia
  'Aurea'
Milium effusum 'Aureum'
  (Bowles' golden grass)
Origanum vulgare 'Aureum'
  (golden marjoram)
Phygelius × *rectus* 'Sunshine'
Tanacetum parthenium
  'Aureum' (golden feverfew)

SILVER FOLIAGE

Anaphalis (pearl everlasting)
Artemisia (wormwood);
  A. 'Powis Castle'
Celmisia
Cerastium tomentosum
  (snow-in-summer)
Convolvulus cneorum
  (silverbush)
Cynara cardunculus
  (cardoon)
Euphorbia myrsinites;
  E. rigida (syn.
  E. biglandulosa)
Geranium renardii
Leuzea centauroides
  (syn. *Centaurea*
  'Pulchra Major')
Lychnis coronaria
Macleaya (plume poppy)
Melianthus major (honeybush)
Romneya coulteri
  (Californian poppy)
Santolina
Stachys byzantina;
  syn. *S. lanata* (lamb's ears)
Tanacetum haradjanii
Tropaeolum polyphyllum
Verbascum olympicum

Above: *Two contrasting silver foliages: the filigree* Artemisia *'Powis Castle' and the furry* Stachys byzantina.

Right: *The purple foliage of* Anthriscus sylvestris *'Ravenswing', which is overlaid with silver, is strikingly beautiful. Not surprisingly, this plant makes a valuable contribution to many planting schemes.*

USING COLOUR

Choosing a Colour Scheme

Perennials are available in a wonderful range of colours, which gives gardeners tremendous scope when they design their planting schemes. It is important to remember that colour is provided not only by the flowers, but also by the foliage. The range of colours varies from the bright and brash to the soft and muted. If all these colours were mixed together, without much thought, it would be fun for a while, but the border would soon begin to look untidy and unpleasant to look at.

GROUPING COLOURS

Rather than randomly scattering colours, it is much better to use them in drifts, placing individual plants so that each has a harmonious relationship with its neighbour. When this is done, the eye can move effortlessly along the border, enjoying the subtleties of the border as it passes over a thoughtfully blended whole.

This harmonious relationship depends largely on how different colours relate to each other. Artists and designers use what is known as a colour wheel, in which colours that are situated next to each other on the wheel have a sympathetic bond and will work well together. Purple and blue as well as blue and green, for example, look good together. On the other hand, colours on opposite sides of the wheel are contrasting and may clash with each other. Purple and yellow, for instance, are in stark contrast with each other, and a border in which these two colours are close to one another is likely to be jarring on the eye.

There are, however, occasions when combining opposing colours can be used to create a focal point or to add life to an

Above: *Orange and blue are both powerful colours. Used in together in a planting scheme, they produce an agreeable tension as is shown by these bright blue agapanthus and orange crocosmia.*

Above: *This unusual juxtaposition of purple and brown works very well and emphasizes the advice that you should always be keen to try unusual combinations.*

otherwise bland scheme. A splash of yellow in a purple border, for example, would certainly draw the eye. Red and green are also contrasting colours, and a plant with brilliant red blooms, such as Jerusalem cross (*Lychnis chalcedonica*), can look extraordinarily dramatic against a dark green yew hedge.

Pastel colours have a romantic quality, and are often suitable for a rather dull, grey climate. Even so, a garden devoted entirely to pale colours such as these can be rather boring. Hot colours – the flame reds and oranges – on the other hand, are lively and will bring a dash of excitement to a border.

Unless you have set your heart on a monochromatic border, the basic principle is to blend colours. If you want to use two colours that oppose each other on the colour wheel in close proximity, you can sometimes find another colour that will link them. Blue and red are in stark contrast with each other, and you may prefer to keep them apart by placing a purple plant between them, which will greatly improve the appearance of the border. Incorporating foliage in suitable colours is often an excellent way of linking and separating blocks of colour.

When you are buying plants, always try to see them in flower if you are doubtful about the colour. If the plant is a true variety, its colour should be fixed in most cases, but plants grown from seed can vary greatly in colour. A carefully thought-out colour scheme can be ruined if plants turn out to be pink or white instead of the expected blue, so take care when you are selecting or growing plants.

Right: *Yellow primroses are charmingly set off by their own green foliage and enhanced by a fountain of yellow Bowles' golden grass,* Milium effusum *'Aureum'.*

Below: *The combination of these perennials, including* Sedum telephium maximum *'Atropurpureum' and* Heuchera micrantha diversifolia *'Palace Purple', makes the most of the beautiful subtlety of their colours.*

Hot Colours

Odd as it may seem, colours have temperatures – some colours, like the reds, are regarded as hot, while others, such as the blues, are seen as quite cold. This phenomenon is most noticeable when you are decorating, because the whole mood of a room can change, depending on whether you are using colours based on reds or on blues. It is exactly the same when you are designing and planning a garden.

THE HOT COLOUR PALETTE

The really hot colours are those that are on the orange side of red. They include the flame reds, the oranges and the golden-yellows. Alter the emphasis, and the feeling also changes. For example, yellows that contain a touch of green, rather than orange, are cool. Similarly, reds that contain a lot of blue are not as warm as a lively, hot orange-red, and caution should be used in mixing the two.

It is possible to create a border containing nothing but red flowers, but it is always more interesting to have one that incorporates other hot colours as well. If it suits your personality, you may even want to fill the whole garden with these bright colours. Particularly in a very small garden, where there is not space to create more than one mood, this can produce a very striking effect. However, most people are more comfortable with a balance of hot and cooler areas. Going to a few lively parties is most enjoyable, but go to one every night and they will soon become a bore, and you will be thinking of excuses to stay at home.

Use hot colours with some discretion. Confine them to one border, possibly as a centrepiece,

but use softer colours in the other beds to ring in the changes and to provide a more tranquil planting area. The contrast will be all the stronger, in fact, if the red border is surrounded by less lively colours. However, many people prefer to use a limited number of hot-coloured perennials in the middle of a less adventurous border, where they will act as a strong focal point.

Hot colours also have a tendency to "advance" – that is, they seem much closer than they really are – so if you want to make a long border appear shorter than it is, plant the hot colours at the far end.

Left: *The Chilean glory flower* (Eccremocarpus scaber), *with its bright orange, tubular flowers, can be used to create a splash of colour against a wall or fence.*

Above: *The crimson-red flowers of the flame creeper* (Tropaeolum speciosum) *look very striking as they weave their way over a bright yellow-green conifer.*

PERENNIALS WITH HOT-COLOURED FLOWERS

RED FLOWERS

Canna
Crocosmia 'Lucifer'
Dahlia
Geum 'Mrs J. Bradshaw'
Hemerocallis 'Berlin Red';
 H. 'Ed Murray';
 H. 'Little Red Hen';
 H. 'Red Precious';
 H. 'Stafford'; H. 'Wally
Nance'
Kniphofia (red-hot poker)
Leonotis ocymifolia,
 syn. *L. leonurus* (lion's ear)
Lobelia tupa
Lychnis chalcedonica
 (Jerusalem cross, Maltese
 cross)
Mimulus cupreus
 'Whitecroft Scarlet';
 M. 'Wisley Red'
Monarda 'Cambridge
 Scarlet'
Paeonia (peony)
Penstemon barbatus;
 P. 'Flame'; P. *jamesii*;
 P. 'Rubicundus'; P. *superbus*
Potentilla 'Gibson's Scarlet'
Tropaeolum speciosum
 (flame creeper)

ORANGE FLOWERS

Anthemis sancti-johannis
 (St John's chamomile)
Canna 'Orange Perfection'
Crocosmia (montbretia);
 C. paniculata
Dahlia
Eccremocarpus scaber
 (Chilean glory flower)
Euphorbia griffithii
Geum 'Borisii';
 G. coccineum
Hemerocallis (daylily)
Kniphofia (red-hot poker)
Ligularia (leopard plant)
Papaver orientale
 (oriental poppy)

Potentilla 'William Rollison'
Primula bulleyana
 (a Candelabra Primula)
Rudbeckia hirta
Trollius (globeflower)
Zauschneria californica

YELLOW–GOLD FLOWERS

Achillea (yarrow);
 A. 'Coronation Gold';
 A. *filipendulina* 'Gold Plate'
Anthemis tinctoria
 (golden marguerite)
Aster linosyris
Aurinia saxatilis,
 syn. *Alyssum saxatile*
 (gold dust)
Bupthalmum salicifolium
Canna
Centaurea
 macrocephala
Chrysanthemum
Coreopsis verticillata
Dahlia
Erysimum 'Bredon';
 E. 'Jubilee Gold'
Geum 'Lady Stratheden'
Helenium (sneezeweed)
Helianthus (sunflower)
Heliopsis (ox eye)
Hemerocallis (daylily)
Hieracium (hawkweed)
Inula
Ligularia (leopard plant)
Lysimachia nummularia
 (creeping Jenny);
 L. punctata (garden
 loosestrife)
Oenothera (evening
 primrose)
Primula
Ranunculus
 (buttercup, crowfoot)
Rudbeckia
 (coneflower)
Solidago (golden rod)
Trollius (globeflower)
Tropaeolum polyphyllum

Right: *Kniphofias have several alternative names, of which red-hot poker aptly describes the colour of many of them. These shafts of hot colours are useful not only for their brightness, but also their shape.*

Below: *The flat flowerheads of* Achillea *'Coronation Gold' form a sea of hot yellow, floating above the green foliage.*

Above: Zauschneria californica *has hot orange flowers, but the softness of the foliage tends to take away some of the heat. Soft foliage is often used for this purpose in a border.*

Pastel Colours

If hot colours are jazzy and lively, pastel shades are soft and romantic. They produce a wonderful, hazy effect, which is tranquil and peaceful. The colours in this part of the spectrum include the soft blues, yellows, whites and pinks. They are not the complete opposite of the hot colours, since, in theory, they would simply be the cold or cool colours, but pinks, and those blues that are tinged with red, are warm in temperature. The overall effect, however, is one of cool calm.

COMBINING THE PASTELS

Pastel colours create a misty effect, which means that they can be mixed together and even dotted around. An even better effect can be achieved by using drifts of colour rather than dots, merging or blending one drift into another. Restricting your choice to one specific colour can create an interesting effect, but a border of, for example, only pale blues or pale yellows can look a little wishy-washy, and expanses of these colours should only be used in moderation.

Soft green foliage can provide an effective link in borders and beds filled with pastel colours, whereas dark green, at least in any great quantity, can be too stark. Silver can look stunning when mixed with pinks and pale blue, and, perhaps surprisingly, it can also be extremely effective with pale and greeny yellows. Blue foliage, which can be found in some grasses and hostas, can also be useful in linking or separating blocks of colour.

Many of the pale colours, especially white and blue, stand out well at twilight, and perennials in these colours are particularly useful to plant near an area where you eat in the evening. As the light fades, they will shine out and be seen in ghostly outline, even after it has become quite dark.

Soft, cool colours make objects seem further away, just as, on a misty day, the horizon always seems more distant than it does on a bright day. Designers and gardeners often use this principle in order to make a border seem

Above: Allium christophii *and* Linaria purpurea *'Canon Went' provide a good combination of colours and shapes.*

longer than it actually is, and placing pale colours at the far end of a border creates a surprising optical illusion.

Above: *Using soft yellows and whites together creates a more striking, even starker, contrast than the combination of other pastel shades.*

Right: *Cream, soft mauve and softly variegated foliage blend to create a soothing effect.*

PERENNIALS WITH PALE FLOWERS

BLUE–MAUVE FLOWERS

Aconitum (monkshood; this plant is poisonous)
Agapanthus (African lily)
Ajuga reptans (common bugle)
Anchusa azurea
Aquilegia flabellata
Aster (Michaelmas daisy)
Baptisia australis (blue false indigo)
Brunnera macrophylla, syn. *Anchusa myosotidiflora*
Campanula (bellflower)
Catananche caerulea
Delphinium
Echinops ritro
Eryngium (sea holly)
Galega officinalis (goat's rue)
Gentiana (gentian)
Geranium (cranesbill)
Hosta
Iris
Linum narbonense (flax)
Meconopsis (blue poppy)
Myosotis (forget-me-not)
Nepeta (catmint)
Omphalodes (navelwort)
Penstemon heterophyllus
Perovskia atriplicifolia
Platycodon grandiflorus (balloon flower)
Polemonium caeruleum
Primula
Pulmonaria (lungwort)
Salvia (sage)
Scabiosa caucasica
Tradescantia × *andersoniana*
Verbena rigida
Veronica (speedwell)

YELLOW FLOWERS

Achillea 'Moonlight'
Anthemis tinctoria 'Sauce Hollandaise'
Asphodeline lutea (syn. *Asphodelus luteus*)
Cephalaria gigantea
Coreopsis verticillata 'Moonbeam'
Digitalis lutea (straw foxglove)
Erysimum suffrutescens
Helenium (sneezeweed)
Helianthus (sunflower)
Heliopsis (ox eye)
Hemerocallis (daylily)
Hieracium (hawkweed)
Iris pseudacorus (yellow flag)
Kniphofia 'Little Maid'
Oenothera stricta 'Sulphurea'
Paeonia mlokosewitschii
Potentilla recta
Primula
Ranunculus (buttercup, crowfoot)
× *Solidaster luteus*
Thalictrum flavum glaucum
Trollius × *cultorum* 'Alabaster'

PINK FLOWERS

Anemone × *hybrida* (Japanese anemone)
Armeria (thrift, sea pink)
Aster (Michaelmas daisy)
Astilbe
Bergenia cordifolia
Dianthus (carnations, pinks)
Diascia
Dicentra
Erigeron 'Charity'
Filipendula (meadowsweet)
Geranium (cranesbill)
Lamium maculatum 'Roseum'
Linaria purpurea 'Canon Went'
Lychnis flos-jovis
Malva moschata (musk mallow)
Monarda 'Croftway Pink'
Penstemon 'Hidcote Pink'
Persicaria (knotweed)
Phlox paniculata (perennial phlox)
Phuopsis stylosa
Primula
Sedum (stonecrop)
Sidalcea (prairie mallow)

Above: *Pink is a very good colour to use in pastel schemes. These pinks (Dianthus) are a particularly good choice because they often have a soft, romantic perfume as well.*

Above: *Mauves and silvers in the foreground combine with other soft colours to create a tranquil cottage garden.*

White and Cream Perennials

White is a symbolic colour, and, since the earliest days of gardening, white flowers have had a special significance. Many gardeners are sufficiently under its spell to devote whole borders to the colour. White imparts a sense of purity and tranquillity, and these are two of the qualities that flowers of this colour will bring to a garden. There is something serene about an area of white flowers that is difficult to capture in any other way. It is a good idea to place a seat in an area devoted to white flowers, because it is the perfect place in which to relax.

THE WHITE GARDEN

In has become fashionable to devote whole borders, even whole gardens, to white flowers. Although they are usually referred to as white gardens, there are usually at least two colours present, because most white-flowered plants have green leaves. A third colour, in the form of grey or silver foliage, is also often added.

It is not as easy as it may seem to create a white garden, because there are, perhaps surprisingly, many different shades of white, and they do not always mix sympathetically. On the whole, it is better to stick to pure whites, since the creamier ones tend to "muddy" the picture. Creams are soothing in themselves, and, with care, a border can be created from them, as an alternative to pure white. Many white and cream flowers, particularly members of the daisy family, have bright yellow centres, and it is best to avoid these if you are planning a white border. They do, however, mix better with cream flowers.

White and cream go well with most other colours, and they can be used to lighten a colour scheme. When used with hot oranges and reds, pure white can create a dramatic effect, whereas creams add a slightly mellower feel. White and blue is always a popular combination, and it can be particularly effective to combine different shades of white and cream with a mixture of pastel colours. White is visible until well after dark, and so it is a good colour to plant where you eat evening meals.

Above: *Planting* Arabis alpina caucasica *'Flore Pleno' against the dark purple-brown foliage of* Euphorbia dulcis *'Chameleon' accentuates the whiteness of the flowers.*

Left: Tanacetum parthenium *with* Galega × hartlandii *'Alba'. The yellow centres of the tanacetum flowers soften the stark effect of having so many white-flowered perennials together.*

WHITE AND CREAM PERENNIALS

Achillea ptarmica 'The Pearl'
Aconitum napellus vulgare
 'Albidum' (poisonous)
Agapanthus campanulatus
 albidus
Anaphalis margaritacea
Anemone × hybrida
 'Honorine Jobert';
 A. nemorosa (wood anemone)
Anthemis punctata cupaniana
Anthericum liliago
 (St Bernard's lily)
Aquilegia vulgaris 'Nivea'
Arabis (rock cress)
Argyranthemum frutescens
 (marguerite)
Artemisia lactiflora (white
 mugwort)
Aruncus dioicus (goat's
 beard)
Aster novae-angliae
 'Herbstschnee'
Astilbe × arendsii 'Irrlicht'
Bellis (daisy)
Bergenia 'Silberlicht'
Campanula latiloba 'Alba'
Centranthus ruber 'Albus'
Cerastium tomentosum
 (snow-in-summer)
Cimicifuga cordifolia;
 C. simplex
Convallaria majalis
 (lily-of-the-valley)
Crambe cordifolia
Dianthus 'Haytor White';
 D. 'Mrs Sinkins'
Dicentra spectabilis 'Alba'
Dictamnus albus
Echinops sphaerocephalus
Epilobium angustifolium
 album
Eryngium eburneum
Galium odoratum, syn.
 Asperula odorata (woodruff)
Geranium phaeum 'Album';
 G. sanguineum 'Album'
Gypsophila paniculata
 'Bristol Fairy'
Hosta

Houttuynia cordata
Iberis sempervirens
Iris
Lamium maculatum
 'White Nancy'
Leucanthemum × superbum
 'Everest'
Lilium (lily)
Lupinus (lupin)
Lychnis coronaria 'Alba'
Lysimachia clethroides
 (gooseneck loosestrife);
 L. ephemerum
Malva moschata alba
 (white musk mallow)
Myrrhis odorata (sweet cicely)
Osteospermum ecklonis
Paeonia (peony)
Papaver orientale
 'Perry's White'
Penstemon serrulatus 'Albus';
 P. 'White Bedder'
Phlox paniculata 'Fujiyama'
Physostegia virginiana 'Alba'
Polygonatum × hybridum
 (syn. *P. multiflorum*)
Pulmonaria officinalis
 'Sissinghurst White'
Ranunculus aconitifolius
 (bachelor's buttons)
Rodgersia
Romneya coulteri
 (Californian poppy)
Sanguinaria canadensis
 (bloodroot)
Silene uniflora, syn.
 S. maritima (sea campion)
Smilacina racemosa (false
 spikenard); *S. stellata*
 (star flower)
Thalictrum (meadow rue)
Trillium grandiflorum
 (wake robin)
Verbascum chaixii 'Album'
Veronica gentianoides 'Alba'
Viola cornuta Alba Group;
 V. odorata 'Alba'
Zantedeschia aethiopica
 (arum lily)

Above: *The flowers of* Crambe cordifolia *create a white haze, a quite different effect from that produced by plants with more "solid" flowers.*

Above: *The clusters of small flowers of* Eupatorium album *'Braunlaub' produce a foam-like effect, rather like waves breaking on a seashore.*

PERENNIALS THROUGH THE YEAR

Spring

Although the working year in the garden begins in winter, it is spring that heralds the start of the new flowering season. Because most perennials are herbaceous, they have spent time below ground and now emerge as clumps of new foliage. Some plants, however, will have been around all winter. The lungworts (*Pulmonaria*), for example, have been in leaf constantly and now produce masses of blue, red, pink or white flowers. The hellebores are in full swing, as are the primulas, of which the humble primrose (*Primula vulgaris*) is still one of the best loved.

SPRING COLOURS

As the days begin to lengthen and the air and ground become warmer, the early-comers, such as hellebores, winter aconites and primulas, move into the background as other plants begin to emerge. Indeed, it is a good idea to grow the early plants towards the back of the bed or border so that they show up in early spring, when they are in flower, but then disappear behind later-flowering plants for the rest of the year. Among the next phase of plants are the bleeding hearts (*Dicentra spectabilis*) and other dicentras, which need light shade and will grow happily under trees that have yet to open their leaves. Wood anemones (*Anemone nemorosa*), which are available in a range of white and delicate blues, pinks and yellows, also make use of the temporary light under deciduous trees and shrubs.

At this time of year everything feels fresh. The soil is often still damp, and the foliage and flowers are brightly coloured. One of the most ubiquitous colours of spring is sunny yellow. Apart from bulbs such as crocuses and daffodils, many perennials put in an appearance, including leopard's bane (*Doronicum*), with its brilliant golden daisies, and kingcups (*Caltha*), which are a must for any bog or waterside planting. *Paeonia mlokosewitschii*, one of the earliest peonies to flower, has delicate yellow flowers (which are followed in autumn by scarlet and black seeds). This

Left: *The bright yellow flowers of* Anemone ranunculoides *'Pleniflora' can be used to illuminate a shady spot.*

Above: Euphorbia polychroma *creates a perfect dome, which is effective in any spring border.*

yellow is intensified in association with the acid green of *Euphorbia polychroma*, which forms beautiful mounds.

LATE SPRING FLOURISHES

As spring passes, the number of plants in leaf and flower increases, until, just on the juncture with early summer, the garden almost seems over-burdened and it is difficult to keep pace with the newcomers. At this time of year, the foliage also still looks crisp and lush, before the strong sun drains away its colour and freshness.

Many gardeners like to plant in spring, but it is important not to get too carried away and to plant only those plants that are in flower or of interest at the time. Remember to include some that will provide something to look at later in the year.

Above: *Primroses are ideal for a cottage garden.*

Below: *The purple foliage and blue flowers of* Veronica peduncularis *'Georgia Blue' form spectacular spring carpets.*

SPRING-FLOWERING PERENNIALS

Ajuga reptans
 (common bugle)
Anemone blanda;
 A. nemorosa (wood anemone)
Arabis (rock cress)
Bergenia (elephant's ears)
Cardamine (bitter cress)
Dicentra
Doronicum (leopard's bane)
Erythronium
 (dog's-tooth violet)
Euphorbia polychroma
Helleborus (hellebore)
Lamium maculatum; *L. orvala*

Meconopsis cambrica
 (Welsh poppy)
Myosotis (forget-me-not)
Primula
Pulmonaria (lungwort)
Pulsatilla
 (pasqueflower)
Ranunculus ficaria
 (lesser celandine)
Symphytum (comfrey)
Trillium (wood lily)
Veronica peduncularis
 'Georgia Blue'
Viola

Right: *The delicate flowers of dicentras bring freshness to a spring border. Here, they are planted with forget-me-nots.*

Summer

Summer always seems to arrive unannounced. One minute it is spring, the next it is summer, and the borders are bursting with life. Summer is the height of the perennial year. It is a season of colour and scents, humming bees and fluttering butterflies. It is also a time when gardeners should be able to relax and enjoy the fruits of their labours.

THE STAGES OF SUMMER
Although this season is usually regarded simply as "summer", in gardening terms there is quite a difference between early summer, midsummer and late summer. Early summer carries on where spring left off, with plenty of fresh-looking foliage and bright colours. Lupins, poppies, peonies and delphiniums add to the delights and are vital parts of any display at this time of year.

As midsummer approaches, the colours change subtly and flowers with more muted tones unfurl, including *Catananche* (sometimes known as cupid's dart), penstemons, baby's breath (*Gypsophila*) and phlox.

By late summer the colours are fading and the foliage is starting to look a little tired. The colours begin to swing towards the autumnal ones of deep golds and russet reds, as perennials such as achilleas, heleniums and inulas come into their own.

There are perennials with flowers in all colours throughout the summer, and so you can control the appearance of the borders by choosing whatever colours you need. Some plants flower throughout the season – various hardy geraniums, for example, will supply colour for months on end, and a number of red-hot pokers (*Kniphofia*) can supply displays of red and orange spikes throughout the entire summer and well into the autumn.

BED AND BORDER CARE
As the display changes, it is important that the beds and borders are kept tidy and well-maintained, so that dead and dying material does not mar the appearance of what is currently in flower. The flowers of each plant should be dead-headed as soon as they go over. This not only removes an eyesore, but also prevents the plant's energy from being spent on seed production. Instead, the energy is channelled back into the plant, which may then produce a second, later crop of flowers.

Some plants benefit from being cut right back to the ground, which encourages a flush of new leaves, so they can then act as foliage plants. Lady's mantle (*Alchemilla mollis*), for example, not only looks tired and tatty if it is left, but it also seeds itself everywhere. If it is sheared back to its base after flowering, however, it will produce a set of beautiful new foliage and self-sowing will have been prevented.

Although constant attention to the borders is needed to keep them looking their best, there is little point in producing a magnificent garden if you do not allow yourself any time to relax in it and admire the results of all your labours. Make a point of strolling around your garden, perhaps in company, or, better still, sit back and simply admire what you have achieved. Your garden will more than repay the effort you have put into it.

Left: *This cottage garden, shown in early summer, is full of freshness and vitality, as the borders begin to fill out with lush vegetation and flowers.*

SUMMER-FLOWERING PERENNIALS

Acanthus (bear's breeches)
Achillea (yarrow)
Aconitum (monkshood; this plant is poisonous)
Alchemilla (lady's mantle)
Aster amellus; A. × frikartii
Astilbe
Baptisia (false indigo)
Campanula (bellflower)
Catananche (cupid's dart, blue cupidone)
Centaurea (knapweed)
Dianthus (carnations, pinks)
Digitalis (foxglove; this plant is poisonous)
Echinops (globe thistle)
Erigeron (fleabane)
Eryngium (sea holly)
Euphorbia (spurge, milkweed)
Geranium (cranesbill)
Gypsophila (baby's breath)
Helenium (sneezeweed)

Hemerocallis (daylily)
Heuchera (coral bells)
Hosta
Inula
Iris
Kniphofia (red-hot poker)
Leucanthemum
Ligularia (leopard plant)
Lilium (lily)
Lupinus (lupin)
Macleaya (plume poppy)
Monarda (bergamot)
Paeonia (peony)
Papaver (poppy)
Penstemon
Phlox
Rodgersia
Scabiosa (scabious, pincushion flower)
Stachys
Veronica (speedwell)
Viola

Above: *The hardy geraniums are one of the mainstays of the summer border. There is a vast range from which to choose.*

Above: *The achilleas with their flat heads bring an air of calm as well as a splash of bright colour to the summer border.*

Above: *Perennial varieties of wallflower (*Erysimum*) make colourful subjects for the early summer border, but, unfortunately, they are not perfumed like the ones treated as annual bedding plants.*

Above: *This summer border, with its delightful combination of fresh yellows and greens and the addition of some bright red highlights, has been beautifully planted.*

Autumn

Apart from looking at the calendar, it is not always possible to say when autumn starts in the garden. High summer usually slips quietly into autumn and there is little apparent change, but, as winter approaches, the differences become much more noticeable.

AUTUMN HUES

Autumn can be a beautiful month in the garden. The colours may be becoming more muted, but there are still plenty of bright tones left. Many plants run on into the autumn from earlier seasons – the penstemons and Japanese anemones (*Anemone* × *hybrida*), for example – but true autumn has its own distinctive flora. The Michaelmas daisies (*Aster*) are one of the mainstays of the autumn garden, as are the chrysanthemums, while ice plants and stonecrops (*Sedum*) are invaluable for attracting the last of the butterflies and bees.

Yellows and oranges are quite common at this time of year, with the coneflowers (*Rudbeckia*) and sunflowers (*Helianthus*) in flower, but there are also deep purple ironweeds (*Vernonia*) and Michaelmas daisies to add variety.

Lilyturf (*Liriope*), with its blue spikes of berry-like flowers, is a good autumn plant. It is useful because it is one of the few autumn-flowering plants that will grow in shade. The toad lily (*Tricyrtis*) and kirengeshoma, which bloom in late summer and early autumn, are also well worth growing. Many grasses are at their best in autumn, especially the large, statuesque pampas grasses (*Cortaderia*) and miscanthus.

AUTUMN MAINTENANCE

It is important to keep on top of maintenance at this time of year. A general lassitude often seems to set in and maintenance tasks are left to the winter. Unfortunately, the dead material often masks plants that are still flowering, so if dead and dying plants are cleared away regularly, the autumn border will look all the better. A few dead stems add to the beauty of the autumn and winter border, however, and the dead stems and seedheads of the sea hollies (*Eryngium*), in particular, are well worth leaving.

If you are planning a major replanting of a border, it is often worth sacrificing a couple of weeks' flowering, so that you can start work on the border in the autumn. This will give the ground an opportunity to weather and any remaining weeds that reappear can be dealt with before planting begins in spring.

Above: *Autumn is a time of rich golds, as this* Rudbeckia fulgida deamii *shows. Its appearance is a reminder that the gardening year is coming to an end.*

Left: *Many of the autumn-flowering sedums are doubly valuable, working well as foliage plants in the summer, before their softly textured flowers emerge in autumn.*

Above: *Autumn-flowering sedums are excellent for attracting late flying butterflies and bees as well as providing colour for the border.*

Above: *There are a number of autumn bulbs that are usually regarded as perennials. This beautiful, but nearly upronounceable,* Schizostylus coccinea *is one of them.*

Right: *Asters are one of the mainstays of autumn. However, some, such as this* Aster × frikartii 'Mönch', *flower over a very long period, from midsummer right through to late autumn.*

AUTUMN-FLOWERING PERENNIALS

Anemone × *hybrida*
 (Japanese anemone)
Aster (Michaelmas daisy)
Boltonia
Chelone (turtle head)
Chrysanthemum
Cimicifuga (bugbane)
Helianthus (sunflower)
Kirengeshoma
 palmata
Liriope (lilyturf)

Leucanthemella serotina
Nerine (this is a bulb)
Ophiopogon
Rudbeckia (coneflower)
Schizostylis coccinea
 (Kaffir lily; this is a bulb)
Sedum (stonecrop); *S. spectabile*
 (ice-plant)
Solidago (golden rod)
Tricyrtis (toad lily)
Vernonia (ironweed)

Winter

Many gardeners like to hibernate in the winter, not poking their noses out into the garden until the worst of the weather is over. This is a mistake. Not only is there plenty to see and enjoy in the garden at this time of year, but an hour's work done now is worth several later on.

A WINTER GARDEN

Several plants flower in the winter, including a number of perennials. Although it might not be a good idea to fill busy summer borders with them, they can still be grown at the back of the bed where they will emerge later, while remaining hidden during the summer. If you have the space, it is a good idea to create a "winter garden" where you can enjoy these plants in an area specially devoted to them.

If you can, plant beneath deciduous trees and shrubs, where there is plenty of light during the perennials' growing season, but where they will be out of sight for the rest of the year. Even under-planting a single bush will create a small winter garden.

WINTER PERENNIALS

Hellebores (*Helleborus*) are one of the mainstays of the perennial scene in winter. Perhaps they would not be so important if they flowered later in the year, but their flowers are most welcome during the winter months. They are available in a wide range of colours, and there are also an increasing number of double varieties. *Helleborus purpurascens* is the earliest to flower, usually appearing before midwinter, but the so-called Christmas rose (*H. niger*) usually flowers later than this.

One doesn't normally expect irises to be in flower in winter, but the Algerian iris (*Iris unguicularis*) starts flowering in late autumn and goes on until early spring, taking little notice of the weather. Its mauve or purple flowers are deliciously scented. It also grows best in

Above: *Many perennials, such as this houseleek* (Sempervivum) *growing on the roof of a porch, are evergreen, which makes them very useful for providing winter decoration and interest.*

Above: *Winter aconites* (Eranthis hyemalis) *are true harbingers of spring. Once they have pushed up through the ground, sometimes even in the snow, you know that winter is almost over.*

poor soil and is a particularly good plant to grow in rocky soil near the house. It is, however, irresistible to slugs, and these should be kept at bay if you want flowers. It is the only winter plant that needs an open position.

The lungworts (*Pulmonaria*) are really spring flowers, but in most years they will flower in winter as well, sometimes in early winter. Primroses (*Primula vulgaris*) often flower sporadically at this time of year, too, and sweet violets (*Viola odorata*) will flower in warm spots, often providing an indoor display for early winter.

WINTER-FLOWERING PERENNIALS

Anemone nemorosa
(wood anemone)
Eranthis hyemalis
(winter aconite)
Euphorbia rigida
Helleborus niger
(Christmas rose);
H. orientalis (Lenten rose);
H. purpurascens
Iris unguicularis
(Algerian iris)
Primula vulgaris
(primrose)
Pulmonaria rubra
(lungwort)
Viola odorata (sweet violet)

Above right: *Wood anemones* (Anemone nemorosa*) come through the soil before anything else is stirring, and briefly clothe the ground with leaves and flowers.*

Right: *Many varieties of hellebores and pulmonarias start to flower very early in the year, often before midwinter.*

BULBS

Mention the word bulbs, and most people think of
spring flowering plants, yet bulbs can provide
wonderful flowers for every season of the year.
As soon as midwinter has passed, *Eranthis hyemalis*
(winter aconite) begins to thrust up its first shoots.
Early spring welcomes daffodils, hyacinths and
tulips. More irises follow in early summer, then
it is time for gladioli, begonias and lilies.
Finally, there are delicate flowers that appear in
autumn, such as cyclamen and autumn crocuses.
The choice of bulbs is huge and varied and although
most prefer a sunny position and well-drained soil,
others do prefer a shadier home. Once established,
many bulbs will largely take care of themselves,
particularly if naturalized, reappearing with
welcome regularity each year.

Left: *Drifts of daffodils, naturalized under trees, produce a
brilliant display in the spring.*

BULBS

What is a Bulb?

Many of the bulbs mentioned in this book are not true bulbs at all. Plants that grow from corms, tubers, and rhizomes are also included because they are often collectively referred to as bulbs. You can buy the plants mentioned from bulb merchants or bulb specialists, although a few are also sold as growing plants or in pots.

BULBS
Bulbs are dormant storage organs, most of which can be lifted from the ground and sold dry, although a few, such as snowdrops, transplant best if lifted in the green, i.e. still with leaves. A few of the plants included, such as agapanthus, which have fleshy roots, and *Hemerocallis* (day lilies), with their rhizomatous roots, are often thought of as ordinary herbaceous plants and are usually bought pot-grown. As they qualify on technical grounds, however, we have included them here.

BOTANICAL CHARACTERISTICS
A true bulb is formed from swollen leaves and resembles an onion, with distinct layers or scales clearly visible if it is cut in half. Usually these are encased in an outer papery skin, but in lilies the individual scales may be separate and more clearly exposed.

A corm is formed from the swollen base of the stem, and is replaced by a new one each year. It is similar in shape to a true bulb, normally with a symmetrical outline, but the flesh is solid when cut and not composed of scales.

Tubers are swollen roots, and are usually more irregular in shape than corms, with more than one "eye" or growth bud (these are not always clearly visible). They also lack the distinctive layers or scales that are so visible in bulbs.

Rhizomes are swollen horizontal stems that grow below or just above the surface of the soil. Roots grow from the bottom of the rhizome, with leaves from the side or top.

WAYS WITH BULBS
Many spring bulbs are at their best when naturalized in grass or under trees, where they will multiply to create large drifts of colour. Daffodils, crocuses, snowdrops and snake's-head fritillaries are ideal for this, and woodland areas carpeted with bluebells are an unforgettable sight. Spring bulbs can also be used in bedding schemes, tulips being especially popular in this setting, and many also work well in herbaceous or mixed borders. They are also excellent in window boxes and other containers, particularly when added to a winter arrangement of heather, ornamental cabbage, ivy or capsicum – the bulbs will then make a welcome appearance just when you may have forgotten they were there.

An anemone tuber.

A galtonia bulb.

A gladiolus corm.

Most of the summer bulbs combine well with other plants in herbaceous or mixed borders. Those that are hardy enough to be left to grow and multiply will often make large and imposing clumps. Crocosmias, for example, make large clumps of glowing orange or red flowers that can become a strong focal point. Others, such as agapanthus, cannas, lilies and alliums, are big enough to create a dramatic impact as single plants or small groups. Some summer and autumn bulbs are at home in the rock garden, or in containers, and lilies are ideal for the edge of a woodland area or planted among shrubs. A few summer bulbs, such as dahlias, can even be used to create a bold, brash effect when a whole border is planted with them.

A TOUCH OF THE TROPICAL

Cannas, with their tall spikes of orange, red, pink or yellow flowers, are often used for sub-tropical bedding in public parks, but they will add a touch of the exotic planted towards the back of a herbaceous border. You could also try planting a drift of caladiums (*Caladium bicolor* hybrids) with their almost paper-thin, heart-shaped leaves variegated pink, red, green and white.

One of the most exotic plants that you can grow is the climbing lily (*Gloriosa superba*). It has strongly reflexed petals that combine yellow and red in a way that resembles a glorious dancing flame.

CUTTING FOR THE HOME

Bulbs provide some outstanding cut flowers. There is a large cut-flower trade in gladioli, for example, which in many ways are more successful cut and used in arrangements than in herbaceous and mixed borders. Dutch irises are also more often seen as cut flowers than as garden plants, even though they make a pleasing – albeit brief – display in the garden.

Right: *The large bright dahlias are popular cut flowers, widely used in floral art. They also make pleasing plants for a border.*

Below: *Crocosmias are ideal plants for herbaceous borders, making large clumps that shout their presence when in bloom.*

The World of Bulbs

These packages of pent-up beauty waiting to be released that we call bulbs show immense diversity, and are suitable for many different climates and soil types. Some like to be baked in hot sun, others need moist soil or woodland shade. Although they are grown commercially on a large scale in relatively few countries, such as Holland, the USA and South Africa, they are native to many different parts of the world. Most bulbs are fortunately frost-hardy, but some of the summer-flowering ones are tender and should be given winter protection.

CONDITIONS

Understanding the conditions that bulbs require is important to a successful display. Spring and Autumn bulbs are generally hardy and tolerant of a wide range of conditions. The summer-flowering bulbs, however, are often more temperamental and demand a more in-depth knowledge of their requirements. Many of them grow naturally in South Africa, tigridias and *Polianthes tuberosa* come from Mexico among other places, caladiums from tropical South America, and gloriosas from Africa. These are very diverse climates, and temperatures, soils, rainfall and humidity may be vastly different to what they will receive in your garden.

In relatively warm climates such as California, the majority of bulbs mentioned in this book can be grown outdoors all the year round, but in cooler climates some will require lifting for winter protection. A few are best grown permanently in pots in a greenhouse or conservatory, though they can also be used as short-term house plants.

SIGNS OF GOOD BREEDING

Breeders have changed many popular bulbs to pinnacles of perfection far removed from the species from which they derive. Nowadays, we do not grow in our gardens true species of dahlias, for example, but use instead the hybrids that have been developed by generations of gardeners and breeders. Most of the gladioli that we grow are the result of the hybridist's skills, and although many true species of lilies are grown it is the hybrids that have helped to make them so popular.

There are specialist societies for enthusiasts of plants such as dahlias, gladioli, and lilies. Dahlias are often grown as exhibition blooms, and show classes are held for gladioli and lilies too. New varieties are constantly being developed, as breeders strive to produce ever-more striking and interesting flowers. Indeed, when tulips were first introduced into Europe, certain flowers, particularly the striped and unusually shaped ones (now known to have been caused by a virus), were so prized that whole fortunes were made and lost through the breeding and sale of the bulbs.

Above: Erythronium dens-canis *in grass.*

Above: *The pretty star-shaped flowers belong to the* Anemone nemorosa.

Left: *Lilies are extensively hybridized, producing a wonderful array of beautiful blooms from which to choose. This one is 'Cover Girl'.*

Below: Tulipa *'Golden Melody' in a formal border with* Bellis perennis.

Above: *Tulip breeders have tried for years to produce a truly blue flower, and this one is, perhaps optimistically, known as 'Blue Parrot'.*

The International Bulb Trade

Holland is the centre of an international trade for spring-flowering bulbs. It has the ideal soil and climate, and the Dutch growers have tremendous expertise in the propagation and production of bulbs. Around the world there are other centres of excellence for specific bulbs – the USA is famous for its lily production – while a small number of bulbs are grown in other countries, such as the UK.

CULTIVATED OR WILD?

Today, most bulbs are propagated and grown in nurseries, and are then exported for sale around the world. Some, however, are collected from the wild, especially plants such as *Cyclamen coum*. Cheap labour in the countries where such wild plants are plentiful makes it economic to pay the transport costs, while giving native workers an income. But collecting from the wild also depletes scarce wild stocks and will eventually endanger the bulbs.

International concern over this wild bulb trade has put pressure on the bulb importers to select only cultivated stock, and many reputable bulb merchants now make a point of labelling relevant bulbs 'from cultivated stock'. If you see this tag, you can confidently buy, knowing that wild plants are not being depleted.

In some areas where collection from the wild used to be practised, the bulb collectors are being retrained to propagate and cultivate the plants so that they still have an income – but one that will not eventually result in the extinction of wild plants.

A WIDE RANGE OF BULBS

The vast majority of bulbs are bred, propagated and distributed by specialist growers, particularly in Holland. They are sometimes sold direct, but usually are distributed world-wide through bulb merchants who distribute in individual countries. Although some popular varieties may be available in many different countries, the number of varieties is so great that not all are universally available, and each year a few are dropped to make way for new ones. If a particular variety mentioned in this book is unavailable, you will almost always be able to buy a very similar one.

The varieties mentioned are just examples of the enormous range that is currently available. A single supplier may offer over 100 different daffodils and 50 crocuses, for example, and specialist growers might offer a dozen varieties of the common snowdrop (*Galanthus nivalis*), and many more hybrids. Some of the variations are minor, however, and the popular, widely available names are most likely to be the best for general garden use.

Above: *A display like this, with a mix of tulips and forget-me-nots, is as colourful as any summer bedding, but do plant closely for maximum impact.*

Left: *The Lisse area of Holland is where many of the Dutch bulbs are grown, and in spring the flowers stretch for almost as far as the eye can see. Although some are allowed to flower, the blooms are sometimes removed to divert all the plant's energy into producing much bigger bulbs.*

Left: *Hardy cyclamen such as this* Cyclamen coum *is one type of bulb that used to be widely collected from the wild, but nowadays this is discouraged. Reputable bulb merchants only sell cultivated stock.*

BULBS THROUGH THE SEASONS

Winter

Winter is usually a bleak time in the garden. The ground may be frozen, branches are bare of leaves, and there is very little colour to be seen. Amid this scene, the appearance of the earliest bulbs – snowdrops, crocuses, scilla – is always a delight, bringing colour and new life to the garden and reminding us that spring is only just around the corner.

WINTER-FLOWERING BULBS

Despite their dainty appearance, winter-flowering bulbs are hardy survivors. They do not waste energy growing to great heights, but keep their heads down out of cold winter winds; most do not grow above 10 cm (4 in).

One of the most popular plants to provide a colourful start to the year is the crocus. *Crocus chrysanthus*, one of the first to flower, has blooms in shades of yellow, cream, blue and purple, as well as white. Many have outer petals striped or flushed in a contrasting colour. Just slightly taller, and another very early flowerer, *C. tommasinianus*, a frail-looking, silvery-lilac crocus, is amazingly tough. Like so many other late winter bulbs, the crocus is excellent for naturalizing in short grass, and looks best in large groups.

Nobody could think of winter flowers without thinking of snowdrops (*Galanthus nivalis*). Despite their small stature, these early blooming bulbs make a big impact, and tiny groups of these delicate-looking plants can look stunning. They are also the natural partner for many other bulbs that make a winter appearance: try grouping them with *Cyclamen coum* for a dainty display. Although the flowers of the *C. coum* resemble the tender florist's cyclamen in shape, these tiny flowers are totally hardy and will make their appearance from late winter (sometimes before) to early spring. The flowers appear before the leaves, in various shades of lilac and purple-blue. There is also a white.

Another excellent partner for the cyclamen is *Scilla mischtschenkoana*. This delicate looking plant, with its open blue flowers, is an ideal bulb for the rock garden, but also grows well in partial shade around trees and shrubs.

Two further plants make a welcome winter appearance. The bright yellow *Eranthis hyemalis* (winter aconite), which enjoys a damp border, is a natural partner for two dwarf irises – *Iris danfordiae* and *Iris histrioides* – which often start to flower in late winter. *Iris danfordiae* is the brightest of the two, the vivid yellow signalling its presence across the garden. Because of its small size, the delightful scent is more likely to be appreciated when the plants are grown in pots to flower indoors. *Iris histrioides* 'Major' is the most commonly grown. It has delightful purple flowers with distinctive yellow and white markings.

Finally, bringing some golden cheer to the frosty garden, the first daffodils appear. *Narcissus* 'January Gold' is just that – golden yellow cups which will brighten even the dreariest January day. Finally, when the season changes to early spring, the garden will be full of bright yellow daffodils, sweetly scented hyacinths, and colourful, vibrant early tulips.

Above: *A carpet of blue scillas makes a stunning effect in late winter and early spring when combined with the subtle colours of hellebores.*

Above: *Winter aconite* (Eranthis hyemalis*) gives a welcome splash of yellow in late winter.*

Above: *When the flowers of* Crocus tommasinianus *open in the morning sunshine, they reveal gorgeous orange stamens in the centre. The contrast is brilliant and certainly worth repeating in containers as well as garden borders.*

Above: *Snowdrops (*Galanthus*) multiply quickly where they are growing in damp woodland and will eventually spread to carpet vast areas. Plant them under shrubs and enjoy a similar, if scaled-down, effect.*

Right: *The common snowdrop* (Galanthus nivalis) *is the most common of all the snowdrop species grown in gardens. It is found widely throughout Europe, from Spain to western Russia. It occurs naturally both with single and double flowers, all with a sweet honey scent.*

Below: *The various shades of pink* Cyclamen coum *make an exquisite combination with bright yellow and deep purple crocuses, the whole enhanced by the silver marking on the cyclamen foliage.*

Above: Galanthus *'Magnet' has taller, larger flowers than* Galanthus nivalis *(common snowdrop). Here, it forms a marvellous carpet beneath the witch hazel* Hamamelis × intermedia *'Pallida'*.

Above: *The leaves of* Cyclamen coum *are variably patterned with intricate silver veining or blotches. These create the perfect background for the tiny flowers, which appear in many appealing shades of light and dark pink.*

Above: *A striking contrast of colours occurs with this planting of* Galanthus elwesii *against the dark foliage of* Ophiopogon planiscapus *'Nigrescens'*.

Above: Galanthus *'Sam Arnott'* has droplet-like white flowers. It looks especially delicate in association with the lime-green flowers of the hellebore, Helleborus orientalis.

Early Spring

With the winter weather over, the ground begins to warm up, and there is the sweet smell of spring in the air. Flowers appear all over the garden – drifts of daffodils filling whole beds and surrounding trees, dainty plantings of spring snowflakes, and eye-catching groups of tulips and forget-me-nots. With this burst of new colour, the garden starts to really come alive.

SPRING-FLOWERING BULBS
One of the bulbs considered synonymous with spring is the daffodil, of which one of the most widely planted species is *Narcissus cyclamineus*. Plant in drifts in moist ground in partial shade, where it can be left undisturbed to bring charm and delight to the garden in late winter and early spring. The hybrids such as *N.* 'February Gold' and *N.* 'Peeping Tom' are among the earliest to flower (sometimes in late winter), but others bloom in early or mid-spring.

There is a wide range of different flower forms and colours from white to orange, including two-coloured varieties. The popular 'Cheerfulness' has small very fragrant cream-coloured double flowers. It is often forced for early indoor flowering, but grows happily outdoors unless winters are severe, though some of the other double varieties, such as 'Soleil d'Or', are more tender and need frost protection. 'Tête-à-tête' is another very popular small variety, with standard yellow daffodil-type flowers, excellent in containers and in borders.

A bed full of early tulips, with their colourful blooms in shades of red, pink, yellow and orange, is a welcome sight in spring. *Tulipa kaufmanniana* varieties have long buds, often cream flushed with pink, that open into stars of oval petals, exposing different colour combinations. They can look like different varieties in bud and flower. Their small stature makes them ideal for the rock garden and formal beds, and they are among the earliest tulips to flower. Other early tulips are the *T. fosteriana* hybrids, which have very large flowers, usually in strikingly bold colours. 'Madame Lefeber', also known as 'Red Emperor', is one of the best early red tulips, sure to give a dazzling display in beds or containers. To complete the picture, interplant them with some *Chionodoxa luciliae* (the delicate blue-and-white blooms look superb with the red-and-pale-pink *T.* 'Heart's Delight') and some *Leucojum vernum*, the spring snowflake, with its white, bell-shaped flowers with green-tipped petals.

Sweetly smelling hyacinths are many people's favourite spring bulbs, and early forced varieties bring a welcome note of spring inside the home. The species *Hyacinthus orientalis* is not normally seen: the highly bred hybrids, sometimes known collectively as Dutch hybrids, are the popular kind. Most are single, but they come in a colour range that includes many shades of blue, pink, purple, mauve, yellow and white. Double varieties have extra petals, but the number varies. Some varieties have just a few extra petals, others have more fully double ones with rosette-like,

Left: Scilla sibirica, *often known as the Siberian squill, is at home in sun or shade but prefers well-drained soils. Here, it makes a charming picture in short grass with wild primroses.* S. sibirica *'Spring Beauty', an improved form, has large, deep blue flowers.*

individual blooms. Doubles are most effective when grown in bowls or raised beds, where the flower formation can be more easily appreciated.

Hyacinths sold as multifloras are ordinary varieties grown by the producers in a way that encourages the production of many stems (albeit with more widely spaced bells) instead of one stout, densely packed stem. Multiflora hyacinths make an impressive display, and some gardeners prefer their looser growth. Try growing hyacinths with *Scilla siberica*. This robust plant is utterly reliable and easy to grow. It self-sows and is ideal for drifts that can be left undisturbed. Blue is the normal colour, with 'Spring Beauty' being a particularly dark blue, but there is also a white form.

One flower that emerged in late winter and is now in full flower is *Anemone blanda*. This little plant has daisy-type flowers usually in blue, though some varieties are white or pink. Mixtures are very popular, but a single-colour planting is usually more striking. This plant prefers partial shade or full sun.

A good self-propagator to consider for the early spring garden is *Corydalis solida*. This charming, neglected, bulbous plant is more at home in a rock garden or at the front of a herbaceous or mixed border rather than part of a bedding display. The long spurred flowers are dull purple in the species, and there are also red and pink varieties. It multiplies freely and naturalizes well in both the sun or in semi-shade. For a glorious display of colour, plant the dull purple species with some Dutch crocuses or some reticulated irises, whose colours of blue, purple and yellow will provide the perfect match.

Above: Chionodoxa luciliae *will naturalize in borders or beneath trees, where it will produce several flower spikes per bulb. Up to three star-shaped, blue flowers, 1–2 cm (½–¼ in) wide, and with white centres, are borne in racemes.*

Above: *The yellow and red flowers of* Tulipa *'Corona' in association with the yellow pansies (*Universal Series*) are uncompromising in their bold brashness.*

Right: *The snowflake (*Leucojum aestivum*) likes damp conditions where it soon multiplies to create a large clump of tall, graceful, white flowers, each petal tipped with a distinctive green blotch.*

Above: Narcissus *'Jumblie' is a dwarf yellow daffodil with narrow golden cups and slightly reflexed petals. The flowers are borne on multiple stems and each stem can bear several miniature flowers which look in different directions, hence their jumbled appearance and name.*

Above: *Siberian squill (Scilla sibirica) grows to 15 cm (6 in) in height and can be used in pots, but it looks best where it has been planted in garden borders and allowed to colonize. Its nodding rich blue flowers look much stronger en masse than as individuals or small groups. The white centre looks lovely with small, grey-leaved plants.*

Left: Narcissus *'Jenny' is growing here through the foliage of* Geranium × oxonianum *'Winscombe'. The pale flowers against the rich greens create a tranquil effect.*

Above: Narcissus *'Quail'*, *a short, multi-headed golden daffodil, may produce two to three scented flowers on each stem. It is a dainty daffodil, ideal for borders or containers.*

Above: *Tulips are suitable for a wide range of planting schemes, including in the rock garden, formal bedding and containers. This one, 'Chopin', with its distinctive markings on both flowers and foliage, makes an elegant cut flower.*

Above: Hyacinthus orientalis *'Pink Pearl' is one of the old favourites, both for its scent and colour. Blues and pinks always look lovely together, and here the combination of H.o. 'Blue Jacket' with the pink hyacinths is particularly charming. A group of just a few of each colour would work just as well as this mass planting.*

Mid- to Late Spring

As spring progresses, the bulb garden is dominated by masses of tulips and daffodils creating a wonderfully colourful display. There can be few sights more cheering and more likely to banish any winter blues.

LATE SPRING BULBS

Many daffodils flower from early through to mid-spring, and the early tulips are now replaced by later ones. Single tulips are the most popular and widely available type, and come in both early and late varieties. They are ideal for beds and borders, and are also perfect as cut flowers for the house.

Double tulips, since they tend not to be so tall, are also suitable for pots, tubs and window boxes, or for bedding in exposed gardens. The amount of doubleness differs among the varieties, but all are generally long-lasting in bloom.

Triumph tulips are mid-season ones that bridge the gap between the early and late singles, and are mainly the result of hybridizing those two types. There is a huge colour range, and many are beautifully marked or shaded. They are ideal for bedding, and make quite superb cut flowers.

Lily-flowered tulips are distinctive and elegant: the reflexed petals are long and pointed, with the buds tapering towards the top. Tall, wiry stems add to the impression of grace and elegance. The open flowers are like large, colourful stars. These dramatic looking flowers are suitable for late spring bedding in sheltered areas and also make excellent cut flowers.

All the tall-growing tulips can sometimes look rather leggy, so experiment by interplanting them with other bulbs or spring bedding plants that will hide their stems. Red or pink tulips look wonderful with bluebells (*Hyacinthoides*), forget-me-nots or *Chionodoxa luciliae*; other colours can be complemented by wallflowers. Try out different combinations until you find the one you like best.

An alternative to hiding the tall stems of tulips is to choose low-

Below: *The brilliant red veining of* Tulipa *'Striped Bellona' is accentuated by combining them with deep rust-red wallflowers.*

growing ones instead. Varieties and hybrids of *T. greigii* are among the best of the low-growing tulips for mid- to late spring. The colour range is brilliant and varied, the centre of the open blooms often presents a striking contrast, and the foliage is beautifully mottled, often with wavy edges. They are suitable for containers and the rock garden as well as formal bedding. A favourite member of this group, 'Red Riding Hood', has scarlet urn-shaped flowers, black at the base of the petals. Another excellent one is 'Plaisir', with pinkish-red flowers edged with pale yellow and with black and yellow bases to the petals.

Bluebells are another very popular spring visitor, although these bulbs are more likely to be welcome in a woodland setting than when they are invading your garden. The English bluebell (*Hyacinthoides non-scripta*) will tolerate full sun, but does best in light shade. Blue is the dominant colour, but there are both pink and white forms. Plant 50–100 bulbs to 1 sq m (1 sq yd) to create a colony for naturalizing, but beware: they are successful self-seeders and will soon spread to take over any available space. The Spanish bluebell (*Hyacinthoides hispanica*) is slightly taller than the English bluebell, and has

wider leaves and stiffer, more upright flower stems. Besides blue, there are pink and white forms. This is an ideal bulb for naturalizing in a shady or partially shady area near trees or shrubs.

Grape hyacinths are great spring favourites and look very effective interplanted with other bulbs or spring bedding plants, or used simply in large drifts for impact. *Muscari armeniacum* is a most amenable bulb that seems ready to make its home anywhere. It thrives in most places and multiplies freely. The flowers are compact and unobtrusive, about 23 cm (9 in) tall and come in various shades

of blue, including a double. A slightly smaller version at 15–20 cm (6–8 in) high, *M. aucheri* has sky-blue flowers at the top of the spike, and navy-blue ones below. It is an easy and reliable plant that makes a good display. Smaller still at 15 cm (6 in) are *M. azureum*, whose flowers are a light, bright blue that shows up well despite the plant's small size, and *M. botryoides*, of which the white variety 'Album' is perhaps more widely grown than the blue species. A more unusual grape hyacinth is *M. comosum* 'Plumosum', which has feathered violet plumes in late spring. It is sometimes called the feather hyacinth or tassel hyacinth

Above: Narcissus *'Pinza'* is a striking daffodil, with its rich yellow petals and deep red cup. It looks even more striking planted against a dark green background or with rich blue grape hyacinths (Muscari).

Right: Narcissus *'Saint Patrick's Day'* is a delicate pale-yellow daffodil with the cups edged in slightly darker yellow. This is a delightful daffodil for borders or grassland.

because of its unusual heads of thread-like flowers, and is sometimes listed under its other varietal name of 'Monstrosum'. A final muscari to consider is *M. latifolium*, which always stands out and demands attention. Slightly larger than the grape hyacinths at 25 cm (10 in) tall, it bears a spike of dramatically blackish-violet urn-shaped flowers, with smaller and paler-coloured flowers at the top of the spike.

Now that the snowdrop has finished flowering, if you want white in your garden consider *Allium neapolitanum*, with its loose heads of star-shaped flowers; *Anemone nemorosa* (wood anemone), which thrives beneath deciduous trees, and whose simple white flowers show up pleasingly against fern-green foliage; or *Leucojum aestivum*, the snowflake, which is an ideal border plant, making a large, bold clump if left undisturbed. It can be naturalized in wild parts of the garden too, and looks particularly pleasing by a pond or at the edge of a stream. *Ornithogalum nutans* and *O. umbellatum* are also perfect for naturalizing around trees and shrubs. Both have white, star-shaped flowers, and the latter is known as star of Bethlehem.

A miniature companion for these white flowers would be the pinkish-purple *Bulbocodium vernum* (just 2.5–5 cm/1–2 in), a charming, unusual plant that almost always attracts attention. The bulb is related to the colchicums, the crocus-like flowers that bloom in the autumn. Its funnel-shaped flowers are almost stemless. Of similar colouring is *Erythronium dens-canis*, the dog's-tooth violet, which is best naturalized in short grass. The bulbs grow best in partial shade and thrive in woodland soil.

Fritillaries make their appearance in mid-spring, and they range from the imposing *F. imperialis* to the diminutive *F. michailovskyi*. *F. imperialis*, the crown imperial, is a most majestic bulb – a clump in a bed or border will stand out across the garden. Orange-red is the dominant colour, although there are varieties with red or yellow flowers, and some have variegated leaves. In contrast to this 1.5 m (5 ft) giant, *F. meleagris* grows to just 25–30 cm (10–12 in). This charming, pink-flowered, dainty plant (also known as the snake's-head fritillary or checkered lily, because of the unusual markings on the petals) is best left undisturbed in short grass, or in clumps in a rock garden. Finally there is *F. michailovskyi* at just 15 cm (6 in). This distinctive and fascinating fritillaria must be viewed at close range to be appreciated. The

Above: *Wood anemone* (Anemone nemorosa*), snake's-head fritillary* (Fritillaria meleagris*) and* Narcissus cyclamineus *are all flourishing in the shade beneath deciduous trees.*

Above: Ornithogalum, *known as star of Bethlehem, bears delicate, star-like flowers which close their petals at night. Note that all parts may causes severe stomach ache if ingested and the sap may irritate the skin.*

purple-brown, nodding, bell-shaped flowers are flushed bright yellow at the ends of the petals. Though sometimes grown as a pot plant in an alpine greenhouse, it can be grown in a rock garden or even at the front of a border.

If you have a taste for the unusual, and a warm, sunny position, then *Hermodactylus tuberosus* might be for you. Sometimes called the widow iris because of its sombre appearance, it has translucent green flowers with an almost black patch on each of the three large outer petals. The flowers grow to a height of 20–40 cm (8–16 in), and have a delightful, delicate fragrance.

If you want to plant some bulbs in shady places in leafy soil, for instance beneath deciduous trees, then trilliums are ideal. *Trillium cuneatum* is the garden plant usually known as *T. sessile*, but the true plant of that name is not as attractive and is seldom cultivated. *T. cuneatum* has dark crimson-maroon flowers, a colour closely reflected in the mottled foliage. Since the rhizomes resent disturbance, allow them to form large clumps if possible. *T. grandiflorum*, the wake robin, has white flowers held well clear of the green leaves. This showy plant is perhaps the easiest trillium to grow. *T. g.* 'Flore Pleno' has double flowers.

Above: Fritillaria michailovskyi *is one of the smallest of the fritillaries at just 15 cm (6 in) tall. Its scale is best appreciated in the rock garden or maybe to the front of the flower border.*

Above: *This grape hyacinth* (Muscari) *is one of the prettiest of all the blue bulbs and looks wonderful as a mass planting beneath roses, with double tulips, or along a path.*

Above: *The woodland is a wonderful picture now that the* Hyacinthoides non-scripta *(English bluebell) is in full flower, looking like a sheet of blue beneath a canoply of leaves. Bluebells look lovely in small areas, too, and any shrubby patch in the garden is suitable. They will also grow beneath fruit trees. Bluebells have a sweet, heady perfume, which can be overpowering on a large scale.*

Above: *Formal patterns with matching colour schemes can look extremely bright and cheerful. The exquisite lily-flowered* Tulipa *'West Point' vies for attention with red and yellow polyanthus, all bordered with the dark blue forget-me-not,* Myosotis sylvatica *'Music'.*

Above: Tulipa *'Christmas Marvel', a Viridiflora hybrid, is especially successful when it is planted in clumps, repeated along a path among herbaceous plants.*

Above: *The blowsy, soft pink* Tulipa *'Hermione' is underplanted to good effect with forget-me-nots (*Myosotis*).*

Above: Fritillaria imperialis, *commonly known as the crown imperial, produces a stout stem topped by impressive umbels of three to six pendent bells, which may be orange, yellow or, more often, red, out of which a crown of glossy, leaf-like bracts emerges. Both the bulbs and flowers have a distinctive foxy smell.*

Above: Tulipa *'Christmas Marvel' can always be relied upon to make a colourful impact in beds and borders.*

Above: *Spring is an explosion of colour in the bulb garden as this border shows. Yellow* Tulipa *'Monte Carlo' and bicoloured* T. *'Tender Beauty' make a dramatic combination.*

Late Spring

As spring moves on towards summer, most of the daffodils and tulips have died down to be replaced by an exciting range of late spring bulbs. Some tulips are still to put on their show, however, and these include the single late varieties, which are tall growing and so excellent for cutting, and the double late varieties, which are often more fully double and taller than the double earlies.

LATE SPRING BULBS

The double late tulips are sometimes listed as peony-flowered tulips. Two unusually decorative tulips also appear now: the fringed tulip and the parrot tulip. The name of the fringed tulip is descriptive: the petals are edged with a conspicuous fringe, and these unusual, attractive varieties look equally stunning in the garden or as cut flowers. Finally, parrot tulips look like the clowns among tulips: showy and extrovert, big and attention-grabbing, with large, lacerated, wavy, crested petals. They are not to everyone's taste, but are seldom ignored. They make excellent cut flowers, but are well worth growing in the garden if a sheltered spot can be found, because they are vulnerable to wind damage.

One late-flowering daffodil puts on its show now: *Narcissus poeticus*, sometimes called the poet's narcissus or pheasant's eye, is one of the most distinctive of the tall-growing daffodils. The very small yellow cup, rimmed red or orange-red, looks like an eye set in the centre of the large white petals. It is good for naturalizing or for creating a cottage-garden planting in borders, and has a lovely fragrance. Perfect planting partners for this late daffodil are the camassias from North America. *Camassia quamash* is the shortest at 60 cm (2 ft). It has spikes of bright violet-blue flowers, giving the impresssion of a blue haze from a distance. *C. cusickii*'s 75-cm (30-in) tall spikes of lavender-blue flowers make an eye-catching clump. It is ideal when naturalized in grass in semi-shade, but it also makes a good border plant. Taller still at 90 cm (3 ft) is *C. leichtlinii*, which is similar to *C. cusickii*, but with creamy white to purple-blue flowers.

Meanwhile, bluebells will still be providing their carpet of flowers, and borders will be enlivened with *Anemone coronaria* hybrids in red, white and blue, and Dutch irises in purple, blue, white and yellow.

Right: *Camassias are eye-catching plants. The taller varieties work well in the border, while the shorter ones are at their best naturalized in grass in semi-shade. This is* C. leichtlinii.

Left: Tulipa *'New Design'* is a beautiful pink tulip that grows to 50cm (20in). It is particularly pretty with the light behind it, when its petals have a translucent appearance. Its leaves are edged with white, making it a favourite with garden designers. Enjoy it simply on its own in a pot or underplanted with forget-me-nots (Myosotis).

Above: Tulipa *'Queen of Night'* is a stunning dark purple tulip, which lasts for many weeks. It looks beautiful beneath an arch of yellow laburnum flowers or against a wall of pale blue wisteria. A underplanting of forget-me-nots is ideal in a container.

Right: *The glorious flame-coloured flowers of* Tulipa *'Lightning Sun' are very effective when underplanted with forget-me-nots in both deep blue and white varieties.*

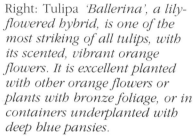

Left: *A bed of* Tulipa *'Dr. Plesum' creates a sea of fiery red, underplanted with pink* Bellis perennis.

Right: Tulipa *'Ballerina', a lily-flowered hybrid, is one of the most striking of all tulips, with its scented, vibrant orange flowers. It is excellent planted with other orange flowers or plants with bronze foliage, or in containers underplanted with deep blue pansies.*

Left: *The colours in this mixed border have obviously been carefully chosen.* Tulipa *'Appledorn Elite' and* T. *'Jewel of Spring' stand out beautifully against the purple berberis.*

Above: The Spanish bluebell (Hyacinthoides hispanica) *bears racemes of up to 15 bell-shaped, unscented flowers all the way around the stem. They might be planted beneath rhododendrons and azaleas for good colour associations, or with small silver foliage plants in a container. There is also a white form, 'Album'.*

Above right: Narcissus poeticus *is a late flowering daffodil. It is a tall-growing, fragrant variety with a distinctive small yellow cup set in large white petals.*

Right: *Any one of the camassias makes an excellant planting partner for* Narcissus poeticus *(above). This one is* C. cusickii, *whose lavender-blue spires reach to 75 cm (30 in).*

Early Summer

Most of the bulbs that play a central role in the garden are over by now, and annuals and perennials will be flowering in abundance. However, there are many summer bulbs which combine happily with other plants in mixed borders.

Below: The tall and stately Allium hollandicum *'Purple Sensation', with its rich purple, star-shaped flowers, towers over a sea of purple* Lavandula stoechas *(French lavender). This allium also looks wonderful beneath long trails of wisteria and laburnum. The seedheads will remain a special feature for many weeks.*

EARLY SUMMER BULBS

The stars of early summer are the alliums, with their impressive heads of pink and purple flowers. *Allium christophii*, sometimes called star of Persia, is one of the most popular of all the ornamental onions. The large spheres of star-shaped purple flowers are 15 cm (6 in) or more across, and can be dried for winter flower arrangements. Many of the most spectacular alliums for the herbaceous border are hybrids with very large drumstick heads. 'Globemaster' and 'Globus' are two fine examples. Both have large heads of rosy-purple flowers that make a pleasing focal point within the border. If you have a space at the back of a border, preferably in full sun, then choose *A. giganteum*, at 1.5–1.8 m (5–6 ft) the largest and most striking of the alliums, with 15 cm (6 in) heads of pinkish-purple flowers in early summer. Finally, for the front of the border there is *A. karataviense*, a compact species only 20–30 cm (10–20 in) tall with globular heads of light purple-pink, set against broad, greyish-purple leaves. It needs a sunny position and good drainage.

To offset the impressive purple heads of the alliums you could interplant them with some *Homeria ochroleuca*. This South African plant has cup-shaped yellow flowers, about 60 cm (2 ft) tall, with spreading petals. The flowers; are short-lived but open in succession to provide a couple of weeks of bloom. It too needs well-drained soil in full sun, and the corms should be lifted for the winter in areas where frosts occur.

Some delicately coloured candidates for the early summer bulb garden are *Hymenocallis × festalis* (spider lily or Peruvian daffodil), which resembles a white daffodil, with extra spidery petals; *Incarvillea delavayi*, whose trumpet-like pink or white flowers appear in early summer, above a basal rosette of foliage; and the diminutive *Oxalis adenophylla*, which manages to combine beautiful, striking pink and white flowers with feathery-looking, grey-green foliage that is highly attractive in its own right.

For the middle of the border, choose *Ixiolirion pallasii*, whose loose heads of blue, funnel-shaped flowers appear on very long, thin stems and make the most attractive cut flowers. Grow it in a clump for maximum effect. At the front of the border, or in front of shrubs, purple-flowered *Scilla peruviana* has an impact far beyond its small, compact size. It is hardy to about -5°C (23°F), but is only likely to thrive where winters are relatively mild and penetrating frosts are quite uncommon.

Above: *The tall flowerheads of* Allium rosenbachianum *sway elegantly above an underplanting of* Epimedium rubrum *'Purple King'*.

Above: *The martagon lily (*Lilium martagon*) should be grown in sun or partial shade. It has glossy, nodding, scented, pink to purplish-red flowers with dark purple spots. The flowers are 5cm (2in) across.*

Right: *This North American plant is known as* Triteleia laxa. *The loose heads of funnel-shaped, pale blue flowers on wiry stems are long lasting and make good cut flowers.*

Above: Allium christophii *creates a striking contrast to the flower spikes of* Salvia sylvestris *'Lye End'. An underplanting of* Geranium sanguineum *'Album' lightens the purple palette of this border.*

Left: *The strappy leaves of agapanthus look good with tall grasses. Blue* Agapanthus *'Ben Hope' forms a wonderful large grouping in front of the frothy masses of* Chionochloa conspicua *(plumed tussock grass).*

Above: Scilla peruviana *is a Mediterranean plant and blooms from early summer.*

Right: *Fiery orange* Crocosmia masonorum *contrasts stunningly with the blue agapanthus, together with* Allium senescens *var.* calcareum *and daylilies (*Hemerocallis*) in pale and deep salmon-pink.*

Below: Agapanthus *'Ben Hope' has rounded umbels of open, bell-shaped, rich blue flowers which make a magnificent display when grown in containers. Agapanthus need protection from frost and flower best when overcrowded.*

Above: Lilium *'Mellon Time', with its burnt-orange flowers, seems to be basking in the summer sunshine.*

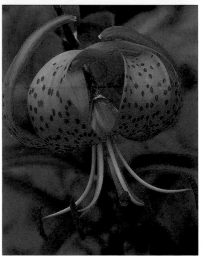

Above: *The tiger lily* (Lilium lancifolium *syn.* Lilium tigrinum) *has vibrant orange flowers with maroon spots and anthers.*

Mid- to Late Summer

The summer bulb garden is a riot of colour. Crocosmias and canna lilies in orange, red and yellow, begonias and gladioli in many colours, and stately lilies in white, salmon pink and yellow all combine to make the border an impressive sight. Many summer bulbs grow to imposing heights; place these at the back of the border where they can make an eye-catching backdrop to lower-growing bulbs and summer bedding plants.

LATE SUMMER BULBS

A beautiful herbaceous, tuberous-rooted climber is *Tropaeolum tuberosum* which will reach 2–3 m (6–10 ft). Its leaves are like those of the annual nasturtium, but smaller, and lobed, with small, spurred, orange-yellow flowers. It needs a lime-free soil and winter protection in areas where frost is likely. Another climber, reaching slightly shorter at 1.5–1.8 m (5–6 ft) is *Gloriosa superba*, a breathtakingly beautiful plant from tropical Africa and Asia, with exotic-looking flowers that have reflexed petals in a mixture of yellow and red – like leaping flames. Its common names include flame lily, glory lily and climbing lily. It is best grown in pots in a conservatory and taken outside just before it flowers. The form usually grown is *G. superba* 'Rothschildiana', often sold as *G. rothschildiana*.

Further candidates for the back row of the herbaceous border are cannas, dieramas and the lilies, all of which grow up to 1.5–1.8 m (5–6 ft) tall. Exotic looking *Canna* hybrids have been described as the lazy gardener's delight. They come into bloom early and continue until the first frost, combining spectacular red, orange or yellow flowers with interesting foliage. Mostly the leaves are dark bronze or purple-bronze, but some are brightly variegated. Being tender, they have to be lifted in winter like dahlias, but they are not difficult to grow. *Dierama pulcherrimum*, one of the most graceful of the iris family, deserves to be more widely planted. Two common names, angel's fishing rod and wandflower, give an indication of its elegant arching shoots, from which the pink to purple funnel-shaped flowers nod in a breeze. They do not transplant well and resent disturbance, so buy pot-grown plants if possible. Since the foliage is almost evergreen, they are seldom offered by bulb specialists as dry corms; some specialist nurseries sell them as growing plants.

A display of stately lilies will always draw attention, whether among other flowers in a border or planted in containers. Their trumpet-shaped flowers, often sweetly fragrant, are borne on elegantly tall stems, and have a grace that is hard to match. *Lilium regale* is sure to make an impression on a border if grown

Left: *The angel's fishing rod or wandflower,* Dierama pulcherrimum *from South Africa, lives up to its evocative common names with its long, graceful stems of purple flowers.*

Left: *The species of* Oxalis *illustrated is* O. triangularis *ssp.* papilonacea. *It must be planted outdoors only where the temperature is unlikely to fall below -7°C (20°F).*

Below: Lilium regale *(regal lily) bears large, white, scented, trumpet-shaped flowers that are streaked with purple on the outside. It grows well in sun or partial shade and sets seed easily. It is a lime-tolerant, stem-rooting lily which is suitable for a sunny border among lavender or roses.*

in a large clump. The flowers are mainly white, with a yellow inside throat, flushed purple-pink outside. There can be 20 or more fragrant flowers per stem. It is perhaps the best trumpet lily for the garden, and even a beginner should succeed with it. American hybrids such as *Lilium pardalinum* are tough and reliable, and can usually fend for themselves for years. The famous 'Bellingham Hybrids' were introduced in 1933 in the USA. Today there are other hybrids, mainly with spotted yellow, yellow-red or orange nodding flowers. The trumpet hybrids have yellow, white or pink flowers with a distinctive trumpet shape, and make pleasing border plants. The oriental hybrids (slightly smaller at 75–150 cm/30–60 in) vary in appearance due to the different species used in their hybridization. Some have the open shape of *L. auratum*,

others have more bowl-shaped flowers, or even flat or recurved shapes. Finally there are the Asiatic hybrids, some of which have upright flowers, some outward-facing, others pendent. Although they vary in appearance, all come in the usual range of lily colours, such as yellows, pinks, reds and whites, and make reliable garden plants for the border. The compact varieties also do well in patio pots.

Clumps of lilies are very effective alternated with blue agapanthus hybrids, whose ball-shaped flower heads in shades of blue, sometimes white, make splendid features. Another white plant of similar height (1–1.2 m/ 3–4 ft) is *Galtonia candicans*. The so-called summer hyacinth is a South African plant, best seen in a herbaceous or mixed border where its bold spikes of white bells can make a

statement in mid- or late summer. Leave undisturbed if possible to make a large clump. Where winters are cold, and the soil is likely to freeze deeply, the bulbs should be lifted for the winter and replanted in the spring.

For eye-catching, colourful blooms on thrusting stems it

would be hard to beat the gladiolus. Spike height and flower size varies with variety, and some are very big and bold. They are popular cut flowers, but can be rather stiff in a border unless planted in bold clumps with low-growing plants in front to hide the base of the stems. The colour range is very varied. Although there are a few long-established varieties, many new ones are introduced regularly, and some are available only from a few specialist bulb companies. The flowering period ranges between midsummer and early autumn, depending on the variety and planting time. In areas where frosts penetrate to the depth of the corms, they should be lifted in autumn. Slightly smaller are butterfly gladioli, with flowers 5–10 cm (2–4 in) across. There are many varieties, in a wide range of colours, usually with a contrasting blotch on the lower segments. Butterfly gladioli are used for cutting and floral art. Treat in the same way as large-flowered varieties.

Crocosmias are outstanding summer border plants and look excellent planted in great clumps with gladioli. Many gardeners are only aware of the old cottage garden favourite *C.* × *crocosmiiflora* (montbretia), but there are a number of modern hybrids derived from South African species. They are sometimes a little less hardy and many need winter protection in cold areas, but they have larger and bolder flowers, and a large clump can be one of the highlights of the late summer border. There are many varieties, in shades of orange, red and yellow.

Peruvian lilies and calla lilies, both of which grow to 60–90 cm (2–3 ft) high, are ideal for the centre of the border. *Alstroemeria* hybrids, or Peruvian lilies, are not true lilies: they grow from tubers, not bulbs. The showy flowers are often multi-coloured and are excellent for cutting. Where winters are severe they should be lifted and replanted the following spring. Dutch, English and Spanish irises need to be planted in a clump, with low-growing plants in front, to look really impressive. The flowering period is short, but by growing all three kinds it is possible to spread the period of interest. The calla lily (*Zantedeschia aethiopica*) is hardy only to about -7°C (20°F), which limits its use in the garden in cold areas, though it makes a fine conservatory or greenhouse plant with its distinctive white flowers. It can be grown in a border, as a pondside or bog plant, or even covered with up to 30 cm (1 ft) of water. 'Crowborough' is considered to be hardier than other forms of the plant, and 'Green Goddess' has very unusual and attractive green and white spathes.

Irises, growing to a height of 60 cm (2 ft), are another good choice for the centre of the border. Dutch irises, hybrids derived from species such as *Iris xiphium* and *I. tingitana*, flower in early summer. Spanish irises, derived from *I. xiphium*, follow on from the Dutch irises, flowering in early to mid-summer, and English irises, derived from *I. latifolia* (*I. xiphioides*), flower in mid-summer.

The dense flower spikes of *Liatris spicata* normally have pinkish flowers, but they can range from white to violet according to variety. At a similar height (60–75 cm/24–30 in) is *Polianthes tuberosa*, a Mexican bulb valued for its waxy white flowers and sweet, heady fragrance. Lift for the winter

Above: *Hybrids of American species such as this* L. pardalinum *are very reliable and easy to grow. The plant above is the famous* 'Bellingham Hybrid'.

Above: *The Asiatic hybrid lilies include many varieties in bold, bright colours and are ideal for creating hot-coloured borders*

where frosts are likely, and plant in a warm, sunny position.

The front of the border needs low-growing plants, around 30 cm (1 ft) high, and with enough colour and variety to draw some attention from the back of the bed. *Tulbaghia violacea* is worth planting because its sprays of bright lilac, scented flowers bloom for a long period in summer. × *Hippistrellia* 'Red Beauty' is an uncommon bulb that is the result of crossing a hippeastrum with a sprekelia. The glowing red flowers resemble a hippeastrum. Plant in a very sheltered part of the garden in mid-spring, or grow in pots started off in the greenhouse. Another uncommon bulb is *Chlidanthus fragrans*, whose yellow flowers resemble a small daffodil. They have a lily-like fragrance. The bulbs are best lifted before the first frost arrives. They can also be grown in pots. In either case, leave the neck of the bulb exposed when planting.

Finally, no summer display could be complete without the reliable and long-flowering begonias. Of the many different types of begonias, only tuberous hybrids are considered here. Sometimes grouped as *Begonia* × *tuberhybrida* varieties, they come in shades of pink, red, orange, yellow and white. Most of those sold by bulb companies are vegetatively propagated. Also popular are the seed-raised tuberous types that flower quickly, such as the popular Non-Stop range. These types are suitable for massed bedding. They flower all summer until cut back by frost in the autumn.

Below: *The exotic tiger flower,* Tigridia pavonia, *produces a succession of brilliantly coloured, if short-lived flowers. The blooms are iris-like in appearance, with three large, outer petals.* Tigridia *is not fully hardy and should be lifted in autumn and replanted in spring.*

Above: *The African corn lily* (Ixia) *is half hardy, and can be planted in spring to flower later in summer.*

Above: Tulbaghia violacea *is a semi-evergreen plant, producing clusters of purple-pink flowers through summer and autumn.*

Above: *Some of the* Crocosmia *hybrids are a little less hardy and may need winter protection in cold areas, but they have larger and bolder flowers, and a large clump can be one of the highlights of a border.*

Above: Crocosmia *hybrids make outstanding border plants.*

Above: Canna *hybrids are exotic looking plants from North and South America.*

Left: *The* Canna *hybrids are valued as much for their dramatic foliage, in shades of purple or bronze, or sometimes brightly variegated, as for their elegant flowers. Here, the colouring is accentuated by the purple* Cotinus *growing behind. Cannas are tender plants, but not difficult to grow.*

Above: *A small, dainty looking plant, this* Allium oreophilum *is a good choice for a rock garden.*

Above: Liatris spicata *produces dense spikes of bright purple flowers that emerge from grasslike foliage.*

Above: *This* Crinum × powellii *is a magnificent late-flowering bulb, probably a hybrid between two South African species. The common name sometimes used is Cape lily. The large pink trumpet flowers span from mid- to late summer into autumn. Provide a warm sunny position and, in colder areas, a protective winter mulch. Avoid planting them in very cold areas.*

373

Late Summer

As the days begin to shorten, and the end of summer is approaching, the garden will still be a glorious sight, with upright stems of brightly coloured dahlias, masses of begonias and canna lilies still holding on until the frost. Other bulbs are just beginning to flower now, to extend the summer into autumn: *Amaryllis belladonna*, *Crinum* × *powellii*, *Eucomis bicolor* and *Lilium auratum*.

LATE SUMMER BULBS

Dahlias have such bright, summery flower heads, that they seem to carry the warmth of that season with them. Since they can last well into autumn, they can be a very cheering sight when all the herbaceous perennials are dying down around them. There are many different kinds of dahlia to choose from. Cactus dahlias have double flowers and narrow petals that taper to a point, with the edges curved back for more than two-thirds of their length, giving them a spiky appearance. Semi-cactus dahlias have fully double flowers, with petals that curve backwards towards the tips, but they are flatter and broader towards the base than ordinary cactus varieties. Decorative varieties have double flowers with flat petals that incurve a little at the edges, often reflexing back towards the stem. The group of decoratives described as waterlily varieties generally have fewer petals, which are flat and broad, giving the flower a flatter appearance than normal decoratives. Both pompon and ball dahlias have spherical blooms with tightly packed petals that are almost tubular at the base. Pompons are smaller with flowers no more than 5 cm (2 in) across. Common varieties include 'Candy Cupid', a miniature ball variety, 'Key Helen' (pompon) and 'Wootton Cupid' (miniature ball). Finally there are Lilliput dahlias which can be used as edgings or in tubs, troughs and large window boxes. Most have single flowers, in all the usual dahlia colours, such as red, orange, pink, cream and white.

When the beautiful lilies of early to mid-summer have died down, there is still the golden-rayed lily (*Lilium auratum*) to enjoy, with its large, fragrant white flowers, usually banded yellow and spotted red. There are two other late-flowering

Above and right: *The impressive, funnel-shaped flowers of* Lilium Golden Splendor Group *are a rich golden yellow. The back of each petal is beautifully marked with maroon stripes. Here, it is planted with eupatorium.*

bulbs that look excellent interplanted with the golden-rayed lily, both bearing large pink trumpets. *Amaryllis belladonna*, a native of South Africa, flowers on leafless stems, the glossy strap-like leaves appearing when the flowers have finished. The magnificent *Crinum × powellii* (Cape lily) also carries its large pink trumpet flowers into autumn.

Eucomis bicolor is an invaluable plant to bring interest to a border in late summer and early autumn. In mild areas it will begin to flower in late summer, probably continuing into autumn, but in cold areas is best regarded as an autumn flower. This is one of several interesting species and hybrids that are available, most with green or greenish bell-like flowers, densely borne on thick spikes. Even before the flowers appear, the tuft of leaf-like bracts on top of the flower stem nestles in the centre of the plant like a pineapple (hence its common name, pineapple lily). The tuft of bracts remains on top of the spike as it elongates, and flowering lasts for several weeks, followed by seed heads that are really quite attractive.

Below: *The luscious white blooms of this tall gladiolus make a winning contribution to this summer scene, cool and elegant and quite at home among the softer shapes of* Cosmos *'Sonata Pink' and* Astrantia major *'Ruby Wedding'.*

Above: Galtonia candicans *(Cape hyacinth) grows to 1.1 m (3 ft 6 in) and bears tall spikes of creamy white, pendent flowers. Plant bulbs in early spring in bold groups towards the back of the herbaceous border, where the flowers will add height and grace.*

Above: Crinum × powellii *grows to about 1 m (39 in) and produces a rosette of broad, bright green, fleshy leaves. These are followed by a stout stem with pretty, funnel-shaped flowers, usually pink; 'Album', shown here, is a white variety. It is a focal point of the autumn garden but requires lower planting companions to hide the untidy leaves.*

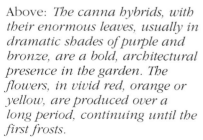

Above: *The canna hybrids, with their enormous leaves, usually in dramatic shades of purple and bronze, are a bold, architectural presence in the garden. The flowers, in vivid red, orange or yellow, are produced over a long period, continuing until the first frosts.*

Right: *Dahlias can be relied upon to brighten up the garden when the borders are beginning to look tired. They come in an enormous range of flower shapes and colours. The variety shown here, 'Video', is one of the type known as cactus dahlias, because of their spiky appearance.*

Right: *This golden-rayed lily is a Japanese species of great beauty, with large, fragrant white flowers, usually banded yellow and spotted red. The flowering period is late summer and early autumn, when a large clump can fill the air with fragrance.*

Above: Dahlia *'Kidd's Climax'is a member of the group known as decorative.*

Above: *'Hamari Katrina', one of the semi-cactus dahlias, is a beautiful clear yellow.*

Autumn

Many people are unaware that they can brighten up the autumn garden with bulbs. There are plenty of plants to choose which will introduce long-lasting colour into beds and borders at this time of year.

AUTUMN BULBS

Colchicums are remarkable plants from western and central Europe that look like huge crocuses, and are sometimes referred to as autumn crocuses. *Colchicum speciosum* bloom in early autumn, before the leaves, which appear in spring and grow to twice the 15 cm (6 in) height of the flowers. The bulbs have the curious characteristic of being able to bloom even if they are not planted and are without water; they live by drawing upon reserves in the bulb. There are varieties in various shades of pink, as well as white. They are best grown beneath shrubs in semi-shade, or rough grass, provided it is not too long and wild. There are other colchicum species that flower at the same time, such as *C. autumnale*, as well as the hybrids. One true crocus, *Crocus speciosus*, happily shares the same growing sites as the colchicums, and shares many of their characteristics, flowering in autumn before the leaves appear. The flowers are smaller, however, only about 10 cm (4 in) tall. They come in shades of purple, lilac and white.

Another valuable plant for the autumn garden is *Cyclamen hederifolium*, one of the best-known of the hardy miniature cyclamen. This Mediterranean species is tough and hardy and blooms prolifically in early autumn, continuing for months. The delicate flowers have the same distinctive form as the larger florist's cyclamen, with sharply swept-back petals, and come in various shades of pink and white, usually with a darker colour at the centre. The leaves have attractive silver markings. This is a useful plant because it thrives beneath trees, provided the ground receives some moisture in winter. You may find this species listed in catalogues under its older name of *C. neapolitanum*. It will self-seed, and naturalizes well.

The nerines, from South Africa, produce a delightful display in autumn, sometimes continuing into early winter. The spidery-looking flowers, in shades of pink, salmon, orange, red and white, appear before the leaves. They like a sunny, well-drained site and are not fully hardy, but in cold areas can be grown indoors in pots. *Nerine bowderii* is hardier than most, and should do well in areas where the temperature does not fall below -7°C (20°F), especially if given a little protection.

Left: *Dahlias continue flowering well into autumn, but are not frost hardy. Before frosts penetrate below the ground, the tubers should be lifted, dried off and stored in a frost-proof place until spring. These diminuative dahlias belong to the Lilliput group and the variety shown here is 'Omo'.*

Right: *Colchicums flower very quickly after planting, appearing early in the autumn even if only planted in the summer. This is C. speciosum.*

Below: *Colchicums bear a strong resemblance to true crocuses, and are sometimes known as autumn crocuses. This is C. speciosum 'Alba'.*

Right: *Colchicums flower before the leaves appear. Their goblet-shaped blooms can be as large as 20 cm (8 in), as with this variety, 'The Giant'.*

Above: *Many excellent dahlias do not fall neatly into any of the more formal classifications, and are placed in a miscellaneous group by enthusiasts. These plants are in no way inferior, and there are many superb varieties such as this 'Bishop of Llandaff'.*

Above: *The flowers of* Canna *'Wyoming' are of a beautiful rich orange, which together with dahlias of a similar colour create a wonderful effect in the autumn sunshine. The dahlia shown here is 'David Charles'.*

Left: Dahlia *'Clair de Lune' has delicate, pale yellow flowers and belongs to the collerette group, with a collar of smaller, narrow petals in front of the broad outer ones.*

Above: *Nerines, like colchicums, flower before their leaves appear. The blooms appear in mid-autumn, in colours from white through pink to red, and can last into the winter. Some varieties are semi-evergreen and not all are fully hardy. This is N. 'Pink Triumph'.*

Above: *Both pompon and ball dahlias have spherical blooms with tightly packed petals. Pompons are smaller with flowers no more than 5 cm (2 in) across. 'Candy Cupid', shown here, is a miniature ball variety in a rich pink colour.*

Right: *Cyclamen hederifolium makes its first welcome appearance from early autumn and continues to flower through much of the winter, providing splashes of hot colour, offset by lovely variegated foliage, at what can be a dull time of the year.*

DISPLAYING BULBS

Bulbs in Patio Tubs

Most bulbs can be grown in pots. Choose bulbs that will provide the brightest, longest or most interesting displays.

BULBS FOR CONTAINERS

Most bulbs do not have a long enough flowering period to make it worthwhile devoting a container to them, but spring bulbs can be very effective when added to a winter container, for example, with winter-flowering pansies or heathers and perhaps autumn cyclamen as well.

However, some bulbs, such as tuberous begonias and dahlias, do flower for longer, and there are some others, such as lilies, which are so magnificent when in flower that it is well worth giving them pride of place in a large container for their brief season of glory.

There are also some bulbs which are not fully hardy, and you may choose to grow them in pots in cold areas so that they can be moved indoors during the winter. Also note that a few, such as nerines, are best left in the pot for a few years before they flower well.

Above: *The beautiful double blue flowers of the* Anemone coronaria *Saint Brigid Group 'Lord Lieutenant' look stunning when teamed with containers in a contrasting shade of blue.*

Above: *Although the modern hybrid lilies, and especially the dwarf varieties, are likely to be brighter and bolder, some of the taller species, like these* Lilium regale, *create a cool elegance that has its own special charm.*

PLANTING LILIES IN A PATIO POT

1 The more lilies that you can pack into the pot, the bolder and more spectacular the display, so choose a pot at least 25 cm (10 in) across, preferably more. Make sure it has a drainage hole, which should be covered to prevent the potting soil washing through.

2 Place a layer of gravel or coarse grit in the bottom of the pot to ensure good drainage, since lilies, like most bulbs, prefer a free-draining soil. You could also use pebbles, broken pots or even polystyrene plant trays.

3 Place sufficient potting soil in the base to raise the level to a height that will allow the bulbs to be covered with twice their own depth, and still leave a good 12–25 mm (½–1 in) gap between the soil and rim of the pot to allow for watering.

4 Plant about three or five bulbs, depending on the size of the pot and bulbs, then cover them with more potting soil, firming it gently between the bulbs. An odd number of plants will generally look more effective than an even number.

5 A slow-release fertilizer will ensure strong growth. Granules are best mixed with the potting soil, but pellets like these can be placed beneath the bulbs or pushed into the soil after planting them. Cover the surface with a mulch of gravel and label. Water thoroughly and allow to drain.

Above: *Transform patios with a well-placed pot plant, such as this attractive* Lilium regale.

Colour in Containers

Summer containers are usually planted with bedding plants, since there are so many available and they tend to have a longer flowering season than most bulbs. However, there are a few bulbs that can definitely hold their own against the competition.

SUMMER BULBS

One of the most popular bulbs for summer containers, and with good reason, are the tuberous-rooted begonias. These come in a wide range of colours, including pink, orange, yellow, red and white, and different flower shapes, including almost rose-like double flowers. There are also trailing varieties ideal for hanging baskets. All of these give a reliable and abundant display of flowers throughout the summer, right up to the first frosts. The tubers can then be kept over the winter for flowering the following year. Allow them to dry out, and store in a frost-free place, either still in their pots or in boxes of dry sand, peat or peat substitute.

Another excellent choice for containers are the smaller varieties of dahlias. These bold, bright plants make a great contribution to the garden, but many gardeners are unaware of their potential for containers, thinking of them only as tall, late-flowering plants for the border. However, some of the modern varieties are quite compact, and most of these will be in flower by midsummer. With regular feeding and deadheading, they will continue flowering until the first frosts. Like begonias, the tubers can then be stored over the winter, in the same way as you would do with dahlias planted in the garden. Look for varieties described as Patio or Lilliput dahlias, but check the height. Some are very compact, growing to about 30 cm (1 ft), and are suitable for window boxes. Others may grow to about 45 cm (1½ ft), and are more suitable for large patio pots. The dahlias will look better if grown on their own.

Above: *Tuberous-rooted bedding begonias provide a long-lasting display in a container, usually blooming until the first frost.*

Left: *Autumn-flowering crocuses require little or no soil in order to flower. A charming effect has been achieved here by planting them in an old trug, covered with moss and leaves.*

Planting a Window Box or Trough

Fill empty window boxes with bulbs for a spring fling before the boxes are required again for next summer's bedding. Complex arrangements using several different kinds of bulbs can be disappointing unless flowering times coincide. A densely planted display of just one or two kinds of bulb is usually more reliable, being likely to give a bolder show.

Above: *Hyacinths should be packed close together for maximum impact. Plant up each container with just one variety if you want to be sure of them flowering simultaneously.*

SPRING BULBS IN WINDOW BOXES

1 Check that there are drainage holes, and cover them with a layer of broken pots or pebbles to ensure free drainage, and to prevent the soil being washed away.

2 Add enough potting compost (potting soil) to cover the bottom 2.5 cm (1 in). Provided the bulbs are planted out in the garden after flowering, old potting soil, or garden soil, can be used as the bulbs do not require high nutrient levels during winter.

3 To pack in plenty of bulbs and extend the flowering period, try planting in two layers. If you use two different kinds, place the larger bulbs on the bottom layer. The deeper ones will flower later.

4 Cover with potting soil and position the smaller bulbs on top, between the larger ones below, if possible. Choose, say, dwarf daffodils and scillas or crocuses, but avoid tall daffodils with dwarf bulbs.

5 Top up with more potting compost (potting soil), firming it between the bulbs, leaving about 1–2.5 cm (½–1 in) at the top of the window box to facilitate watering.

The Natural Look

Bulbs naturalized in grass can look wonderfully inspiring, especially once they have multiplied and formed large clumps and drifts of colour. Daffodils are sometimes planted in grassland and in orchards, or on banks and roadside verges, to provide a breathtaking display in early or mid-spring. Planted en masse they create an eye-catching, yellow carpet.

NATURALIZING BULBS

When planting bulbs for naturalizing, it is best to scatter them at random over the ground and plant them where they fall, to create a natural look. In grass, an area of turf can be lifted and small bulbs planted below it before replacing the turf. With larger bulbs, it may be easier to plant them individually using a bulb planter.

Once planted, naturalized bulbs can simply be left to multiply, and only require lifting and dividing very infrequently.

BULBS TO NATURALIZE

Anemone blanda
*Anemone nemorosa**
Chionodoxa
Crocus
Eranthis hyemalis
*Galanthus nivalis**
*Hyacinthoides**
Narcissus

* Best in woodland or beneath deciduous shrubs or trees.

Above: *Daffodils planted in grass will multiply until they form a thick, abundant carpet of brilliant colour. They will occasionally need lifting and dividing to prevent them becoming too congested, as they would eventually cease to flower well.*

Right: *A stunning display of bluebells.*

PLANTING LARGE BULBS

1 Scatter the bulbs on the ground in a group, fairly close together, to be planted where they fall.

2 Use a bulb planter, a trowel, or long-handled trowel if you find it easier, to remove a core of grass and soil. Make the hole about three times the depth of the bulb you wish to plant.

3 Sprinkle some loose soil around the bulb to ensure that there are no large air pockets around it, then replace the core of grass. It may be necessary to remove some soil from the base for the plug to fit.

PLANT LISTS

For all gardeners, making the right selection of plants
is the single most important ingredient for successful
gardening. To do this, you must be informed on several
different levels: you need to be able to identify the overall
look you are hoping to achieve and the kind of garden you
want to create, and you also need to understand the
conditions that determine which plants will grow
successfully. Perhaps the most important lesson for any
novice gardener is to grasp that you cannot grow exactly
what you want wherever you please. Although you always
want to try and manage nature, or at least influence it as
much as you dare, the most successful gardeners are those
who look at how plants grow in their natural habitat, and
apply this to their own garden, working with nature
wherever possible. The greater your understanding of
where plants grow best, and what their individual needs
are, the easier it becomes to grow them.

Left: *French marigolds* (Tagetes patula*) are half-hardy annuals, and
if planted in a sunny position in fertile, well-drained soil will flower
happily until the first frosts. Shown here are 'Striped Marvel'
and 'Cinnabar'.*

Shrubs List

Lists of shrubs for specific purposes (e.g. ground cover) are given in the relevant sections

d = deciduous
e = evergreen

YELLOW-FLOWERED SHRUBS

Azara (e)
Berberis (d & e)
Buddleja globosa (d)
Chimonanthus (d)
Colutea arborescens (d)
Cornus mas (d)
Coronilla (e)
Corylopsis (d)
Corylus (d)
Cytisus (d)
Forsythia (d)
Fremontodendron californicum (e)
Genista (d)
Halimium (e)
Hamamelis (d)
Helianthemum (e)
Hypericum (d)
Jasminum (d & e)
Kerria japonica (d)
Mahonia (e)
Phlomis (e)
Piptanthus (e)
Potentilla (d)
Rhododendron (d & e)
Senecio (d)

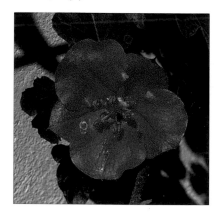

Fremontodendron californicum

Azara lanceolata

ORANGE-FLOWERED SHRUBS

Berberis (d & e)
Buddleja x weyeriana (d)
Colutea orientalis (d)
Embothrium coccineum (e)
Helianthemum (e)
Potentilla (d)
Rhododendron (d & e)

Fuchsia 'Genii'

RED-FLOWERED SHRUBS

Callistemon citrinus (e)
Calluna (e)
Camellia (e)
Chaenomeles (d)
Crinodendron hookerianum (e)
Desfontainia spinosa (e)
Erythrina crista-galli (d)
Escallonia (e)
Fuchsia (d)
Helianthemum (e)
Hydrangea (d)
Leptospermum (e)
Rhododendron (d & e)
Ribes speciosum (d)
Weigela (d)

PINK-FLOWERED SHRUBS

Abelia (e)
Andromeda (e)
Buddleja (d)
Calluna (e)
Camellia (e)
Chaenomeles (d)
Cistus (e)

Chaenomeles speciosa 'Moerloosii'

Calluna vulgaris 'Darkness'

Clerodendrum bungei (d)
Cotinus coggygria (d)
Cytisus (d)
Daphne (d & e)
Deutzia (d)
Erica (e)
Escallonia (e)
Fuchsia (d)
Hebe (e)
Helianthemum (e)
Hibiscus (d)
Hydrangea (d)
Indigofera (d)
Kalmia (e)
Kolkwitzia (d)
Lavatera (d)
Leptospermum (e)
Lonicera (d)
Magnolia (d & e)
Nerium (e)
Prunus (d)
Rhododendron (d & e)
Ribes sanguineum (d)
Spiraea (d)
Syringa (d)
Viburnum (d & e)
Weigela (d)

Ceanothus impressus

BLUE-FLOWERED SHRUBS
Buddleja (d)
Caryopteris (d)
Ceanothus (d & e)
Ceratostigma (d)
Hebe (e)
Hibiscus (d)
Hydrangea (d)
Lavandula (e)
Perovskia (d)
Rhododendron (d & e)
Rosmarinus (e)
Vinca (e)

Syringa vulgaris

PURPLE-FLOWERED SHRUBS
Buddleja (d)
Elsholtzia stauntonii (d)
Erica (e)
Hebe (e)
Hydrangea (d)

Rhamnus alaternus 'Variegata'
with *Campanula pyramidalis*

Lavandula stoechas (e)
Rhododendron (d & e)
Salvia officinalis (e)
Syringa (d)
Vinca (e)

WHITE-FLOWERED SHRUBS
Aralia (d)
Berberis thunbergia (d)
Buddleja (d)
Calluna (e)
Camellia (e)
Carpenteria californica (e)
Chaenomeles (d)

Choisya (d)
Cistus (e)
Clerodendrum trichotomum (d)
Clethra alnifolia (d)
Cornus (d)
Cotoneaster (e)
Crataegus (d)
Cytisus (d)
Daphne blagayana (d)
Erica (e)
Escallonia (e)
Eucryphia (d & e)
Exochorda x *macrantha* (d)
Fuchsia (d)
Gaultheria (e)
Halesia (d)
Hebe (e)
Helianthemum (e)
Hibiscus (d)
Hoheria (d)
Hydrangea (d)
Itea (d & e)
Jasminum (d & e)
Leptospermum (e)

Ligustrum (e)
Magnolia (d & e)
Myrtus (e)
Olearia (e)
Osmanthus (e)
Philadelphus (d)
Pieris (e)
Potentilla (d)
Prunus (d)
Pyracantha (e)
Rhododendron (d & e)
Romneya (d)
Rubus 'Tridel' (d)
Sambucus (d)
Skimmia (e)
Spiraea (d)
Stephanandra (d)
Syringa (d)
Viburnum (d & e)
Vinca (e)

GREEN-FLOWERED SHRUBS
Daphne laureola (e)
Garrya elliptica (d)

Carpenteria californica

SHRUBS FOR DRY SHADE
Aucuba japonica (e)
Ilex (d & e)
Pachysandra terminalis (e)
Buxus sempervirens (e)
Daphne laureola (d & e)
Elaeagnus × ebbingei (e)
Gaultheria shallon (e)
Hypericum × inordum 'Elstead' (d)
Lonicera pileata (e)

SHRUBS FOR MOIST SHADE
Camellia (e)
Clethra (d & e)
Corylopsis (d)
Crataegus laevigata (d)
Enkianthus (d)
Fatsia japonica (e)
Fothergilla (d)
Mahonia aquifolium (e)
Osmanthus decorus (e)
Pieris formosa var. *forrestii* 'Wakehurst' (e)

Rhododendron (d & e)
Salix magnifica (d)
Sarcococca ruscifolia (e)
Skimmia japonica (e)
Viburnum davidii (e)
Vinca major (e)
Vinca minor (e)

SHRUBS FOR SUNNY AND DRY AREAS
Caryopteris × clandonensis (d)
Cistus (e)
Convolvulus cneorum (e)
Cytisus (d & e)
Hamamelis mollis (d)
Helianthemum nummularium (e)
Santolina chamaecyparissus (e)
Senecio (e)
Yucca (e)

SHRUBS FOR ACID SOIL
Azalea (d & e)
Calluna vulgaris (e)
Camellia (e)
Corylopsis pauciflora (d)
Daboecia (e)
Enkianthus (d)
Erica cinerea (e)
Fothergilla (d)
Gaultheria mucronata (e)
Halesia carolina (d)
Hamamelis (d)
Kalmia latifolia (e)
Pieris (e)
Rhododendron (d & e)
Ulex europaeus (e)

SHRUBS FOR CHALKY SOIL
Berberis darwinii (e)
Buddleja davidii (d)
Ceanothus impressus (e)
Choisya ternata (e)
Cistus (e)

Clematis (d & e)
Cotoneaster (d & e)
Deutzia (d)
Helianthemum (e)
Lavandula (e)
Nerium oleander (e)
Paeonia suffruticosa (d)
Potentilla (shrubby species) (d)
Pyracantha (e)
Rosa rugosa (shrub species)
Syringa (d)
Viburnum tinus (e)

SHRUBS FOR SANDY SOIL
Calluna vulgaris (e)
Ceanothus thyrsiflorus (e)
Cistus (e)
Cytisus scoparius (d)
Erica arborea alpina (e)
Gaultheria mucronata (e)
Genista tinctoria (d)
Lavandula (e)
Rosa pimpinellifolia (d)

Below: *Rosemary* (Rosmarinus) *has a distinctive scent.*

Below: *The foliage of* Pieris japonica *changes through the year.*

Below: Helianthemum *'Wisley Pink' has unusual silver leaves.*

Rosmarinus officinalis (e)
Spartium junceum (d)
Yucca gloriosa (e)

SHRUBS FOR CLAY SOIL
Clethra alnifolia (d)
Cornus alba 'Sibirica' (d)
Kalmia latifolia (e)
Magnolia (some) (d & e)
Salix caprea (d)
Sambucus racemosa (d)
Viburnum opulus (d)

SHRUBS FOR GROUND COVER
Cotoneaster cochleatus (e)
Erica carnea (e)
Euonymus fortunei (e)
Hypericum calycinum (e)
Juniperus horizontalis (e)
Lonicera pileata (e)
Pachysandra terminalis (e)
Persicaria affinis (e)
Rosa (ground cover species)

Thymus (e)
Vinca minor (e)

SHRUBS THAT ATTRACT WILDLIFE
Buddleja davidii (d)
Cotoneaster species (d & e)
Hebe (e)
Lavandula (e)
Ilex (e)
Pyracantha (e)

SHRUBS WITH FRAGRANT FLOWERS
Buddleja davidii (d)
Chimonanthus praecox (d)
Choisya ternata (e)
Cytisus battandieri (e)
Daphne mezereum (d)
Lavandula (e)
Lonicera fragrantissima (d & e)
Philadelphus (d)
Rosa (d)

Sarcococca (e)
Syringa (d)
Viburnum × bodnantense (d)
Viburnum carlesii (d)

SHRUBS WITH SCENTED FOLIAGE
Aloysia triphylla (d)
Artemisia abrotanum (d)
Helichrysum italicum (e)
Hyssopus officinalis (d)
Lavandula (e)
Pelargonium (scented-leaved forms) (e)
Rosmarinus officinalis (e)
Salvia officinalis (e)

SHRUBS FOR HEDGES AND WINDBREAKS
Berberis darwinii (e)
Buxus sempervirens (e)
Cotoneaster simonsii (d)
Elaeagnus × ebbingei (e)

Escallonia (e)
Euonymus japonicus (e)
Griselinia littoralis (e)
Lavandula (e)
Ligustrum ovalifolium (e)
Lonicera nitida (e)
Photinia × fraseri 'Red Robin' (e)
Pittosporum tenuifolium (e)
Prunus laurocerasus (e)
Prunus lusitanica (e)
Tamarix ramosissima (d)

SHRUBS FOR EXPOSED SITES
Elaeagnus pungens 'Maculata' (e)
Erica cinerea (e)
Euonymus japonicus (e)
Genista hispanica (e)
Hibiscus rosa-sinensis (e)
Hippophäe rhamnoides (d)
Lavandula 'Hidcote' (e)
Pyracantha coccinea (e)
Senecio 'Sunshine' (e)
Viburnum tinus (e)

Below: Choisya ternata *'Sundance'* *has fragrant white flowers.*

Below: Pyracantha *has very decorative autumn berries.*

Below: Salvia officinalis *'Icterina'* *or sage is often used in cooking.*

Climbers List

Plant lists for specific types of climbers (e.g. fragrant climbers) are given in the relevant sections.

Where only the genus is given several species and cultivars are suitable.

ac = annual climber
c = climber
wf = wall fruit
ws = wall shrub

YELLOW-FLOWERED CLIMBERS AND WALL SHRUBS

Abutilon megapotamicum (ws)
Azara dentata (ws)
Billardiera longiflora (c)
Clematis (c)
   C. 'Moonlight'
   C. 'Paten's Yellow'
   C. rehderiana
   C. tangutica
   C. tibetana

Clematis tangutica

Eccremocarpus scaber (c)
Fremontodendron californicum (ws)
Humulus lupulus 'Aureus' (c)
Jasminum (c & ws)
Lathyrus (ac & c)
Lonicera (c)
Magnolia grandiflora (ws)
Piptanthus laburnifolius (ws)
Rosa (c)
   R. 'Dreaming Spires'
   R. 'Emily Grey'
   R. 'Gloire de Dijon'
   R. 'Golden Showers'
Thunbergia alata (ac)
Tropaeolum (ac)

Lonicera japonica *'Halliana'*

ORANGE-FLOWERED CLIMBERS AND WALL SHRUBS

Bignonia capreolata (c)
Bougainvillea spectabilis (c)
Campsis (c)
Eccremocarpus scaber (c)
Lonicera (c)
Rosa (c)
   R. 'Autumn Sunlight'
   R. 'Danse du Feu'
Tropaeolum (ac)

RED-FLOWERED CLIMBERS AND WALL SHRUBS

Akebia quinata (c)
Bougainvillea spectabilis (c)
Callistemon citrinus (ws)
Camellia (ws)
Chaenomeles (ws)

Clematis *'Madame Julia Correvon'*

Clematis (c)
   C. 'Niobe'
   C. 'Ruby Glow'
Clianthus puniceus (ws)
Crinodendron hookerianum (ws)
Desfontainea spinosa (ws)
Eccremocarpus scaber (c)
Erythrina crista-galli (ws)
Lathyrus (ac & c)
Lonicera (c)
Phaseolus coccineus (ac)
Rhodochiton atrosanguineum (c)
Ribes speciosum (ws)
Rosa (c)
   R. 'American Pillar'
   R. 'Danny Boy'
   R. 'Excelsa'
   R. 'Galway Bay'
   R. 'Symphathie'
Tropaeolum (ac & c)

Clematis *'Duchess of Albany'*

Clematis *'Comtesse de Bouchard'*

PINK-FLOWERED CLIMBERS AND WALL SHRUBS

Bougainvillea spectabilis (c)
Camellia (ws)
Chaenomeles (ws)
Cistus (ws)
Clematis (c)
   C. 'Comtesse de Bouchard'
   C. 'Hagley Hybrid'
   C. 'Margot Koster'

Lathyrus grandiflorus

Hoya carnosa (c)
Jasminum beesianum (c)
Jasminum x *stephanense* (c)
Lapageria rosea (c)
Lathyrus (ac & c)
Lonicera (c)
Malus (wf)
Mandevilla splendens (c)

Nerium oleander (ws)
Prunus (wf)
Rosa (c)
  R. 'Albertine'
  R. 'Bantry Bay'
  R. 'New Dawn'
  R. 'Pink Perpétue'
  R. 'Zéphirine Drouhin'

Vinca major

BLUE-FLOWERED CLIMBERS AND WALL SHRUBS
Aloysia triphylla (ws)
Ceanothus (ws)
Clematis (c)
  C. 'Beauty of Richmond'
  C. 'Lady Betty Balfour'
  C. macropetala
  C. 'Mrs Cholmondeley'
  C. 'Perle d'Azur'
Hydrangea aspera villosa (ws)
Ipomoea (ac)
Lathyrus (ac & c)
Passiflora caerulea (c)
Plumbago capensis (c)
Rosmarinus officinalis (ws)
Solanum crispum (ws)
Solanum jasminoides (c)
Sollya fusiformis (c)
Teucrium fruticans (ws)
Vinca major (c)
Wisteria (c)

PURPLE-FLOWERED CLIMBERS AND WALL SHRUBS
Clematis (c)
  C. 'Etoile Violette'

Clematis *'Lasurstern' and* Clematis *'Nelly Moser'*

  C. 'Gipsy Queen'
  C. 'The President'
Cobaea scandens (ac)
Lathyrus (ac & c)
Rosa (c)
  R. 'Bleu Magenta'
  R. 'Veilchenblau'
  R. 'Violette'
Solanum dulcamara 'Variegata' (c)

Vitis vinifera *'Purpurea'*

GREEN-FLOWERED CLIMBERS AND WALL SHRUBS
Garrya elliptica (ws)
Hedera (c)
Itea ilicifolia (ws)
Ribes laurifolium (ws)
Vitis (c)

Clematis *'Mrs George Jackman'*

WHITE-FLOWERED CLIMBERS AND WALL SHRUBS
Camellia (ws)
Carpenteria californica (ws)
Chaenomeles (ws)
Cistus (ws)
Clematis (c)
  C. 'Edith'
  C. 'Miss Bateman'
  C. 'Snow Queen'
Clianthus puniceus (ws)
Cotoneaster (ws)
Dregea sinensis (c)
Fallopia baldschuanica (c)
Hoheria (ws)
Hoya carnosa (c)
Hydrangea anomala petiolare (c)
Jasminum (c & ws)

Clematis florida *'Sieboldii'*

Lathyrus (ac & c)
Mandevilla suaveolens (c)
Myrtus (ws)
Nerium oleander (ws)
Pileostegia viburnoides (c)
Prunus (wf)
Pyracantha (ws)
Pyrus (wf)
Rosa (c)
  R. 'Albéric Barbier'
  R. 'Kiftsgate'
  R. 'Mme Alfred Carrière'
Solanum jasminoides 'Album' (c)
Trachelospermum (c)
Wisteria (c)

Rosa *'Iceberg' and* Clematis tangutica

Clematis *'Marie Boisselot'*

CLIMBERS FOR DRY SHADE
Hedera canariensis (c)
Lapageria rosea (c)
Parthenocissus tricuspidata (c)

CLIMBERS FOR MOIST SHADE
Humulus lupulus 'Aureus'
   (h & c)
Hydrangea petiolaris (c)
Lonicera tragophylla (c)
Pileostegia viburnoides (c)
Schizophragma
   integrifolium (c)

Trachelospermum
   jasminoides (c)

CLIMBERS FOR ACID SOIL
Berberidopsis corallina (c)

CLIMBERS FOR CHALKY SOIL
Campsis radicans (c)
Celastrus orbiculatus (c)
Clematis (all)
Eccremocarpus scaber (c & a)
Hedera (c)
Lonicera (some) (c)

Passiflora caerulea racemosa (c)
Rosa banksiae 'Lutea' (c)
Rosa 'Albertine' (c)
Trachelospermum jasminoides (c)
Wisteria sinensis (c)

CLIMBERS FOR SANDY SOIL
Vitis vinifera 'Purpurea' (c)

CLIMBERS FOR CLAY SOIL
Humulus lupulus 'Aureus' (c)
Rosa filipes 'Kiftsgate' (c)
Vitis coignetiae (c)

CLIMBERS FOR QUICK COVER
Hedera helix (small cvs) (c)
Hydrangea petiolaris (c)
Polygonum
   baldschuanicum (c)
Trachelospermum
   jasminoides (c)

Below: Rosa *'Iceberg' is a beautiful, highly fragrant rose.*

Below: *Hops* (Humulus lupulus) *are good at disguising eyesores.*

Below: Passiflora *is a stunning climber that loves walls.*

CLIMBERS FOR GROUND COVER

Hedera colchica 'Dentata Variegata' (c)
Schizophragma hydrangeoides (c)
Vitis coignetiae (c)

CLIMBERS WITH FRAGRANT FLOWERS

Azara (c)
Clematis montana 'Elizabeth' (c)

Itea ilicifolia (c)
Jasminum (most) (c)
Lathyrus odoratus (c & a)
Lonicera (many) (c)
Osmanthus (c)
Passiflora (c)
Trachelospermum (c)
Wisteria (c)

CLIMBERS WITH ARCHITECTURAL FOLIAGE

Hedera colchica 'Dentata Variegata' (c)

Schizophragma hydrangeoides (c)
Schizophragma integrifolium (c)
Vitis coignetiae (c)

CLIMBERS FOR CONTAINERS

Eccremocarpus scaber (c)
Hedera helix and cvs (c)
Ipomoea (some) (c & a)
Lathyrus (climbing species) (c & a)
Passiflora (c)

CLIMBERS FOR EXPOSED SITES

Euonymus fortunei (c)
Hedera helix (c)
Wisteria sinensis (c)

Below: Campsis radicans *is a beautiful late summer climber.*

Below: Rosa *'Zéphirine Drouhin' is adaptable and has no thorns.*

Below: *The flowers of* Clematis *'Perle d'Azur' open in summer.*

Annuals List

Choose from this list of annuals for specific purposes such as lime or chalk (alkaline) soil.

YELLOW-FLOWERED ANNUALS

Argemone mexicana
Calendula officinalis 'Kablouna'
Chrysanthemum segetum
Chrysanthemum tenuiloba 'Golden Fleck'
Coreopsis 'Sunray'
Glaucium flavum
Helianthus annuus
Limnanthes douglasii
Lonas annua
Oenothera biennis
Sanvitalia procumbens
Tagetes 'Gold Coins'

Chrysanthemum segetum *and* Dahlia *'David Howard"*

ORANGE FLOWERED ANNUALS

Alonsoa warscewiczii
Calceolaria 'Kentish Hero'
Emilia coccinea
Erysimum cheiri 'Fire King'
Impatiens 'Impact Orange'
Nemesia 'Orange Prince'
Osteospermum hyoseroides 'Gaiety'
Rudbeckia hirta 'Goldilocks'
Tithonia rotundifolia 'Torch'
Tropaeolum majus 'Alaska'

Papaver rhoeas *'Mother of Pearl'*

RED FLOWERED ANNUALS

Amaranthus caudatus
Antirrhinum 'Scarlet Giant'
Begonia semperflorens 'Lucifer'
Cosmos bipinnatus 'Pied Piper Red'
Dianthus chinensis 'Fire Carpet'
Impatiens 'Tempo Scarlet'
Lathyrus odoratus 'Airwarden'
Lobelia erinus 'Red Cascade'
Nicotiana 'Crimson'
Papaver rhoeas
Petunia 'Red Star'
Tagetes patula 'Cinnabar'
Tropaeolum majus 'Empress of India'
Verbena 'Sandy Scarlet'

PINK FLOWERED ANNUALS

Alcea rosea 'Rose'
Begonia semperflorens 'Pink Avalanche'
Callistephus chinensis
Cleome 'Pink Queen'
Cosmos 'Versailles Tetra'
Crepis rubra
Clarkia grandiflora 'Satin Pink'
Helichrysum bracteatum 'Rose'
Lavatera trimestris 'Pink Beauty'
Nicotiana 'Domino Salmon-Pink'
Oenothera speciosa
Osteospermum 'Lady Leitrim'
Papaver somniferum

BLUE FLOWERED ANNUALS

Borago officinalis
Campanula medium
Centaurea cyanus
Consolida ambigua
Echium vulgare
Limonium sinuatum 'Azure'
Myosotis
Nemophila menziesii
Nicandra physalodes
Nigella damascena
Salvia farinacea 'Victoria'

Osteospermum hyoseroides

Cloeme hassleriana

PURPLE AND VIOLET FLOWERED ANNUALS

Ageratum 'North Star'
Antirrhinum 'Purple King'
Centaurea cyanus 'Black Ball'
Eschscholzia californica 'Purple-Violet'
Galactites tomentosa
Heliotropium
Hesperis matronalis
Limonium sinuatum 'Midnight'

Osteospermum *'Tresco Purple'*

Nigella damascena *'Miss Jekyll'*

Lunaria annua
Senecio ciliocarpa
Silene armeria 'Electra'
Trachelium caeruleum

WHITE AND CREAM-FLOWERED ANNUALS
Antirrhinum 'White Wonder'
Argemone grandiflora
Centaurea moschata 'The Bride'
Clarkia pulchella
   'Snowflake'
Digitalis purpurea alba
Gypsophila elegans 'White
   Elephant'
Hibiscus trionum
Iberis crenata
Lobularia maritima
Nemesia 'Mellow White'
Nemophila maculata
Nicotiana sylvestris
Osteospermum
   'Prostratum'
Tagetes 'French Vanilla'

ANNUALS FOR LIME OR CHALKY SOIL
Ageratum houstonianum
Calendula officinalis
Callistephus chinensis
Chrysanthemum
Erysimum
Gypsophila

Digitalis purpurea alba

Lavatera trimestris 'Silver Cup'
Limonium sinuatum
Lobularia maritima
Matthiola
Salvia viridis
Tagetes
Zinnia

ANNUALS FOR SANDY SOIL
Antirrhinum majus
Brachycome iberidifolia
Coreopsis tinctoria
Dimorphotheca
Helichrysum bracteatum
Limnanthes douglasii
Limonium sinuatum
Lobularia maritima
Mesembryanthemum
Papaver rhoeas
Schizanthus
Tagetes
Tropaeolum

Lunaria annua variegata

Nasturtiums with Tagetes *'Suzie Wong'*

Tagetes patula *'Safari Tangerine'*

Osteospermum ecklonis *var.* prostratum

Amaranthus

ANNUALS WITH FRAGRANT FLOWERS
Brachycome iberidifolia
Centaurea moschata
Dianthus barbatus
Erysimum
Heliotropium
Iberis umbellata
Lathyrus odoratus
Limnanthes douglasii
Lobularia maritima
Matthiola incana
Nicotiana alata
Oenothera biennis
Reseda odorata
Scabiosa atropurpurea

ANNUALS WITH SCENTED FOLIAGE
Salvia sclarea

ANNUALS FOR CUT FLOWERS
Amaranthus caudatus
Callistephus chinensis
Centaurea cyanus
Centaurea moschata
Gypsophila elegans
Helipterum roseum
Lathyrus odoratus

Salvia sclarea *var.* turkestanica

Limonium sinuatum
Matthiola
Moluccella laevis
Zinnia elegans

ANNUALS FOR DRIED FLOWERS
Amaranthus caudatus
Centaurea cyanus
Gypsophila elegans
Helichrysum bracteatum
Limonium sinuatum
Moluccella laevis
Onopordum acanthium
Salvia viridis
Scabiosa atropurpurea

ANNUALS FOR FOLIAGE
Abutilon megapotamicum
  'Variegatum'
Atriplex hortensis 'Rubra'
Beta vulgaris
Brassica oleracea
Canna
Coleus blumei
Euphorbia marginata
Helichrysum petiolare
Medicago echinus
Melianthus major
Onopordum acanthium
Ricinus communis
Senecio cineraria
Tropaeolum majus 'Alaska'

ANNUALS FOR EXPOSED AND COASTAL SITES
Antirrhinum majus
Calendula officinalis
Clarkia amoena
Coreopsis tinctoria
Eschscholzia californica
Helichrysum bracteatum
Limnanthes douglasii
Matthiola
Tagetes

ANNUAL CLIMBERS
Asarina erubescens
Cobaea scandens
Convolvulus tricolor

Zinnia *Giant Double mixed with* Tithonia rotundifolia *'Torch'*

Canna *'Wyoming' and 'Striata'*, Ricinus communis *'Zanzibariensis' and mixed* Dahlias *'Rigoletto'*

Early chrysanthemums with Helianthus *'Valentine' and* Eupatorium purpureum

Perennials List

A list of perennials for specific purposes such as colour schemes and particular soils.

YELLOW-FLOWERED PERENNIALS
Achillea 'Coronation Gold'
Anemone ranunculoides
  'Plentiflora'
Caltha palustris
Doronicum
Eranthis hyemalis
Helianthus
Kirengeshoma palmata
Lysimachia punctata
Milium effusum 'Aureum'
Paeonia mlokosewitschii
Rudbeckia
Solidago
Verbascum olympicum

ORANGE-FLOWERED PERENNIALS
Asclepias tuberosa
Eccremocarpus scaber
Euphorbia griffithii 'Fireglow'
Helenium 'Wyndley'
Hemerocallis 'Golden Chimes'
Kniphofia caulescens
Kniphofia triangularis
Strelitzia reginae
Zauschneria californica

RED-FLOWERED PERENNIALS
Astilbe 'Montgomery'
Cosmos atrosanguineus
Kohleria eriantha
Lobelia 'Cherry Ripe'

Euphorbia griffithii *'Fireglow'*

Doronicum

Lychnis chalcedonica
Monarda bradburyana
  'Cambridge Scarlet'
Papaver orientale
Rheum palmatum
  'Atrosanguineum'
Schizostylis coccinea 'Major'
Tropaeolum speciosum

Tropaeolum speciosum

Meconopsis

PINK-FLOWERED PERENNIALS
Anemone huphensis
Astilbe arendsii 'Venus'
Centaurea pucherrima
Dicentra spectabilis
Eupatorium purpureum
Filipendula rubra
Lupinus 'The Chatelaine'
Mirabilis jalapa
Salvia involucrata
Schizostylis coccinea 'Sunrise'
Sedum spectabile
Tanacetum coccineum 'Brenda'

BLUE-FLOWERED PERENNIALS
Agapanthus 'Dorothy Palmer'
Agapanthus praecox orientalis
Aster × *frikartii* 'Mönch'
Convolvulus sabatius
Gentiana asclepiadea
Mertensia pulmonarioides
Pulmonaria angustifolia
Veronica peduncularis
  'Georgia Blue'

PURPLE-AND-VIOLET FLOWERED PERENNIALS
Acanthus spinosus
Campanula lactiflora
  'Prichard's Variety'
Clematis 'Etoile Violette'
Geranium phaeum
Helleborus purpurascens
Heuchera micrantha
  'Palace Purple'
Iris unguicularis
Liriope muscari
Monarda fistulosa
Verbena patagonica

WHITE-AND-CREAM FLOWERED PERENNIALS
Anaphalis margaritacea
Anemone nemorosa
Caltha introloba
Convallaria majalis
Crambe cordifolia
Dicentra spectabilis 'Alba'
Dictamnus albus
Eupatorium album 'Braunlaub'
Galium odoratum
Gypsophila paniculata

Liriope muscari

Eupatorium purpureum

Convallaria majalis

Helleborus niger
Ranunculus aconitifolius
Rodgersia podophylla
Salvia argentea
Tanacetum parthenium

GREEN-FLOWERED PERENNIALS
Alchemilla mollis
Euphorbia amygdaloides
 var. *robbiae*
Euphorbia cyparissias
Euphorbia polychroma
Kniphofia 'Percy's Bride'
Thalictrum lucidum

PERENNIALS FOR DRY SHADE
Alchemilla mollis
Brunnera
Euphorbia amygdaloides
 var. *robbiae*
Iris foetidissima
Kohleria digitaliflora
Streptocarpus saxorum
Tradescantia zebrina
 'Quadricolor'
Viola

PERENNIALS FOR MOIST SHADE
Aconitum
Anemone × *hybrida*
Aruncus dioicus
Bergenia
Convallaria majalis
Digitalis orientalis
Helleborus foetidus
Helleborus niger
Helleborus orientalis
Hosta

Clematis *'Etoile Violette'*

Helleborus orientalis *hybrid*

Ligularia
Ranunculus
Rodgersia

PERENNIALS FOR ACID SOIL
Cypripedium reginae
Drosera
Liriope
Lupinus
Meconopsis
Nepenthes
Sarracenia flava
Trillium
Uvularia

PERENNIALS FOR ALKALINE OR LIME SOIL
Acanthus spinosus
Achillea filipendulina
  'Gold Plate'
Alyssum
Aubrietia
Bergenia
Campanula
Dianthus
Doronicum
Erysimum
Gypsophila paniculata
Salvia nemorosa

Campanula Latiloba *'Percy Piper'*

Scabiosa
Verbascum

PERENNIALS FOR SANDY SOIL
Acanthus spinosus
Alstroemeria
Cryptanthus zonatus
Eryngium × tripartitu
Limonium latifolium

PERENNIALS FOR CLAY SOIL
Aruncus dioicus
Filipendula ulmaria 'Aurea'
Gunnera manicata
Houttuynia cordata
  'Chameleon'
Iris laevigata
Mimulus guttatus
Trollius

PERENNIALS FOR GROUNDCOVER
Alchemilla mollis
Anemone nemerosa
Artemisia frigida

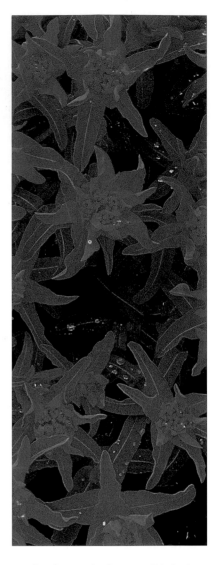

Euphorbia polychroma *'Major'*

Dianthus deltoides
Euphorbia amygdaloides
  var. *robbiae*
Geranium macrorrhizum
Hosta
Lysimachia nummularia
  'Aurea'
Osteospermum jucundum
Persicaria affinis
Pulmonaria
Stachys byzantina

Helleborus × nigercors

Viola

Dianthus *'Haytor White'*

PERENNIALS WITH FRAGRANT FLOWERS
Convallaria majalis
Cosmos atrosanguineus
Dianthus
Galium odoratum
Hesperis matronalis
Iris graminea
Lupinus
Nicotiana sylvestris
Phlox maculata

Saponaria officinalis
Sedum spectabile
Verbena × hybrida 'Defiance'

PERENNIALS WITH SCENTED FOLIAGE
Agastache mexicana
Artemisia alba 'Canescens'
Cestrum parqui
Galium odoratum
Geranium macrorrhizum

Houttuynia cordata
  'Chameleon'
Meum
Nepeta cataria
Pelargonium quercifolium
Tanacetum parthenium

PERENNIALS FOR CUT FLOWERS
Anaphalis
Astrantia major
Chrysanthemum
Helleborus niger
Phlox paniculata
Strelitzia reginae

PERENNIALS FOR DRIED FLOWERS
Astilbe
Catananche caerulea 'Major'
Echinops
Gypsophila paniculata
Limonium
Lythrum
Rodgersia
Solidago
Typha

ARCHITECTURAL PERENNIALS
Angelica archangelica
Cordyline
Gunnera manicata
Heracleum mantegazzianum
Rheum 'Ace of Hearts'

PERENNIALS FOR FOLIAGE
Anthriscus sylvestris
  'Ravenswing'
Artemisia 'Powis Castle'
Crocosmia
Euphorbia mellifera
Ferula communis
Morina afghanica
Osmunda regalis
Phormium tenax
Stachys byzantina

Alstroemeria ligtu *hybrids with* Lychnis coronaria

PERENNIALS FOR COASTAL AND EXPOSED SITES
Anaphalis margaritacea
Anthurium andraeanum
Echinacea purpurea
Erigeron 'Charity'
Euphorbia griffithii 'Fireglow'
Kniphofia caulescens
Phormium tenax
Salvia argentea
Senecio cineraria 'Silver Dust'

PERENNIAL CLIMBERS
Clematis
Eccremocarpus scaber
Tropaeolum speciosum
Vinca major

PERENNIALS FOR HEDGES
Echinops bannaticus
Helianthus atrorubens
  'Monarch'
Macleaya microcarpa
  'Coral Plume'
Rudbeckia 'Goldquelle'

Hosta *'Gold Standard'*

Bulbs List

A = autumn; Sp = Spring; Su = summer; W = winter

YELLOW-FLOWERED BULBS
Begonia, tuberous (some) (Su)
Chlidanthus fragrans (Su)
Crocosmia 'Citronella' (Su)
Crocus (many) (Sp)
Dahlia 'Butterball' (Su-A)
Dahlia 'Early Bird' (Su-A)
Eranthis hyemalis
   'Guinea Gold' (Sp)
Freesia 'Yellow River' (Sp)
Gladiolus 'Green
   Woodpecker' (Su)
Gladiolus 'Moon Mirage' (Su-A)
Gladiolus 'Tesoro' (A)
Homeria ochroleuca (Sp-Su)
Iris danfordiae (Sp)
Lilium 'Amber Gold' (Su)
Lilium 'Connecticut King' (Su)
Lilium Golden Splendor
   Group (Su)
Narcissus (many) (Sp)
Sternbergia lutea (A)
Tropaeolum tuberosum (Su-A)

Tulipa *'Roulette'*

Tulipa (many) (Sp)
Zantedeschia elliottiana (Su)

ORANGE-FLOWERED BULBS
Alstroemeria aurea (Su)
Begonia, tuberous (some) (Su)
Canna iridiflora (Su)
Crocosmia masoniorum (Su-A)
Dahlia 'Chinese Lantern' (Su)
Dahlia 'Highgate Torch' (Su-A)
Fritillaria imperialis (Sp)

Iris danfordiae

Fritillaria recurva (Sp)
Gladiolus 'Carioca' (Su)
Gladiolus 'Deliverance' (Su)
Gladiolus 'Melodie' (Su)
Hippeastrum 'Orange
   Sovereign' (W-Sp)
Hyacinthus orientalis 'Princess
   Maria Christina' (Sp)
Lilium bulbiferum var.
   croceum (Su)
Lilium 'Enchantment' (Su)
Lilium 'Harmony' (Su)
Littonia modesta (Su)
Tulipa (many) (Sp)

RED-FLOWERED BULBS
Alstroemeria 'Margaret' (Su)
Begonia, tuberous (some) (Su)
Canna × *generalis* 'Assault' (Su)

Hyacinthus orientalis

Crocosmia 'Bressingham
   Blaze' (Su)
Crocosmia 'Lucifer' (Su)
Dahlia 'Comet' (Su-A)
Dahlia 'Scarlet Beauty' (Su-A)
Gladiolus 'Rutherford' (Su)
Gloriosa superba
   Rothschildiana' (Su)
× *Hippistrellia* 'Red Beauty' (Su)
Scadoxus multiflorus (Sp)
Schizostylis coccinea (A)
Tulipa (many) (Sp)

PINK- AND PURPLE-FLOWERED BULBS
Allium christophii (Su)
Allium gigantium (Su)
Allium karataviense (Sp-S)
Allium schubertii (Su)

Tulipa *'Mirella'*

Amaryllis belladonna (Su-A)
Begonia, tuberous (some) (Su)
Bulbocodium vernum (Sp)
Chionodoxa luciliae (Sp)
Colchicum speciosum (some) (A)
Corydalis solida (Sp)
Crinum × *powellii* (Su-A)
Crocus (many) (Sp)
Cyclamen coum (W)
Cyclamen hederifolium (A)
Dactylorhiza elata (Sp-Su)
Dahlia 'Athalie' (Su)
Dahlia 'Wootton Cupid' (Su-A)
Dierama pulcherrimum (Su)
Dracunculus vulgaris (Su)
Freesia 'Everett' (W-Sp)
Fritillaria meleagris (Sp)
Fritillaria michailovskyi (Sp)
Gladiolus 'Drama' (Su)
Gladiolus 'Mexicali Rose' (Su)
Gladiolus 'Robin' (Su)
Hyacinthus orientalis
   'Queen of Pinks' (Sp)
Hyacinthus orientalis
   'Violet Pearl' (Sp)

Incarvillea delavayi (Su)
Liatris spicata (Sp)
Lilium 'Magic Pink' (Su)
Lilium 'Star Gazer' (Su)
Nerine bowdenii (A)
Oxalis adenophylla (Sp-Su)
Roscoea auriculata (A)
Tulipa (many) (Sp)

BLUE-FLOWERED BULBS

Agapanthus hybrids (Su)
Allium caeruleum (Su)
Camassia cusickii (Sp-Su)
Camassia quamash (Sp-Su)
Chionodoxa luciliae
    'Gigantea' (Sp)
Chionodoxa sardensis (Sp)

Allium caeruleum

Crocus speciosus (some) (A)
Hyacinthoides
    hispanica (Sp)
Hyacinthus orientalis
    'Blue Jacket' (Sp)
Hyacinthus orientalis
    'Delft Blue' (Sp)
Iris reticulata (Sp)
Ixiolirion pallasii (Sp)
Muscari armeniacum
Muscari aucheri (Sp)
Muscari azureum (Sp)
Muscari latifolium (Sp)
Puschkinia scilloides (Sp)
Scilla mischtschenkoana (Sp)
Scilla siberica
    'Atrocoerulae' (Sp)

VIOLET-FLOWERED BULBS

Iris histrioides (Sp)
Moraea polystachya (A)
Muscari comosum
    'Plumosum' (Sp)
Scilla peruviana (Su)
Tulipa pulchella
    'Violet Queen' (Sp)

LILAC-FLOWERED BULBS

Crocus speciosus (some) (A)
Crocus tommasinianus (W)
Lachenalia archioides var.
    glaucina (Sp)
Tulbaghia violacea (Su)

WHITE-FLOWERED BULBS

Allium neapolitanum (Sp)
Anemone blanda 'White
    Splendour' (Sp)
Anemone nemorosa (Sp-Su)
Begonia, tuberous
    (some) (Su)
Camassia leichtlinii (Su)

Muscari botryoides *'Album'*

Chionodoxa luciliae
    Gigantea Group 'Alba' (Sp)
Colchicum speciosum
    (some) (A)
Convallaria majalis (Sp)
Crinum × powellii 'Album' (Su-A)
Crocus (many) (Sp)
Dahlia 'Angora' (Su)

Dahlia 'Easter Sunday' (Su-A)
Eremurus himalaicus (Su)
Eucharis amazonica (A)
Galanthus nivalis (Sp)
Galtonia candicans (Su)
Gladiolus 'Ice Cap' (Su)
Hippeastrum 'Apple Blossom'
    (W-Sp)
Hyacinthus orientalis
    'White Pearl' (Sp)
Hymenocallis × festalis
    (Sp-Su)
Leucojum aestivum (Su)
Leucojum vernum (Sp)
Lilium candidum (Su)
Lilium longiflorum (Su)
Lilium regale (Su)
Muscari botryoides
    'Album' (Sp)
Nerine bowdenii 'Alba' (A)
Ornithogalum nutans (Sp)
Ornithogalum
    umbellatum (Sp)
Polianthes tuberosa (Su)
Trillium cuneatum (Sp)
Trillium grandiflorum
    'Flore Pleno' (Sp)
Tulipa turkestanica (Sp)
Zantedeschia aethiopica
    'Crowborough' (Su)
Zephyranthes candida (Su-A)

Hyacinthus orientalis

GREEN-FLOWERED BULBS

Eucomis bicolor (Su-A)
Galtonia viridiflora (Su)
Hermodactylus tuberosus (Sp)
Tulipa viridiflora
    'Spring Green' (Sp).

Freesia

INDEX